Appalachian Trail Names

Appalachian Trail Names

Origins of Place Names Along the AT

DAVID EDWIN LILLARD

STACKPOLE
BOOKS

To every volunteer
who has a hand in producing the guidebooks
and maps that keep us safe in the world
between the white blazes

Published by
STACKPOLE BOOKS
5067 Ritter Road
Mechanicsburg, PA 17055
www.stackpolebooks.com

Printed in the United States of America

10 9 8 7 6 5 4 3 2 1

First edition

Cover design by Caroline Stover
Cover painting by Doug Pifer

Library of Congress Cataloging-in-Publication Data

Lillard, David Edwin.
Appalachian Trail names / David Edwin Lillard.—1st ed.
p. cm.
Includes bibliographical references.
ISBN 0-8117-2672-X
1. Appalachian Trail—History, Local. 2. Names, Geographical—Appalachian Trail. 3. Appalachian Trail—Description and travel. I. Title.
F106 .L58 2002
917.4'003—dc21 2001049528

Contents

Acknowledgments

Kitty Clark and Ed Talone joined me in researching this project. Kitty's research abilities, pursuit of leads, and interview skills added immeasurable enrichment to the book. Ed knows more about the Appalachian Trail's history and locations than just about anyone alive. His interviews of AT veterans and his poring over periodicals dating to the earliest days of the trail help bring the AT culture to life.

The Guide to the Appalachian Trail series is a treasure of cultural history, including place-names' origins. The older editions are still among my favorite reading, even if they are no longer accurate for their turns and mileposts. The contemporary guides to the trail in central Virginia and Shenandoah National Park are particularly rich in history and place-name stories and have sparked my interest in the trail's historical context.

Other authors whose work was especially helpful, as well as engaging, include Bob Bistrais, whose thesis project "Place Names on Vermont's Long Trail" was a real find. Allen R. Coggins's very fine *Place Names of the Smokies* and John T. B. Mudge's *The White Mountains: Names, Places & Legends* are gratifying reads for hikers for their treatment of places associated with outdoor recreation. Mudge, in particular, dives deep into names and stories from the early days of trail-building and mountain-retreating in the Whites. Paula Strain's *The Blue Hills of Maryland* is as entertaining as it is thorough.

This project would not have been possible in an entire decade were it not for the place-name histories available on several states traversed by the AT. They include *The Dictionary of Maine Place-Names* by Phillip R. Rutherford, Esther Munroe Swift's *Vermont Place Names: Footprints of History,* Hamill Kenny's *The Place Names of Maryland, Their Origin and Meaning,* and Abraham Epershade's *Pennsylvania Place Names.*

I am deeply appreciative to all the AT stewards who took time to share stories with us, and to the legion of reference librarians and historical society staffs for going those extra steps.

Introduction

I grew up on Washington Avenue, a street named to memorialize Gen. George Washington's march to Brandywine Springs in New Castle County, Delaware. The massive oak under which the future president held council in Brandywine Springs came to be known as the Council Oak—a name it carried until its demise some two centuries later.

Naming the street for George Washington illustrates *commemorative* place naming. The Appalachian Trail corridor has hundreds of commemoratively named places. Some memorialize historical figures, such as Williams Mountain in Massachusetts, named for the founder of Williams College, or Clingmans Dome in the Smokies, named for the statesman, explorer, and scientist who first measured its height.

But for every name that comes from the history books, another comes from a dedicated hiker or trail-builder. Belter's Bump, Roger's Ramp, and Billy's View are just three places in Connecticut named for Appalachian Trail stewards. After more than 75 years, the AT itself is now part of America's story. And for the mountains, popular since the 1880s as a destination for people seeking renewal, the chronicles of mountain recreation are now as remembered as the tales of early settlers who struggled against all odds in the isolated Blue Ridge.

Place names, or toponyms, come in a variety of classifications. George R. Stewart's *Names on the Globe* tells us that every place name fits neatly into one of several broad categories. In addition to the commemorative names, there are *descriptive* names, such as High Point in New Jersey and Georgia's Chatahoochee, which means "sparkling rocks."

Associative names create a relationship between the named place and the character of the landscape. The many variations on Sugarloaf and Haystack along the AT come to mind, as do the places that evoke the Prince of Darkness—Little Devil Stairs, the Devil's Marbleyard, and so on.

Incident names, such as Panther Ford or Dead Womans Hollow, are names that remember specific episodes in time. And there are *mistake* names and folk evolutions—often a name that is slightly different than its original is the result of a misspelling by a map-maker or the slow metamorphosis of a name after thousands of utterances.

Behind each name is a piece of our history's puzzle, an oddity in an era in which sports arenas are named for corporate sponsors. These are times for big projects—bigger ski developments, bigger highways, bigger lights lighting bigger lots—which are often given names that have no connection to the landscape's history or past. This process of losing our history is taking place in the entire landscape surrounding the trail. And so the trail and its history are threatened.

What's in a name? Along the Appalachian Trail there are places whose names recall the rambles of Thoreau, Bartram, Kephart, Guyot, Jefferson, Boone, and Melville. These names remind us that the Appalachians are more than a vital natural resource. These mountains and the trail that weaves through them also embody irreplaceable elements of America's history.

In the past decade, there has been a reawakening of understanding for the ecological values of the Appalachian Trail. People are rallying to protect the trail's ecology as well as its scenic and recreational values.

Now it's time for a reawakening of the trail's cultural history—not just because famed explorers, authors, and statesmen have trod there. The trail's path through time tells a history much deeper than a collection of names we all recognize. The countless forgotten people who lived and died in these mountains and in their shadows live on in a pastoral landscape that, remarkably, people of long ago could still recognize.

And the chronicle of the Appalachian Trail is itself now the stuff of history. Benton MacKaye, Myron Avery, Jean Stevenson, J. Raymer Edmands—their contributions to the American landscape are celebrated by this remarkable pathway.

At the beginning of the 21st century, hikers who have been around since the early days of the trail, especially the 1940s and '50s, are departing this life and too often taking their stories with them. To study the Appalachian Trail is to hear, time and again, that one has arrived a year too late to hear the full story.

On foot in these mountains, no one is bigger than the next hill. No one can cover in a day the distance cars in the valley will cover in a matter of minutes. But, lost in ourselves in the shade of the AT's "long green tunnel," we must try to remember the often irreplaceable things the trail experience represents—an ancient name, a woodland, a farmscape in the valley, a Civil War soldier's story, solitude, early American life, the startling moment when a grouse takes flight, slow and quiet travel, dark skies at night, wildness, safety, and renewal.

Indian Names Along the AT

Indian words and phrases are one of the most dominant characteristics of place names in the Appalachians and along the eastern seaboard. Many names were adopted and handed down by European settlers, while others were bestowed much later to evoke a nostalgia for the original Americans.

Hundreds of tribes, some with dozens of bands, once formed dozens of confederacies east of the Mississippi. Today, many that we typically think of as a single tribe are (or were) confederacies of many tribes or a group of confederacies defined by a common language stock: the Algonquian and Iroquoian families, for example.

Some of the stories of these tribes and nations are offered here through the place names they gave. But all the stories, alliances, wars, and histories, like the tribes, are far too numerous to detail here. Outlined below is a brief account of some of the principal tribes and confederacies that have influenced names along the Appalachian Trail.

Abenaki. The term is derived from "light" and is thought to refer to the morning light, or people of the easternmost Atlantic coast. The term "Abenaki" was used to refer to an Algonquian confederacy centering largely in what is now Maine. Other Algonquian tribes, however, included all of the northeastern tribes in the Abenaki confederacy, including the Passamaquoddy, Malacite, Penobscot, and Kennebec.

Algonquian Family. The term "Algonquian" refers to a linguistic stock that occupied more territory than any other in North America, with tribes in what are now the Midwest, New England, and mid-Atlantic regions. Along the Appalachian Trail, place names appear from many Algonquian dialects, including the Delaware, the Abenaki group, Pennachook, Mohegan, Mahican, and Shawnee.

Cherokee. Formerly occupying mountain territory of the southern Allegheny Mountains in Virginia, North Carolina, Tennessee, and Georgia, the Cherokee were a powerful and prominent tribe at the time of European settlement. Their name is thought to be a Choctaw word for "cave people," because of their homes in the mountains.

Creeks. Occupying the greater portion of Alabama and Georgia, the Creeks are a confederacy of the Muskhogean family. Their name was given by English settlers for the many streams flowing through the tribe's homeland.

Delaware (Lenapi). They called themselves Leni-Lenape or the Lenapi, which means "genuine men." Their confederacy of tribes was at one time the most important of the Algonquian stock, occupying much of the land in the Delaware River basin in New York, New Jersey, Pennsylvania, and Delaware.

Iroquoian Family. The term applies to many tribes, but is primarily associated with the Five Nations of the Iroquois: the Mohawk, Oneida, Onondaga, Cayuga, and Senaca. Later, the Tuscarora, which had broken from one of the confederated tribes some 300 years earlier, became a principal part in the Six Nations. Each nation itself was an independent political unit consisting of tribal leagues, themselves operating as independent political units. Along the AT, the Iroquois ranged from Maryland and central Pennsylvania into New York.

Mahican and Mohegan. An Algonquian tribe that occupied both banks of the upper Hudson River in New York. They extended their range into the Housatonic valley in Massachusetts. At war for many years with the Mohawk, they were eventually forced entirely into Massachusetts. When their territory became too crowded, they sold land to settlers and relocated to Pennsylvania and were eventually subsumed into the Delawares and Munsees.

Mohawk. The easternmost of the Iroquois people. The name, derived from an Algonquian term, translates into "man eaters." They called themselves "flint people."

Passamaquoddy. A small tribe of the Abenaki confederacy that spoke nearly the same dialect of the Algonquian language as the Malacite. A Maine coastal tribe, the Passamaquoddy name means "plenty of pollock."

Pennacook. This confederacy of Algonquian tribes was situated primarily in the valley of the Merrimac River in New Hampshire and Massachusetts, as well as southwestern Maine.

The Entries

A

A. RUFUS MORGAN SHELTER NC
Named for the Rev. Dr. A. Rufus Morgan, an Episcopalian minister born near Franklin, NC, who founded the Nantahala Hiking Club in the 1940s and almost single-handedly maintained the AT in the Smokies during World War II; well into his 70s, he kept clear a 55-mile section. At age 81, Morgan joined a protest walk of 576 hikers who opposed the construction of a road across the Smokies. The hikers won the battle. Morgan was renowned for climbing Mt. LeConte more than a hundred times, the last time after reaching age 90.

ABOL BRIDGE
ABOL POND ME
This is one of the most lyrical place names of the entire AT corridor, but unfortunately one we rarely hear in its original form. From the Abenaki word *Aboljackarnegassic,* meaning "bare" or "devoid of trees," it was shortened by white settlers.

ADAM & EVE MOUNTAINS NJ
Thought to be so named because they were the first two mountains named in the area.

ADAMS MA
Settled by Rhode Island Quakers in 1762, this town was first known as East Hoosuck, later East Township. It was renamed in 1778 for Samuel Adams, Revolutionary War leader, signer of the Declaration of Independence, and governor of MA. In keeping with the American tradition of commercializing history, Adams is now better known by the identification given him by marketers: "brewer, patriot."

ADDIS GAP GA
Named for the Addis family that lived in the area until 1942.

AGONY GRIND NY
A fitting description for the steep southbound climb of Arden Mountain from Route 17. The name is thought to have come from original AT crews in the 1920s.

AIR LINE TRAIL NH
Given this name by its builders, Laban Watson and E. B. Cook, in the 1870s. The trail was built in the White Mountains to follow a ridge line rather than a valley—hence the name. *See* Edmands Col, NH.

ALBERT MOUNTAIN NC
Named for Albert Siler, grandfather of A. Rufus Morgan, who helped establish and maintain the AT in NC. *See* A. Rufus Morgan Shelter, NC.

ALLEGHENY TRAIL VA
Intersecting the AT just south of the Pine Swamp Branch Lean-to, this yellow-blazed trail runs about 340 miles to Ohiopyle, PA. The name is transferred from the Allegheny Mountains and may be a Delaware Algonquian word. Translated literally, it is all adjectives: "alternate motion" *(ghenny)* and "good" *(al).* Somehow, this combination has been translated alternately as "good river" and "endless mountains."

ALLIS TRAIL NY
Named for J. Ashton Allis, pioneer trail builder and president of the New York City–based Fresh Air Club, an all-male group of speed hikers who, in the 1920s,

averaged 30 miles per outing. Allis's experience as a New York City banker came in handy for the still-young AT Conference; he served as one of the group's first treasurers.

AMICALOLA FALLS STATE PARK GA
From the Cherokee *ama* for "water" and *kalola* for "tumbling." Falling some 720 feet over seven cascades, Amicalola Falls is the tallest waterfall east of the Mississippi River.

AMMONOOSUC RAVINE NH
An Abenaki word meaning "fish place."

ANDREW JOHNSON MOUNTAIN NC/TN
Born into poverty in Raleigh, NC, in 1808, the future president headed west in 1825, landing in Greeneville, TN. After training as a tailor, he entered politics, first as an alderman, then mayor, state legislator, and U.S. representative. He was elected to the Senate, then was selected as Abraham Lincoln's vice president in 1864. A pro-Union southerner, he stayed with Lincoln after TN seceded. He became president after Lincoln's assassination, but was considered by many northerners to be too soft on the South during Reconstruction—a perception that would lead to his impeachment by the House in 1868.

ANDROSCOGGIN RIVER NH
Abenaki for "the place where fish are aired."

ANDY LAYNE TRAIL VA
This side trail and former section of the AT is dedicated to trail worker and overseer Andy Layne (1913–91) of the Roanoke AT Club.

ANNAPOLIS ROCK MD
Maryland's state capital is named for Anna Stuart (1655–1714), who became queen of England. How the name was transferred to the rocks after the naming of Annapolis in 1695 remains unknown.

ANTHONY WAYNE RECREATION AREA NY
Named for revolutionary general Mad Anthony Wayne, who received his nickname for his unconventional strategy to capture the fort at Stony Point, on July 15, 1779. Under cover of darkness, one group of colonial troops crept into the British fort and took positions, then began shouting "the fort is ours!" while commanding the "captured" British to remain in their quarters. The startled British, confused and cut off from assistance, resigned themselves to defeat. This allowed a much larger force of armed continental troops to enter the fort unimpeded.

ANTHONY'S NOSE NY
Such an interesting geologic formation is worthy of many toponymic legends. Here are a few. It might be named after Rio St. Antonio, which is what a 16th-century Portuguese sailor named Estevan Gomez had christened the river that would become known as the Hudson. Giving credence to this origin is the fact that the village of Manitou, just north of Bear Mountain Bridge, was formerly known as St. Anthonysville.

Other sources claim the nose was named for Mad Anthony Wayne, the Revolutionary War general who captured the fort at Stony Point in 1779. But this theory is undermined by a letter from Lord Sterling to George Washington written in 1776 on the subject of the Hudson Highlands fortifications. It says in part "Ft. Montgomery is situated on the west bank of the river, which is there about half a mile broad, and the bank one hundred feet high. On the opposite shore is a point of land called Anthony's Nose, which is many hundred feet height, very steep, and inaccessible to anything but goats, or men very expert in climbing."

The most colorful story comes from Washington Irving's *History of New York,* which claims the feature is named for Anthony Van Corlear, or Anthony the Trumpeter, one of Henry Hudson's crew members who had a giant nose. The nose was said to have reflected sunlight so fiercely that the glare once killed a sturgeon in the Hudson that became supper for the crew.

ANTIETAM SHELTER PA
LITTLE ANTIETAM CREEK MD

Built by the Civilian Conservation Corps in 1936, it is named for the nearby creek. The *Indian Bulletin II* of 1868, viewed as an authority at the time of its publication, gives the meaning of Antietam as "swift river." The word is thought to be of Algonquian origin, derived from *ehtan,* or "current." Its spelling has appeared variously through the years, including Odieta in 1721 and Antieatum in 1730. About 12 miles above its confluence with the Potomac River, the creek flows through the town of Sharpsburg, MD, site of one of the bloodiest battles of the Civil War, known today as the Battle of Antietam (southerners call it the Battle of Sharpsburg).

ANTLERS CAMPSITE ME

Named for the Antlers Camps chain of sporting camps that operated here until 1949.

APPALACHIAN TRAIL ME TO GA

Benton MacKaye suggested the name Appalachian Trail in his 1921 article that introduced the idea of the trail, "The Appalachian Trail: An Experiment in Regional Planning."

APPALACHIAN TRAIL (FORMER) ME

According to *The Maine Naturalist,* another trail bearing the AT name was built by the Appalachian Mountain Club in 1887 near Mt. Katahdin, in what became Baxter State Park—some of it following the present-day AT. This trail, 20 to 30 miles in length, was given the name Appalachian because in those days AMC members were called "Appalachians."

APPLE HOUSE SHELTER TN

Built in 1984 on the site of an old barn that was used to store tools for a nearby orchard. The barn was built in 1952, and for a time after it was abandoned it served as a trail shelter itself.

APPLE ORCHARD MOUNTAIN VA

Named not for apple trees, but for the oaks that are so twisted by the region's harsh, icy weather that their appearance resembles an apple tree's. Once known as Lee Mountain, for Gen. Robert E. Lee. The AT does not reach this height again traveling north until Killington, VT.

AQUASHICOLA CREEK PA

A corruption of *Achqucanschicola,* an Indian word meaning "where we fish with the bush net."

ARCADIA LUMBER CO. VA

The AT follows the old railroad grade once used by the company to haul timber. It hit sudden hard times in 1910 when a foreman named Hendricks who had just begun hauling timber with a new $125,000 Shay train engine let his pleasure at commanding the machine override his common sense. He decided to haul ten carloads up the slope at once instead of the typical three. Gravity was more powerful than the engine, however, and the load rushed down the hill out of control. The crew saved themselves by leaping from the train, which crashed into Cornelius Creek, where it remained until 1940.

ARDEN MOUNTAIN
ARDEN VALLEY NY

Railroad magnate Edward Harriman and his wife Mary purchased this tract in 1888 from two brothers, the Parrotts, who owned iron mines and furnaces in the region. The Parrotts had made their fortune manufacturing cannons and shot—including the famed Parrott rifle—for the Union Army. The Parrotts had called their estate Arden, the maiden name of Peter Parrott's wife, Mary Antoinette. The Harrimans retained the name when they purchased the property and absorbed it into their growing holdings, which would later become part of Bear Mountain–Harriman State Park.

ARDEN-SUREBRIDGE TRAIL NY

Blazed in 1921 by J. Ashton Allis, a leader of the Fresh Air and Appalachian Mountain clubs as well as a founder of the Palisades Interstate Park Commission and NY–NJ Trail Conference. He intended the trail to be a shortcut to the Ramapo-Dunderberg Trail between Arden and Surebridge mountains. On a 1921 map, it is labeled "Allis Short Trail." In 1922, it was extended by members of the Green Mountain Club.

ARETHUSA–RIPLEY FALLS TRAIL NH

The trail goes to both waterfalls. Arethusa Falls is named for the poem "Arethusa" by Percy Shelley, which tells the story of a beautiful nymph who is transformed into a fountain. Ripley Falls is named in honor of Henry Ripley, a friend of the Rev. Starr King, who bestowed the honor. King, a Unitarian clergyman, explored this area extensively and wrote the book *The White Hills, Their Legends, Landscapes & Poetry. See* King Ravine, NH.

ARLINGTON–W. WARDSBORO ROAD VT

Also known as Kelly Stand Road. Arlington was probably named for Augustus Fitzroy (1735–1811), the 4th earl of Arlington, in Suffolk, England (an earl is a position of British nobility, one level above a viscount). He was prime minister of England in 1768–70, but lost the job because of unrest in America. Wardsboro is named for William Ward of Newfame, one of the original grantees in 1780.

Kelly Stand was once a small settlement, but little remains of it today. Local tradition says that the village grew up around a logging operation owned by a man named Kelly. There was also a John Kelly who claimed patents on thousands of acres in VT after he was awarded the land by NY colony, which disputed NH colony's claim to the land (VT, at that time, was part of NH). King George III ruled in NY's favor. Because of this, the newly formed VT legislature recognized Kelly's patents in several towns. It is conceivable that Kelly is the same man for whom the logging settlement is presumed to have been named.

ARNOLD TRAIL ME

Between Middle and West Carry ponds, the AT follows about 2 miles of the trail Gen. Benedict Arnold took on his march to Canada in 1775, when he was still on the side of the revolutionaries.

ARNOLD VALLEY VA

Stephen Arnold established a homestead here in 1749.

ARNOLDTOWN ROAD MD

Named for the Arnold family, which owned property in what is now the western edge of Frederick County.

ASHBY GAP VA

Named for Thomas Ashby, who settled here in the early 1800s. It was formerly called both the "Upper Thoroughfare of the Blue Ridge" and "Ashby's Bent" (for its winding road).

ATKINS VA

Variously called Atkins Switch, Atkins Tank, and Atkins, after the Atkins family, who were large landowners. The name Atkins Tank derived from the water tower that once filled steam trains here. The "switch" in Atkins Switch refers to the junction here for a branch line.

AUDIE MURPHY MONUMENT VA
Audie Murphy, said to have been the single most decorated soldier of World War II, was a recipient of the Congressional Medal of Honor. After the war, he became one of the earliest advocates for veterans' causes, especially those of disabled veterans. He died 25 years after the war ended when a small civilian plane in which he was a passenger crashed into the side of this VA mountain, unable to navigate through fog and rain. The monument, placed by friends and family, marks the crash site.

B

B POND ME
B Pond is in Township B, a settlement established by a logging company.

BAGGS CREEK GAP GA
Supposedly named for a Cherokee family named Bagg that lived along the creek until 1819.

BAKER PEAK VT
Probably named for Remember Baker (1737–75), who did the first survey of the Wallingford area in 1770. A native of Woodbury, CT, he went to VT (then called the NH grants) in 1764 and quickly joined with his cousins Ethan and Ira Allen in their efforts to create an independent state. He gained renown as a Green Mountain Boy, fighting NY colonists over lands disputed by NH and NY. Governor Tryon of NY put a bounty on his head. Baker served in the French and Indian War in 1758, and fought the British at Ticonderoga in 1775. Only two months after Ticonderoga, he was killed by Indians while on a scouting mission up the Richelieu River, the outlet of Lake Champlain, near Isle aux Noix.

BAKER STREAM ME
Thought to be named for one of the Baker family that settled south of here in 1773, in what is now Moscow Township, 18 miles south on the Kennebec River. But which of the Bakers is anyone's guess—there were so many Bakers in the area that Moscow, ME, was first called Bakerstown. (The name change occurred when the town was first surveyed, in 1812, the year the Russians defeated Napoleon, so the story goes.)

BALCONY FALLS VA
These James River rapids west of the AT are named for a feature above known as The Balcony.

BALD KNOB VA
Now completely wooded, at one time it had been cleared for pasture land.

BALD PEAK
BALD PEAK TRAIL CT
The trail, which leads to a Mt. Riga–area peak, illustrates a common occurrence in naming evolution. Originally called Ball Peak, after local 18th-century industrialist Daniel Ball, it was mistakenly labeled Bald Mountain by U.S. Geographical Survey cartographers. Once on the official maps, the erroneous name achieved currency and, eventually, official status.

Potomac AT Club

Fungus on a pine tree.

BANGOR & AROOSTOOK RAILROAD BED ME

Bangor is said to have been named for the hymn "Bangor," a favorite of the Rev. Seth Noble, who is credited with naming the town. *Aroostook* is a Micmac word for "beautiful river" or "shining river." The railroad line crossed by the AT here was a spur line connecting two ME towns, Blanchard and Greenville, and was originally the Bangor and Piscataquis Railroad when it was created around 1884.

BANNISTERS FLAT VA

This area upstream from Panther Ford is where freed slave George Bannister grew tobacco. In 1877, Jennings Creek rose and swept Bannister downstream along with $300 in gold coins he had just gotten for his crop. His drowned body washed ashore near Panther Ford; he was buried near where the Jennings Creek Road Trailhead is today. In 1936, Bannister's remains were moved to the Indian Rock Methodist Church.

BARNARD BROOK VT

The name was transferred from Barnard, VT, which was named for Sir Francis Bernard, a grantee of the town. Sometime around 1810, Bernard became Barnard.

BALDY MOUNTAIN MA

Formerly called Bald Mountain Top Pasture, it had been cleared for grazing in the late 18th century.

BALL BROOK CT

Named for David Ball, who operated a metal forge here beginning in 1781. The area is still known by some as Ball's Forge.

BALSAM CORNER NC/TN

Formerly called Big Swag in reference to the ridge gap here—swag being another name for gap. The "corner" in the current name refers to a sharp angle in the county line.

BARRACK MATIFF PLATEAU
BARRACK MOUNTAIN CT

It's impossible to investigate one of these two place names without the other, because various researchers have assigned different meanings to the word "barrack" in each name. There are a couple of theories about the names' origin from a couple of sources. According to one theory, Barrack Matiff Plateau is the northern end of Wetauwanchu Mountain, and the name is a combination of two Dutch words: *matiff,* meaning "steep high cliff" or "hill," and *barrack,* meaning, loosely translated, a haystack with a wooden cover that slides up and down poles. So the name roughly means Haystack Mountain. Another source claims that barrack is a derivation of the Gaelic word for pyramidal. There is agreement that Wetauwanchu is derived from *wanchu,* for "hill" or "mountain," and *wetau,* for "wigwam place." But the meaning changes in the context of Barrack Mountain. Here, *barrack* is said to derive from the German word for dump, *barraka,* and the mountain name to come from an old hermit who lived there in a dumpy shack. Other sources say a farmer named Barrack once owned property that included the mountain.

BARREN MOUNTAIN ME

The name for this densely wooded peak is a misnomer. According to local authorities, it was once called Slate Mountain. Fannie Hardy Eckstrom, a noted ME authority, suggests the name may have been changed after the great Pisquatis fire of 1825. The summit was known locally as "The Copper Plate" because of a triangulation marker on top. A prehistoric Indian battle was fought near here.

BARTLETT BROOK VT

Named for a family that lived in Stockbridge in the 18th century.

BARTRAM TRAIL NC

William Bartram was to the Smokies what Lewis and Clark were to the western U.S. His explorations of FL, GA, NC, and AL, which began in 1775, have sparked the imagination of explorers, naturalists, and historians ever since. In his journal *The Travels of William Bartram,* published in 1791, he documented the plants and animals he observed as he traveled along an Indian trade route from the Cherokee town Nikwasi (present-day Franklin) to the Nantahala River. The book is also an early document of Cherokee life. *Travels* is considered one of the earliest and finest examples of American nature writing, in the spirit of later writers Henry David Thoreau and John Muir. A 118-mile hiking trail through NC and GA, and extending 8 miles into AL, follows Bartram's route, based on references from his journal.

BASCOM LODGE MA

The lodge is named for John Bascom (1827–1912), a professor of philosophy at Williams College in nearby Williamstown and one of the first commissioners of the Mt. Greylock Reservation Commission.

BASIN-CASCADE TRAIL NH

Named for "The Basin," a glacial pothole in the Pemigewasset River formed by sand swirling against the rock. The pothole is 15 feet deep and 30 to 40 feet in diameter.

BASTIAN VA

Its early name was Parkersburg, named for Parker Hornbager, who in 1853 inherited 200 acres along Hunting Camp Creek from his father, Daniel. This land was later donated for the founding of the town. In 1914, it was renamed for F. E. Bastian, a railroad manager. The change was requested by the railroad because the line passed through another Parkersburg, this one in WV—a situation that often confused passengers and railroad workers alike.

BATES LEDGE ME

Although not really known, it is thought to be named for the Bates College Outing Club from nearby Bates College. In July 1934, a Bates work party plotted a trail route from Grafton Notch to Saddleback Mountain, which includes this area.

BAXTER PEAK
BAXTER STATE PARK ME

Named for Percival Baxter, governor of ME in 1921–25, whose gifts of land totaling 201,000 acres established the state park beginning in 1931. When he was governor, he failed to get the state legislature to purchase the land, so he took matters into his own hands by purchasing and donating the first 5,960 acres. He would continue this effort until his death in 1969. Baxter Peak, the northern terminus of the AT at Mt. Katahdin, was called Monument Peak before the AT was established here, in 1933.

BEACON HILL VT

While Boston's Beacon Hill conjures images of Paul Revere, this one has more contemporary origins. It is named for the airport signal lights there.

BEAR MOUNTAIN CT

Because the area's last bear was shot in 1821, speculation is that the original name for the mountain was "bare," derived from its denuded condition after fire or logging. Thanks to contemporary habitat protection and wildlife management practices, there are once again black bears roaming the area.

Edward Talone

Monument erected on Bear Mountain, CT, in 1885. When erected, it was erroneously thought to be the highest point in the state.

BEAR MOUNTAIN NY

Some sources claim it was originally called Bare Mountain, because it was stripped of trees to provide charcoal for the iron industry. But records show it was already known as Bear Hill when granted to Richard Bradley by King George III in 1743. Presumably, the name is derived from the mountain's resemblance to a bear in repose. Viewers from the east of the mountain saw not a bear, but a plate of bread, so the mountain alternately has been known as Bread Tray.

BEAR MOUNTAIN BRIDGE NY

Completed in 1924, and at the time the longest suspension bridge in the world, at 1,600 feet, it is a national engineering landmark. The bridge is also the low-elevation mark along the AT, with an elevation of only 176 feet above sea level. It was privately built and maintained by the Harriman family until 1940, when it was sold to the state of NY. *See* Bear Mountain–Harriman State Park, NY.

BEAR MOUNTAIN INN NY

Notable as the meeting place of AT planners in 1923, including Benton MacKaye, whose article proposing the trail is credited with launching the movement to establish and protect it. The inn was built in 1915 of native stone. *See* Bear Mountain–Harriman State Park, NY.

BEAR MOUNTAIN MONUMENT CT

First erected in 1885, by Robbins Battell of Norfolk, CT, the original monument (now damaged) was a pyramid of stone with a bronze ball atop it. A monument tablet lists the mountain's height at 2,354 feet and calls it the highest point in CT. It is in fact the highest point on a mountain that's entirely in CT. The highest point in the state is on the south slope of Mt. Frissell (2,380 feet), the summit of which is in MA.

BEAR MOUNTAIN ROAD CT
A former charcoal road that led to a blast furnace at Forge Pond, also known as South Pond.

BEAR MOUNTAIN–HARRIMAN STATE PARK NY
The Harriman story is an important part of the history of not only the AT, but of land conservation in America. Edward Harriman bought the Parrott property (*see* Arden Mountain) at auction in 1888, in part because other prospective buyers intended to harvest lumber, and he couldn't bear to see the forest denuded. He bought additional tracts of land throughout the end of the 19th century. In 1896, Harriman organized Arden Farms Dairy Company, which supplied milk to local residents and to the military academy at West Point. He also put in 40 miles of bridle paths and roads through Arden Estate. By 1905, he owned about 30 square miles. His goal was to save the wooded hillsides west of the Hudson River. In 1909, when the state of NY planned to build a prison in the area, he offered a great part of his estate to the state for a park. He wrote then governor Charles E. Hughes, "I plan to set aside about 12,000 acres of what I at present own, and, with this, to donate something like $1,000,000 for the acquisition of the necessary interior properties and the property lying over toward the Hudson River. I feel that if this should be accomplished, the state's prison should be moved again to the other side of the river, so as not to destroy the natural beauty which can never be replaced."

After his death, Harriman's widow, Mary, carried out his plans by donating 10,000 acres to the Palisades Interstate Park Commission. The state provided the land it had acquired for the prison. Subsequently, private individuals gave money and land for the establishment of the park. The first 6 miles of trail established specifically for the new AT were built here between the Ramapo River and Fingerboard Mountain in October 1923. By January 1924, 20 miles of the trail were completed all the way through the park.

Edward Talone

Bear Spring Cabin below the AT in MD.

BEAR SPRING CABIN TRAIL MD
Just before Harrison Krider entered military service in 1940, he left land and a partially built cabin to the Potomac AT Club, which dedicated the finished cabin in 1941. Early settlers knew the spring as a watering hole for black bear.

BEARFENCE MOUNTAIN HUT VA
Built by the Civilian Conservation Corps in 1940, the hut takes its name from Bearfence Mountain. The likely origin of the mountain's name is a pasture that was fenced to keep out the bears.

BEARPEN GAP NC
"Pen" refers to deadfall traps commonly used in the mountains by early settlers to capture bear for food and their hides. A deadfall trap is constructed of heavy, broken tree limbs, which fall when triggered by the weight of the animal. When they fall, they usually pin the animal or strike its head, which usually kills it. Once gone

V. Collins Chew

A sign tacked to a sapling many years ago is devoured by the mature tree. The sign points to Bear Wallow, near Bearwallow Gap, NC/TN.

from much of the eastern U.S. in the early 20th century, bears are now often seen by AT hikers.

BEARS DEN HOSTEL VA

Built as a residence in the 1930s, for many years hikers could enter and, for 10 cents, enjoy the building's view. Later, it was purchased by the Potomac AT Club and eventually became a youth hostel. The former owners had named the residence Bears Den because it was evocative of a hunt club.

BEARTOWN MOUNTAIN
BEARTOWN STATE FOREST MA

Two origin stories tell of men attacked by bears on the mountain. One man, armed with only a pocketknife for protection, had an arm mauled and half eaten. But with his other arm and his teeth, he managed to open his pocketknife and cut the bear's throat. Another pioneer from the town of Lee supposedly killed a bear here using only a knotted rope. Another story of the Beartown name recalls a giant black bear shot there in 1857. In addition to man-eating bears, the mountain was said to be rife with wolves that harassed area farmers.

The mountain was also the longtime home of Levi Beebe, known as Beartown Beebe, who purchased 2,000 acres here in 1850, opened a sawmill, and later developed a weather forecasting system so accurate that farmers throughout New England relied on his forecasts. Beebe wrote a pamphlet, *Meteorology: How to Foretell the Weather for Each Season, for All Time and in All Parts of the World,* published on January 1, 1892.

BEARWALLOW GAP NC/TN

Wallows, whether used by bear, elk, or another critter, are formed by soft humus layered over an impermeable substrate, such as clay. This characteristic makes for a swampy, damp area favored by many kinds of animals.

BEARWALLOW GAP VA

Thought to have been a major buffalo crossing over the Blue Ridge until the mid-18th century—but this doesn't account for the name. The seasonal standing water here provides habitat for the kind of berries and herbaceous foods favored by black bears and other creatures. *See* Bearwallow Gap, NC/TN.

BEE COVE LEAD NC

In the South, a "cove" is a small valley or hollow, and a "lead" is a spur leading off a larger mountain. "Bee" likely is derived from the abundance of blackgum trees here, which have long been used by beekeepers to make hives.

BEECH MOUNTAIN NC

Cherokees called it *Klonteska,* meaning "pheasant," which feasted on the nuts of the beech trees here. The trees led to the current name. It was a favored Indian hunting area. A legend tells of a battle between two Indian tribes fought on Beech Mountain. One tribe's chief was so shamed by the number of men he lost that he hanged himself atop the mountain. The nation's original "interstate highway," an Indian trail known as the Great Trading Path, which connected VA with GA, crossed Beech Mountain. When the town of Beech Mountain was incorporated in 1981, it became the highest town in the eastern U.S.

BELLOWS PIPE MA

The origin is unclear, but the first use of the name is attributed to Henry David Thoreau, who climbed Mt. Greylock in 1844 by way of Bellows Pipe, "a long and spacious valley" so named because "the winds rush up or down it with violence." Indians believed the noise to be the angry voice of the spirit Manitou.

BELLVALE MOUNTAIN NY

Known historically as Bellevale, the name, meaning "beautiful lowland," is a bit of a misnomer for even the most modest of mountains. The nearby village of Bellevale, 3 miles east of the village of Warwick, is the likely source of the name.

BELTER'S BUMP CT

This scenic outlook is named for Willie Belter, who owned the property with his brother Hank. The name was bestowed by Belter's good friend Norm Sills, editor of the AT guide to CT.

BENEDICT POND MA

The 35-acre pond is named for Fred Benedict, who owned a farm here in the early 20th century. Ice cut from the pond was sold locally. The Civilian Conservation Corps dammed the pond in 1933 to enlarge it.

BENNINGTON VT

The first town granted by NH governor Benning Wentworth in the NH grants—land that would become VT. Wentworth issued the grant in 1749, nine years after NH was ceded from MA. In a move that would make even politicians of questionable repute blush, the governor himself was a partner in the grant, along with other family members.

BENTON MACKAYE TRAIL GA

This branch trail is named for the man known as the founder of the AT, who lived in 1879–1976. Construction of the trail, which intersects the AT in GA, was begun by the Benton MacKaye Trail Association in 1980. MacKaye's article, "The Appalachian Trail, an Experiment in Regional Planning," published in 1922, proposed a series of conservation lands along the spine of the Appalachian Mountains, with spurs leading to the Atlantic Ocean. The article served as the inspiration for the AT. MacKaye's concept was based on VT's popular Long Trail.

BERLIN NH

Originally called Maynesborough to honor Sir William Mayne of London in 1771, its name was changed in 1829. The story for years had been that the change was made to recognize Berlin, MA, because many settlers to the area had come from that part of MA. Today, the conventional wisdom is that the town was named for Berlin, in Prussia, Germany, presumably because town elders thought the cosmopolitan name would lure new settlers.

BIG ABRAMS GAP
LITTLE ABRAMS GAP NC/TN

Abram (Abraham) was a Cherokee chief who was said to be of mixed white and Cherokee lineage. To the Cherokee, he was known as *Ooskuah.* When the Cherokee sided with the British during the American Revolution, Abram led the Indians on raids on the Watauga settlements. The Cherokee lived on a bend in the Little Tennessee River, now submerged under Chilhowee Lake.

BIG BALD NC/TN

Sometimes called "Griers Bald," for David Grier, a hermit who lived here in 1802–34 after being rejected by a woman. He was once charged with murder, but acquitted on grounds of insanity. Friends of the victims found Grier and killed him. Indians called the bald *Sasseenohla,* or "white man," presumably referring to Grier.

The Cherokee called all the southern balds *Udawagunda;* in Cherokee legend, the balds were the domain of the *Ulagi* monster, who would come down from the mountain and kidnap children. After the Indians killed the monster, they petitioned the Spirit to keep the summits clear so they could keep watch for other *ulagus.*

BIG BUTT MOUNTAIN NC/TN

Westerners have the gentrified term of "butte," but its meaning is the same as "butt": an isolated protuberance of a mountain.

BIG ISLAND VA

The largest island in the James River, 1 1/2 miles long and 1/4 mile wide.

BIG MEADOWS VA

A vast open area in the central Shenandoah NP near the lodge of the same name. The history of the meadow is complex. It is thought to have begun with lightning-induced fire, which created an open field. Recovery species, such as berries, soon attracted deer and other game. The Indian tribes that summered in the high mountains may have maintained the clearing through controlled burns—creating a hunting ground. Later, when white settlers began grazing cattle in the meadow, it was enlarged, often through a process called deadening, where trees are killed, or deadened, by gashing their bark throughout the circumference. Deadened trees would be leafless but remain standing. The meadow, at one time much larger than it is now, was a patchwork of pasture and gardens. Just before the creation of the park in 1937, the chestnut blight devastated the massive trees surrounding the meadow, making it even larger. For some time after the blight, the meadow offered a haunting view of dead, leafless giants, left standing. Today, the meadow measures only about 300 acres; it's kept open by the National Park Service for historic interpretation. Gradually, however, the wetlands created by the meadow are drying up as the woodlands recover.

BIG NIAGARA FALLS ME

An endearing allusion to the real thing.

BIG STAMP GAP GA
BIG STAMP GAP NC

After a summer of grazing in the summits, cows were herded into the grassy mountain gaps in anticipation of descent. These bovine gatherings were often called "stamps."

BIG WALKER MOUNTAIN VA

Named for colonial-era physician and explorer Dr. Thomas Walker, of Albermarle County, who built a home called Castle Hill near Charlottesville in 1764. The house still stands today.

BILLY'S VIEW CT
Another AT name bestowed by trail activist and guidebook author Norman Sills. Billy Forsyth is the son of the family that owned this property. As a teenager in the 1960s, Billy cleared this site to camp and enjoy the solitude. The family had originally referred to the place as Billy's Campsite, but the name was changed so as not to attract hordes of campers. "Billy's View" is an appropriate name; the site offers splendid prospect on Salmon Kill valley from Wetauwanchu Mountain.

BINGHAM ME
When ferry service is unavailable, it becomes part of the AT experience for hikers to travel the 16 miles south on U.S. Route 201 to cross the Kennebec River. The town is named for William Bingham, who was once the owner of vast holdings in the state of ME.

BLACK CAT MOUNTAIN ME
Visible from Old Blue, it is named for the local term for a fisher.

BLACK GUM GAP NC
Northerners might mistake the name for a sweet licorice treat, but the black gum is a tree common in this part of the South.

BLACK HORSE GAP VA
Named for the Black Horse Tavern, which once stood on the east side of the gap.

BLACK MOUNTAIN NY
The dark lichen growing on exposed rock gives the mountain its name, as it does other features named "black" along the AT. Black Mountain was the subject of a real estate ruse back in 1735, when Spanish explorers arrived by ship and went to the mountain in search of silver. They left the area bearing heavy sacks, claiming they had discovered the precious metal. For years afterward, locals searched the mountain for a silver mine but found only iron ore.

BLACK MOUNTAINS NC
The dense cover of deep green spruce and fir gives these ridges their name.

BLACK ROCK MD
By the time Jacob D. Wolf, whose family gave its name to nearby Wolfsville, had opened the Black Rock Hotel here in the mid-19th century, the name Black Rock was already in currency. The hotel prospered until it burnt in 1880. Shortly afterward, Wolf's wife and daughter died. Despondent, Wolf moved to NY, where he grew wealthy marketing a formula for tapeworm medicine. In 1907, he returned to Wolfsville and rebuilt the hotel. It was considered fine accommodations, but was too remote to prosper once again. It fell into disrepair, then was destroyed by arson in the 1920s. *See* Wolfsville Road, MD.

BLACKBURN TRAIL CENTER VA
Named for Fred and Ruth Blackburn, members of the Potomac AT Club from its earliest days. Both Fred and Ruth served as club president (Fred, 1951–54; Ruth, 1965–67) and were involved in club activities for more than 50 years.

BLACKINTON MA
Sanford Blackinton began manufacturing woolen goods in the area in 1821. In 1893, the family business became the Blackinton Company.

BLACKROCK GAP
BLACKROCK HUT VA
The name probably was chosen because of the lichen-covered rocks found here. The hut was built in 1941 by the Civilian Conservation Corps.

BLACKSTACK CLIFFS NC/TN

Also known as Blackstaff Cliffs, although they are actually composed of white quartzite. The cliffs, like their counterparts in VA, appear black from a distance because of their lichen covering.

BLAIRSTOWN NJ

Named for financier John I. Blair. The town was originally named Smith Mills in 1796, then Gravel Hill in 1828. It was renamed in 1836 for Blair, who opened a general store here at age 13 and went on to make millions running railroads.

BLAND VA

First called Crab Orchard Creek, then Seddon, for James Seddon, a member of Congress who later served as secretary of war for the Confederacy. It became Bland in 1861 in honor of Richard Bland, a member of the Continental Congress and leader of the state's resistance to Great Britain in the years before the Revolutionary War.

BLOOD MOUNTAIN GA

The reddish tint of the local lichen may give the mountain its name, but the Indian folklore is more colorful. Legends describe a terrible battle between Cherokee and Creek Indians, during which the mountain ran red with blood. A Cherokee legend tells of the *Yunwee Chuns Dee* (little folk) who dwelled in caves and made "magic music" heard on the mountain. Also living in the vicinity were the *Nunnehee,* an invisible race of normal-size people "who always aided those lost or injured in the mountains," watching over the Cherokee like guardian angels.

BLOODY BROOK VT

There are two stories about this name. In 1824, Zadock Thompson wrote in the *Gazetteer of Vermont* that the name commemorates a bloody battle fought here during the French and Indian War. Sixty years later, a local historian wrote that the stream was named for someone named Blood, who once lived along it.

BLUE MOUNTAINS PA

As with the Blue Ridge Mountains, the name comes from the blue haze that surrounds the slopes, a phenomenon caused by a combination of soil and vegetation types and climatic conditions, including moisture and wind draft. The Blue Mountains were home to the Wolf Indians, a tribe of the Leni-Lenape Federation, and were once known as *Wisquick Mellatin Kitaspaschi,* or "source of 10,000 springs." *See* Blue Ridge Mountains, GA to VA.

BLUE RIDGE CANAL VA

Over two years, beginning in 1827, the 7-mile Blue Ridge Canal was built to skirt the Balcony Falls Rapids. It was engineered by Col. Claudius Crozet, who also built the famous railroad tunnel under Rockfish Gap in 1854 (and crossed the Alps with Napoleon). The canal ran along the north side of the river, where the AT crosses. In 1841, it was removed with the intention of enlarging it, but new construction did not begin until 1847. For six years, boats on the James River were forced to run the Balcony Falls; many vessels and lives were lost. In 1870, the community of Wayland Crossing, east of the AT, was renamed Crozet.

BLUE RIDGE MOUNTAINS GA TO VA

Named for the bluish haze that hangs over the mountains. The range was first called the Blue Ledge by early visitors. The Blue Ridge Mountains extend from GA to southern PA. In the South, they are a jumbled collection of peaks, sags, and valleys. In the North, the range narrows to two narrow ridgelines through Loudoun County, VA. *See* Blue Mountains, PA.

BLUE RIDGE SWAG GA
"Swag" is a local term for sag, a low saddle ridge.

BLUEMONT VA
Its original name was Snickersville, after Edward Snicker, who sometime before 1764 operated a ferry across the Shenandoah near here. In 1900, town boosters changed the name to Bluemont, thinking it would appeal to tourists. Bluemont was the starting point for many outings sponsored by the Potomac AT Club in the 1930s because the train from Alexandria terminated here.

BLUFF MOUNTAIN VA
In the 1800s, it was also known as Thunder Hill. At one time it might have been a cleared, open bald used for grazing. Unlike today's common meaning of "bluff" as steep and rocky, common usage of the word in the 19th century referred to a high, open, broad, and flat landscape.

BLUFF TRAIL VA
"The Bluff" was the local name for Mt. Marshall, with its steep, rocky, south-facing ledges. The Bluff Trail is listed in early guides as a way to avoid the steep climb over Mt. Marshall. AT history buffs are intrigued that this trail predates the AT but was not chosen as its route up Marshall. Some believe this is an indication of the intent of early trail builders to keep the AT atop the crestline. We can't overlook the fact that AT buffs would choose a mountain named for a chief justice of the Supreme Court over which to hold an argument about intent.

BOARSTONE MOUNTAIN ME
Philip Rutherford's *Dictionary of Maine Place-Names* and the 1936 edition of the *Maine AT Guide* differ on the origin of the name, but each reflects a common occurrence in name creation—visual association and transformation from an Indian language. Rutherford reports that the mountain's name comes from its resemblance to a boar's testicles. To city slickers and suburbanites hiking the trail, this might not conjure a definitive image, but it must have meant something to early settlers. According to the early AT guide, however, the name was an anglicization of an Indian word, the origin of which is lost. The first published reference to Boarstone occurs in 1839, when geologist C. T. Jackson noted it in his "Report on Maine Geology." Borr Mountain appears on several early maps, as does Elliotsville Mountain, associating the peak with the nearby town. Boarstone first appeared on a published map in 1883.

BOBBLETS GAP SHELTER VA
A farmer named Will Bobblet once lived here. The shelter was built by the U.S. Forest Service in 1961.

BODFISH FARM ME
The name supposedly comes from Nymphus Bodfish, who settled here in 1823, cleared the valley, and built a road.

BOILING SPRINGS PA
Named for the springs that bubble up, or boil, from the porous limestone underlying nearby Children's Lake. With a flow of about 24,000 gallons a day, these springs are among the largest in the state.

BONDCLIFF TRAIL NH
The name was transferred from Mt. Bond, which was named for professor G. P. Bond of Harvard, an early explorer here.

BOONESBORO MOUNTAIN ROAD MD
In 1774, William and George Boone, who are said to have been relations of Daniel Boone, settled in the area surrounding what is now Boonesboro. The town was officially named with the opening of its post

Edward Talone

Erected in 1827, the George Washington Monument on South Mountain, east of Boonesboro, MD, was the first monument built to honor Amercia's first president.

office in 1801. Lots were laid out in 1829. The road was for many years known as Wolfsville Road, but with the introduction of the 911 emergency telephone system, a name change was needed to differentiate it from another Wolfsville Road. The change was precipitated when a dispatcher sent fire trucks to the wrong location.

BOOTENS GAP VA
John Booten was an early settler in the area.

BOTE MOUNTAIN TRAIL TN
When a road was to be built from Cades Cove in TN across the Smokies to Tuckasegee, the route was determined by the builders, many of whom were Cherokee Indians who were asked to vote on the road's location. It's rough terrain here, so there was much deliberation over the vote. Because there is no *v* sound in their language, the Cherokees referred to the routing process as taking the "bote." The route chosen, and then the peak, became known as Bote. The losing route was christened Defeat Ridge.

BOULEVARD TRAIL NC
A nearly level sag between Mt. LeConte and the main crest, which carries the AT. Before this trail was cut to provide access to the AT from LeConte, the pass was named for its "avenue terrain."

BOUSQUET SKI AREA MA
Located on Yokum Seat Mountain, the property for this ski area belonged to Clarence J. Bousquet, who allowed the Mt. Greylock Ski Club to use and clear his property for skiing.

BRADLEY FORK NC/TN
Jack Bradley's family settled this tributary of the Oconaluftee River, as well as a portion of its main stem.

BRAGG HILL ROAD VT
Named for a Norwich family named Bragg.

BRANCH POND TRAIL VT
This former AT route, which now is an intersecting side trail, takes its name from Roaring Branch Brook.

BRANCHVILLE NJ
The town derives its name from its location on the main branch of the Paulins Kill. It was laid out by surveyors as an 8-sided polygon to resemble an Indian arrowhead.

BRASSTOWN BALD GA
The Cherokee phrase *Itse'yi* means "town of the green valley" or "place made green with vegetation." The word was confused with the Cherokee word *Untsai'yi,* which

means "brass." In a Cherokee legend reminiscent of the story of Noah, a great flood killed everyone on earth except the few who landed atop this peak in a big canoe. The Great Spirit cleared the summit of trees so the survivors could plant crops until the flood waters subsided.

BREADLOAF MOUNTAIN CT
The view of the mountain from the east inspires the name. But, as with many names, the visual association is in the eye of the beholder. One might ask, for example, does this mountain resemble a baguette or a bialy?

BREAKNECK HILL VT
This is a very steep hill.

BREAKNECK RIDGE NY
Breakneck Ridge is the north portal of the Hudson Highlands (1,220 feet). It was formerly known as "Broken Neck Hill," attributed by some to its jagged cliffs. But a story that ties the name to adjacent Bull Hill is livelier and just as credible. Apparently, a wild bull once roamed the area, trampling crops and creating general havoc among the locals. Farmers with pitchforks chased the bull over what is now Bull Hill and up the ridge, where it fell and sustained the broken neck that killed it.

BRINK ROAD SHELTER NJ
This shelter, originally built in 1933 and rebuilt in 1970, takes its name from a nearby road formerly known as Old Wallpack Road. The new name is descriptive; the road follows the "brink" of the Hudson Highlands.

BROMLEY MOUNTAIN VT
The name was transferred from the town of Bromley, once named Brumley, now known as Peru. There seems to be no Bromley for which the town or the mountain was named. It's thought to be named after a borough south of London, England. *See* Peru, VT.

BROWN MOUNTAIN CREEK VALLEY VA
No one is sure who Brown was, but the valley where the trail passes was bought by a freed slave in 1868. He proceeded to build cabins, which he rented to former slaves who share-cropped the land until 1918. There is no record of the community's name, perhaps because the white establishment outside the valley thought a black community unworthy of documentation. Old stone walls and house foundations still offer evidence of the place. The Brown Mountain Creek shelter was built by the U.S. Forest Service in 1961.

BROWNS GAP VA
Named for Benjamin Brown, whose family owned several plantations in this part of Shenandoah, NP. The west side of the gap was once called "Madisons Gap" after a local family that settled here before 1749. James Madison, the first Episcopal minister in VA, was born here. Brown's Pike was built through the gap in 1805 by Brightberry Brown and William Jarman.

BROWNSVILLE GAP MD
Tobias Brown was one of the first settlers in Washington County. He owned land from the area now known as Gapland to what became Brownsville, which obtained its name when the post office was assigned in 1833. G. T. Brown served as the town's first postmaster. Both Union and Confederate troops used the Brownsville Gap Road during the Civil War. Union general George McClellan, who would challenge Abraham Lincoln in the 1864 election, rested in Brownsville after his failure at the Battle of Antietam (known in the South as the Battle of Sharpsburg). The road is impassable by car but can be

used by hikers to walk down the west side of South Mountain to MD Route 67.

BRUSHY MOUNTAIN VA

The AT follows this ridge along the Smith-Tazewell county line. It is named for the brushy growth on its south side. Many hikers consider this stretch the most annoying on the trail.

BRYANT RIDGE SHELTER VA

Named for the Bryant family, which lived nearby. The shelter was built in 1992 as a memorial to Nelson Garnett, a Catholic University architecture student. The structure was designed by fellow architecture students and built with funds provided by Garnett's family.

BUCHANAN VA

Originally known as Pattonsburg, after Col. James Patton, an early explorer. Later named for John Buchanan, Patton's son-in-law, a local surveyor. *See* Burkes Garden, VA.

BUCHANAN MOUNTAIN NY

Believed to be named for George Briggs Buchanan, born in 1875 in Haverstraw. An executive with the Corn Products Company, makers of Karo Syrup, Buchanan purchased an estate on Cheescoke Mountain. He named his estate Orak, Karo spelled backward.

BUCK HILL ME

Named for the Buck families that settled here sometime before 1880.

BUCKEYE GAP NC/TN

For settlers, it was the abundance of yellow buckeye trees that inspired the name. The Cherokee name is much more colorful, if baffling. They called it *Walasiyi,* or "frog place." Legend says that after the Cherokee captured the magician Shawano during battle, he convinced them to spare his life in return for the capture of *Uktena,* the evil serpent. When the Cherokee and their prisoner entered the gap, they encountered a giant frog, which terrified the captors. Shawano got a big laugh out of their terror. The meaning of the parable is lost.

BUCKLIN TRAIL VT

Probably named for the Bucklin family that lived in the Killington area.

BUENA VISTA VA

The name is Spanish for "beautiful view." It comes from a furnace that supplied cannonballs for the Battle of Buena Vista near Monterrey, Mexico, in February 1847. Because the furnace commenced operation at about the same time the battle occurred, people began referring to it as the Old Buena Vista Furnace. It operated until 1864, when it was destroyed by Union forces. The town of Buena Vista was founded in 1892, but there was disagreement over what the name should be: Buena Vista or Green Forest. Although many people preferred the latter, a land company had already begun selling lots under the name Buena Vista, so founders agreed to it. Present-day locals pronounce the name "bu-no" vista.

BULLS BRIDGE ROAD CT

The road derives its name from both the bridge and village of the same name. The first Bulls Bridge was built in 1777 by William Johnson and David Lewis, who were authorized by the general assembly to charge a toll. The name comes from the Bull family, which had an iron furnace, gristmill, and sawmill nearby. Jacob Bull built an inn at the foot of the bridge. A Quaker, Bull refused to serve in the Revolutionary War and was taken to court for high treason because people thought he harbored deserters and loyalists at his inn. He was released from jail in 1778.

Sketchy details survive of an incident on the bridge involving Gen. George Washington, who is said to have crossed it several times. There is disagreement over whether it was Washington's horse or wagon, or the future president himself, who went over the edge and into the water. Whatever the details, apparently the cost to remove the general or his charges from the river was $215. The second bridge there, a covered bridge, was built in 1842. The village, in Kent Township, had an iron furnace that became known as the Monitor Iron Works during the Civil War because iron made there was used in the construction of ironclad vessels, including the first one, the *Monitor.*

BUNKER HILL VT
When veterans of the Revolutionary War received land grants here, it became known as Bunker Hill in memory of the famed Boston battle.

BURKES GARDEN VA
A long highland valley that was a hunting ground for the Cherokee and Shawnee, it is named for James Burke. The legend surrounding its name concerns a hunting trip in which Burke is said to have led British colonel James Patton there to hunt. According to the story, Burke killed a bear, and while it was roasting, he dug up the potatoes he had planted the previous year. Col. Patton, enjoying the effects of good food and liquor, bestowed the name.

BURNINGTOWN GAP NC
When Gen. Griffith Ruthered ordered the burning of thirty-six Cherokee towns, the Indians had to retreat to the mountains and watch their burning towns from above.

BUTTERFLY MEADOW NY
One of the many place names bestowed by AT hikers and activists. Apparently, John Yrizarry wandered into the 4-acre clearing on a summer morning in 1992. He identified twenty-five butterfly species here; the field is now kept clear for butterfly habitat. *See* Kloiber's Pond, NY.

BUTTERMILK FALLS NJ
Said to be named because of the churning action created by the falls and the creamy consistency of the foam in the pool.

BUTTON HILL VA
The former site of a garment factory dump, buttons are still found in the area.

BUZZARD KNOB MD
Turkey vultures, also known as buzzards, still continually circle above the rocks.

BYRD'S NEST SHELTERS VA
Four of these exist in Shenandoah NP, three on or near the AT. They were built between 1961–65 with federal funds secured by the late Sen. Harry Flood Byrd of VA, one of the principal congressional boosters of park legislation. They were closed a decade later to remove squatters who had taken up residence there.

BYRON REECE MEMORIAL GA
Byron Herbert Reece was a poet from Union County who farmed near Cloestoe. The footpath, constructed by the GA AT Club, provides access to the AT at Neels Gap.

C

CAESAR BROOK CAMPSITE
CEASAR ROAD CT
An old name in this region indeed, but not nearly so ancient as the Caesar betrayed by Brutus. There are Caesars, sometimes spelled Caeser, to this day on mailboxes all over Sharon. Caesar Road crossed the Housatonic River via Young's Bridge in the 18th century.

CALEB'S PEAK CT
Named for 18th-century farmer Caleb Barton, whose farm was located on Skiff Mountain.

CALEDONIA STATE PARK PA
Named for the iron furnace built here in 1837. During the Civil War, it was operated by Thaddeus Stevens, a congressman from PA who would later lead impeachment proceedings against President Andrew Johnson. The furnace was destroyed in 1863 during a Confederate raid led by Gen. Jubal Early. Stevens was so embittered by this act that he drafted Reconstruction-era legislation against Southern power brokers. Stevens was born in Caledonia, VT, and gave the area its name.

CALF MOUNTAIN SHELTER VA
Summer grazing contracts with valley people created a thriving industry here. The mountain's name was likely conjured as a way of marketing the mountain to cattle owners. The shelter was built by the Potomac Appalachian Mountain Club around 1985. Most of it was constructed from chestnut timbers from the Old Shaver Hollow Lean-to, which was removed from the Central District of Shenandoah NP in 1973.

CAMEL GAP NC/TN
Unlike other features named for their resemblance to a hump, this one may be a corruption of Campbell, a family that lived in the area.

CAMP MICHAUX PA
The site of a former Civilian Conservation Corps camp used as a prisoner of war camp for German submarine personnel during World War II. *See* Michaux State Forest, PA.

CAMP SMITH TRAIL NY
Camp Smith, once called Camp of Instruction, was formerly a training ground for the NY Division of Military and Naval Affairs. It was renamed in honor of NY governor Alfred E. Smith.

CAMPBELL SHELTER VA
Tom Campbell was a longtime Roanoke AT Club member who was involved in trail development in the 1930s; he remained active in the club for more than three decades.

CANAAN MOUNTAIN CT
The name comes from Canaan Township, so named in a 1750s marketing strategy to lure new settlers. The biblical Canaan was the land of milk and honey, the promised land. Earlier maps referred to it as Town C.

CANADA HILL NY
Some say it is named for the Canada Mine in Fahnestock State Park, but it's really not that close to the mine. Even so, no one really knows how Canada Mine got its name, either.

CANEBRAKE RIDGE NC/TN
The cane referred to is switch cane (*Arundinaria tecta*), a native bamboo plant once used by farmers as winter forage for

hogs. The cane grows in rich soil near streams here, to the surprise of many, who think of it as an exotic plant.

CANNON MOUNTAIN/PROFILE MOUNTAIN NH

Named Cannon Mountain because of an oblong rock near the summit. The knobs south of the mountain along Kinsman Ridge are known as "cannonballs." The peak is better known as Profile Mountain; near the ridge a profile in rock known as "The Old Man of the Mountain" can clearly be seen. Francis Whitcomb and Luke Brooks, who in 1805 were working on the Franconia Notch Road, tell of the rock profile. By the early 20th century, the Old Man needed a facelift. Today, he's held together by rods, turnbuckles, and epoxy.

CANOPUS HILL NY

Canopus is the name of an Indian chief, as well as the name of his village, which was part of the Nochpeem, a tribe of the Wappinger confederacy located on the east side of the Hudson River. There is record of contact between the Nochpeem and Dutch settlers as early as the 1660s.

CANUTE PLACE TN

Named for an early family that settled here.

CARATUNK ME

Abenaki for "forbidding or crooked stream."

CARL A. NEWHALL LEAN-TO ME

Named for a longtime ME AT Club volunteer who helped build six AT shelters in the state.

CARLISLE PA

Founded in 1751, it is named for Carlisle, England.

CARLS RIDGE PA

Visible east of the AT, this ridge was the route of the AT in the 1970s. It is named for George Carls, who owned 350 acres here.

CARRABASSETT RIVER CARRABASSETT VALLEY ME

Visible from the AT on Little Bigelow, Carrabassett is Abenaki for "small moose place."

CARRIAGE ROAD NH

Built by the Mt. Mooselauke Road Company in the 1840s to allow tourist carriages to reach the Tip-Top House Lodge on the summit of Mooselauke.

CARRY PONDS (EAST, MIDDLE, AND WEST) ME

This is a series of ponds not connected by navigable streams—so canoes and supplies had to be carried from one pond to the next.

CARRYING PLACE STREAM ME

A "carrying place" is where canoes and supplies have to be carried across land from one body of water to another. This name specifically refers to "The Great Carrying Place," the portage between the Kennebec and Dead rivers. The 1792 Bingham Purchase Map tells us that "Great Carrying Place" refers to the "Great Bend of Dead River."

CARSE BROOK CT

David B. Carse lived along the stream and operated a forge there in the early 20th century. The place had been called Forge Brook for the forge run by the two Hutchinson brothers here, who also gave their name to the area near the forge, Hutchinson's Hollow.

Edward Talone

A hiker of the Lynchburg AT Club visits with a Canada jay in the White Mountains of NH.

CARTER MOUNTAIN NH
There are a few stories about the origin of this name. The two most common say that Carter was a hunter who worked this mountain. In one, he is a lone woodsman; in the other, he plies his trade with a companion named Hight. When they become separated, they climb adjoining mountains to look for each other, giving each mountain their respective names. Another story says that the mountain was named for Dr. Ezra Carter, a physician from Concord, NH, who searched this area for herbs and roots. *See* Mt. Hight, NH.

CASH HOLLOW VA
May have been named for Howard Cash, who surveyed here in the 1700s.

CASTLE RAVINE NH
Probably derived from "Castellated Ridge," named for the rocks that resemble the ruins of castles.

CAT ROCKS NY
Like several other similarly named places along the Appalachian chain, this refers to the various species of wild cats, including bobcats and mountain lions, that roamed the hills. (Mountain lions are also called cougars, pumas, catamounts, painters, and panthers.) Both species would have once lived on Peters Mountain Ridge when the area was being settled. Only bobcats remain in the area today—although people regularly report to authorities that they have seen mountain lions, their presence is speculative.

CATAWBA
CATAWBA CREEK
CATAWBA MOUNTAIN SHELTER VA
The Catawba were an Indian people primarily associated with the western Carolinas. Their name is thought to derive from *kataba,* a Choctaw word for "separated" or "cut off," given to the Catawba because steep terrain isolated their territory. They made a wine beverage, called *catawba,* from a native grape similar in appearance to a variety of rhododendron now known as Catawba. The plant is abundant on this mountain.

The shelter was constructed in 1984 by the AT Conference.

CATSKILL MOUNTAINS NY
The Dutch called the mountains *Katsbergs,* owing to the presence of mountain lions. The name Catskill originally identified a creek flowing from the hills, called Katerskills. Its translation from the Dutch is "tomcats' creek."

CAUGHNAWAGA SHELTER VT
Thought to be a made-up moniker bestowed in 1931 by the shelter's builders, who also built Camp Najerog—another manufactured name.

CAVETOWN MD
This small town visible from Catoctin Mountain is named for a quarry cave dating to 1748. The cave's size was truly a wonder—500 feet long, with a lake large

enough for a boat at one end. The cave had a capacity of about a thousand people; for a time it was used as a beer garden, and paid tours were given. Unfortunately, early in the 20th century, mining activity caused the cave to collapse. Today, only a small section remains, closed for safety reasons.

CENTENNIAL TRAIL NH

Constructed in 1976, the 100th year of the Appalachian Mountain Club.

CENTER POINT KNOB PA

The AT was routed here, December 8, 1935, to mark the midpoint of the trail.

CERES VA

Named in 1879 for the goddess of agriculture, but its namer is unknown.

CHAMBERSBURG PA

Named for Benjamin Chambers, who settled here in 1730.

CHAPMAN ROAD NY

This road once connected to the Old Albany Post Road. James Chapman lived at one end (reportedly in the early 19th century), so it became known locally as the road out to Chapman's place, or Chapman Road.

CHARLES TOWN WV

Identifiable from the AT by the glow of its lights, it is named for George Washington's brother Charles.

CHARLIES BUNION NC/TN

This rock sticks out from the surrounding ridge—like a bunion. It was named by famed naturalist and author Horace Kephart for his hiking companion Charlie Conner, who is said to have described this feature as "about the size of this bunion on my foot." Another story tells of Conner resting here to soothe an aching foot while he and Kephart were on a reconnaissance mission to inspect fire and storm damage in the Smokies.

CHATEAUGUAY ROAD VT

Spelled Chateaugay by locals, it is a Natick Indian word that means "swift or principal stream."

CHATFIELD SHELTER VA

Louise Chatfield was a conservationist from NC who helped organize the Piedmont AT Club in 1965. The former Glade Mountain Shelter was renamed for her in 1986, just before she died.

CHATTAHOOCHEE GAP
CHATTAHOOCHEE NATIONAL FOREST GA

One translation claims the word is Cherokee for "corn rock" or "flour rock." Another has *chatta* meaning "sparkling or flowered" and *ochee* meaning "rocks." The river is named for the Cherokee town once located there. The spring here is considered the source of the river. In 1932, a group of GA AT Club hikers determined that the spring was the "highest and most northerly stream source of the Chattahoochee."

CHATUGE LAKE NC

The Cherokee word for "meeting of the waters" was given when the Tennessee Valley Authority created the lake by damming the confluence of Shooting Creek and the Hiwassee River.

CHEOAH BALD NC

This bald was created by the forest service to improve the view and provide grazing for wildlife. Cheoah is the Americanized spelling of *tsiyah,* Cherokee for "otter"—presumably for the presence of the creatures in the creek below. Both the bald and the stream are known locally as Beech Creek.

Bill O'Brien

Much of the landscape surrounding the AT was formerly inhabited. The remains of this old house were found near the AT in the Chattahoochee National Forest.

CHEROKEE NATIONAL FOREST TN

Cherokee is thought to be either a Choctaw word meaning "cave people" or a Creek word meaning "people of different speech." The Cherokee actually called themselves *Yunwiya,* a word of lost origin. The land encompassing the national forest was purchased from timber companies after they stripped it and left its slopes to erode. The forest was established in 1912, when foresters began to assemble parcels from VA, NC, GA, and TN. In 1920, it was formally dedicated as Unaka National Forest; the name was changed to Cherokee in 1936. Today the forest encompasses some 630,000 acres.

CHESAPEAKE & OHIO CANAL MD

George Washington had the idea of transporting goods via the Chesapeake Bay and Potomac River to the Ohio River when he founded the Patowmack Company to build a canal alongside the Potomac. His attempt stalled, but President John Quincy Adams turned the first shovelful of dirt to start another attempt to link east and west in 1828. Completed in 1850, the canal navigated a 605-foot rise with seventy-four locks between Georgetown in Washington DC and Cumberland, MD. Boats on the canal averaged 4 miles per hour, pulled by mules. The vessels were only 8 feet wide but as long as 224 feet.

The canal was barely opened before a railroad connected Baltimore and Pittsburgh. This competition, along with perpetual flooding, closed the C&O in 1924. Politicians in the mid-20th century proposed using the canal's tow path for an automobile parkway, but advocates pushed for designation as a historic landmark. In 1954, Supreme Court Justice William O. Douglas called the editors of Washington newspapers and challenged them to join him on a walk of the canal's entire 184 miles. The attention the walk brought created the momentum that led to the authorization of the canal as a national historical park, in 1971.

CHESHIRE MA

Originally settled in 1766 by Rhode Islanders, this town was for a time called New Providence. After it was chartered in 1793, it was renamed for Cheshire, England. One of the more famous town exports was a 1,235-pound round of cheese, sent to President Thomas Jefferson at the White House, on New Year's Day, 1802. The Cheshire Mammoth Cheese was the idea of John Leland, a MA native who had lived for a time in VA and become acquainted with the future president. Leland later settled in Cheshire.

On July 20, 1801, curds were collected from every local cow. By December, the barrel-shaped cheese was on its way, first transported by sled to the Hudson River, then by boat to New York City, and then on to Washington DC. The gift was a political act: in the accompanying note, the people of Cheshire wrote, "the cheese was procured by the personal labor of freeborn farmers with the voluntary and cheerful aid of their wives and daughters, without the assistance of a single slave." Jefferson skirted this issue in his acknowledgment, saying the cheese "presents an extraordinary proof of the skill with which those domestic arts, which contribute so much to our daily comfort, are practiced by [the citizens of Cheshire]."

CHESHIRE HARBOR TRAIL MA

This area near Cheshire, MA, was once a safe haven, or harbor, for runaway slaves.

CHESTER GAP VA

In 1736, a man named Chester began operating a ferry on the Shenandoah River at Riverton. Nothing else is known about him.

CHESTNUT BALD NC/TN

Named for the American chestnut, once the dominant tree species in the Appalachians, destroyed by blight in the 1920s.

CHESTNUT BRANCH TRAIL NC/TN

According to a 1937 oral history survey, a local woman named Zilphie Sutton claimed that Chestnut Branch was a name invented by the National Park Service when the park was created. According to her, both the creek now called Chestnut Branch and Mt. Cammerer were called "Old Mother" until the establishment of the park. Within a couple of years of the name change, the entire eastern chestnut forest was wiped out by blight.

CHINQUAPIN HILL PA

Located near Quarry Gap, it is named for the chinquapin tree, a brushlike member of the beech family. The word is probably a Delaware Algonquian phrase meaning "big nut."

CHOGGAM BROOK CT

Thought to be derived from the name of an Indian who hunted there.

CHUNKY GAL MOUNTAIN
CHUNKY GAL TRAIL NC

One legend tells of a chubby Cherokee maiden who left her family to be with her lover of another tribe. Other researchers say a more likely origin is that Chunky Gal is the anglicized form of an unknown Cherokee word.

CHURCH POND ME

Named for J. H. Church, superintendent of schools in Shirley Township in 1905.

CITY STREAM VT

The stream flows in the town of Woodford. In the hopes of attracting settlers, locals began calling the place Woodford City after one resident urged townspeople to actively promote an evocative name for the town. Reportedly, he quoted the Bible, saying that "a city that is set on a hill cannot be hid." Although the population of Woodford never boomed, and "City" was dropped from the town's name, the stream running through it still carries the moniker.

CLARENDON GORGE BRIDGE VT
Transferred from the town of Clarendon; the bridge is dedicated to 17-year-old hiker Robert Brugmann, who drowned on Independence Day 1973 while trying to cross the stream after the bridge had been washed out by a flood.

CLARENDON SHELTER VT
The Green Mountain Club built this shelter in 1952 and named it for the nearby town. *See* Clarendon Gorge Bridge, VT.

CLARKS FERRY BRIDGE PA
Clark's Ferry was operated by Daniel Clark during the 1780s about 1 mile south of the bridge. This is the sixth bridge that has spanned the Susquehanna River here. The first bridge was constructed in 1827–28 by the PA Canal Commission as an aqueduct. It was the first of five spectacular wooden covered bridges that carried the canal until 1913. The current bridge was built in 1925.

CLARKSBURG STATE FOREST MA
Borrowed from nearby Clarksburg, whose first settler, Seth Hudson, lent his last name as the original name of the town. In 1769, Nicholas Clark moved into the area; more Clarks followed, eventually leading to the name change. In 1956, the state purchased land here for the state park.

CLEARWATER BROOK TRAIL ME
Formerly part of the AT, the stream for which the trail is named was known locally as Black Brook because of its dark color—a far cry from "Clearwater."

CLINCH MOUNTAINS VA
Two origin stories have been uncovered, but neither seems very credible. In one, a hunter named Clinch is the first settler to explore here. In another, a local Irishman falls from a mountain ledge, breaking bones, and is heard to cry "clinch me!" A more likely source of the name is the appearance of the summits, which seem bent—or clinched—like the tips of nails protruding through wood.

CLINGMANS DOME NC/TN
Called *Kuwa-hi,* or "mulberry place," by the Cherokee, it was said to be the place where bears danced before their hibernation. Settlers called it Smoky Dome. Thomas Lanier Clingman, a former student of Elisha Mitchell, led the party that measured the dome's height in 1858. Clingman would later become a Confederate general and senator from NC. Some blame the untimely death of Mitchell on Clingman. He disputed Mitchell's claim that the mountain which would be named Mitchell was the highest east of the Mississippi. After a public row, the elderly Mitchell returned to the wilds alone to measure his peak; he was found dead on the mountain some time later. *See* Mt. Mitchell, NC.

CLOUD POND LEAN-TO ME
The pond's elevation high in the mountain places it "in the clouds." The original lean-to, built by the ME AT Club in the late 1950s, was notable as one of the last dirt-floor lean-tos on the AT. The new lean-to was built in 1992, also by the ME club.

CLOUDLAND HOTEL (REMAINS) NC/TN
Built in 1885 at the top of Roan Mountain (6,367 feet) by Gen. John Wilder, the hotel was the pinnacle of luxury. Local cherry and maple were used for furniture and paneling. Guests enjoyed golfing, bowling, tennis, horses, and ballroom dancing. The

dining room straddled the NC–TN state line; guests who wanted to drink alcohol sat on the TN side because NC was a dry state at the time. Oddly, the hotel contained only one commode for 250 guest rooms, although each room had its own copper bathtub. Building such a hotel at this altitude today would be considered an ecological disaster.

CLYDE SMITH SHELTER NC/TN
Named for the first national park ranger in Cades Cove, within the Great Smoky Mountains NP.

COG RAILWAY NH
This engineering wonder began operating in 1869, running from the town of Carroll to the summit of Mt. Washington, a distance of 3 miles. It was built by Sylvester Marsh, who adopted the cog system invented by Herrick and Walter Aiken of Franklin. Instead of rails, the cog railway uses a series of slots into which gears, or teeth, fit. At one time called "Jacobs Ladder," the grade reaches 37.4 percent, the steepest railway grade in the world.

COHUTTA MOUNTAIN GA
The name is thought to be derived from the Cherokee word for "frog." Cohutta Mountain was one of the early choices for the southern terminus of the AT.

COLD MOUNTAIN VA
Named Cole Mountain on early U.S. Geological Survey maps when map-makers misunderstood the local dialect, it is thought to have been named for the long duration of its snowy season.

COLD RIVER ROAD VT
The name is transferred from the former name of a nearby settlement, once called Coldriver, which in turn took its name from its proximity to the Cold River. Because of Vermonters' accent, many visitors mistook the name as "Coal Driver," so the town's name was changed. The river kept its name.

COLD SPRING KNOB NC/TN
Early maps noted a year-round water source here.

COLD SPRING SHELTER NC
The Civilian Conservation Corps built this shelter of American chestnut in the 1930s, making lasting use of the tree species that by then was doomed by disease.

COLLINS GAP NC/TN
Robert Collins (1806–63) was a toll keeper on the Oconaluftee Turnpike and guide for Arnold Guyot—a scientist and explorer of the entire Appalachian Mountain chain and a prolific place-namer.

COLUMBUS MOUNTAIN ME
Named for the Columbus Lumber Company, which operated on the southeast side of the mountain.

COMPTON GAP TRAIL VA
The route of the AT to Chester Gap (Route 55) until 1974. The gap is named for the Compton farm site, on which the Indian Run maintenance hut now stands.

V. Collins Chew

Early AT proponents connected the dots to create a trail any way they could, often following roads. This one in southwest VA took the notion to the extreme.

CONGDON SHELTER VT
Built by the Long Trail Patrol in 1967, the shelter was a gift from Stephen Congdon. The camp is named for Herbert Congdon, a Long Trail pioneer.

CONOCOCHEAGUE CREEK PA
The Algonquian pronounced it *GU-ne-uk-is-SHICK*, a close relative of the current *KAHN-oh-ko-CHEEG. Gu-ne* is thought to mean "long or lengthy," with the rest of the word meaning "a dull sound." Together, the meaning would be "a dull sound heard afar off," according to Hammel Kenny in his *Place Names of Maryland*. Whether it was the echo of thunder in the creek valley, the sound of boulders bounding in a flood, or any other sound in nature is unknown.

CONODOGUINET CREEK PA
A corruption of *Gunnipduckhannet*, an Indian word meaning "for a long way nothing but bends."

CONSTITUTION ISLAND NY
The patriotic name actually refers to the British Constitution. It was bestowed to recognize the 18th-century struggle to achieve a constitutional government for the colonies under the crown of England. A fort was built here by colonists in a 1775 effort to gain control of the Hudson River. In 1778, an iron chain was erected to span the river from Sterling Iron Works to West Point. Each link was 2 feet long and weighed roughly 150 pounds; the links were floated into the river on logs. A similar chain between Fort Montgomery and the eastern shore of the river was broken by the British. The Sterling one was not tested. The island was formerly known as Martelaer's Rock Island, for a French family that lived there.

CONTINENTAL ROAD NY
Built in 1779 by Continental troops.

COOLIDGE RANGE VT
Named for Calvin Coolidge, the 30th president and a native of Plymouth. Coolidge, the vice president in the Harding administration, became president at Harding's death. He was visiting his father in Plymouth when word of Harding's death reached him by telegraph in the middle of the night. Coolidge's father, a local justice of the peace, administered the oath of office by the light of a kerosene lamp.

COOPER LODGE VT
The cabin was built in 1939 by the VT Forest Service and named for Charles Cooper, former president of the Green Mountain Club.

COPPER RIDGE BALD NC
Named for a copper mine that once operated on the mountain.

CORNWALL BRIDGE CT
Taking its name from the town in southwestern England, the CT town of Cornwall was established in 1738. Mill and furnace operators were drawn here by the river's power and the presence of a ferry. Milk was the principal agricultural product shipped from the area. Upon the construction of the first span across the river here, the village became known as Lewis' Bridge, for a local resident who some say was the toll taker. A covered bridge spanned the river until it was destroyed by a flood in 1936.

COSBY KNOB SHELTER NC/TN
Smoky Mountains toponymist Allen R. Coggins presents two possibilities: it was named for Cocke County, TN, physician James Cosby or for frontier trapper John Cosby, a contemporary and companion of John English. *See* English Mountain, NC/TN.

COVE MOUNTAIN VA
Probably a descriptive name, given the character of the topography here, with so many deep recesses in the side of the mountain. It was formerly known as Luna Mountain, or Moon Mountain. But some maps of the early 1900s are said to refer to the northern section as Luna and the southern end as Boatland (thought to be a derivation of a German surname). Other maps refer to the entire mountain as Luna. The Cove Mountain Lean-to originally was the Marble Spring Shelter, built north of here in 1960. It was moved to its current site in 1980 after James River Face was designated as a wilderness. This is one of several Cove Mountains in VA; whether any are derived from a family name is not known.

COW CAMP GAP
COW CAMP GAP SHELTER VA
In the 19th century, cattle were taken to the denuded mountains in the higher elevations. In autumn, they were herded into the gap here for the return trip down the mountain to winter pasture or the market. The shelter was built in 1986 by the AT Conference's Konnarock Crew, which dismantled an old shelter called Wiggins Spring Lean-to and moved it to this site.

CRABTREE FALLS VA
Shown as Dwights Falls on an 1863 map, the name is transferred from Crabtree Meadows, which are named for a local family.

CRAG CAMP NH
Built in 1909 and probably named for the rocky outcrop from which it overlooks King Ravine. It was deeded to the Randolph Mountain Club in 1939.

Edward Talone

The Crampton Gap shelter near Gathland State Park, MD, was erected in 1942. The Civilian Conservation Corps is credited with constructing it, but it was actually left half finished in 1942. The Potomac AT Club finished the job in 1943.

CRAMPTON GAP MD
Thomas Crampton had a farm below the gap in Pleasant Valley. Born during his family's crossing of the Atlantic, he grew up in Prince George's County, where his family settled in 1735. Crampton moved to the Pleasant Valley frontier in pursuit of cheap land. He died in 1819.

CRAWFORD PATH NH
The first trail built to the summit of Mt. Washington, in 1819, by Abel and Ethan Allen Crawford. Later they established Crawford House, the first hotel in Crawford Notch. It burned in 1976. The famous Mt. Washington weather observatory, called Summit House, opened in 1870.

CROWN POINT MILITARY ROAD VT
This road from Charlestown, NH, to Crown Point, NY, was constructed in 1759.

CUBE MOUNTAIN NH
Historically called "Cuba" Mountain because the man living at its base had visited Cuba and bestowed the name on his farm. As has happened with countless place names in the Appalachians, its name was transformed by a map-maker's misspelling.

CUMBERLAND COUNTY TRAIL PA
CUMBERLAND VALLEY MD

Here the valley is also known as Antietam Valley, while southward it is both the Shenandoah Valley and the Valley of Virginia. It is known throughout its length as the Great Valley, which carves a path between mountain ranges from northern GA to VT. The name Cumberland is thought to derive from Cumberland County, PA, which was named in 1750 for the duke of Cumberland, who was the son of George I and a military hero in England at the time. The AT follows the route of the Cumberland County Trail in Pine Grove Furnace State Park, PA. Between 1864 and 1940, the South Mountain Railroad hauled iron ore along this corridor from nearby furnaces.

D

DAHLGREN CHAPEL MD

The chapel was built by Madeleine Dahlgren in 1881, after she bought the South Mountain Inn for use as a summer home. Dahlgren was the widow of Adm. John A. Dahlgren, who was commandant of the Washington Navy Yard during the Civil War and is credited with design improvements to the rifled cannon. She was also an author, best known for *South Mountain Magic*, a collection of ghost stories gathered from mountain people. Her stories are illustrative of a time when South Mountain was a veritable wilderness; they feature Indian ghosts who stalked children, a doglike demon known as "snarly yow," and a pale woman who signaled approaching death to those who saw her. Somewhat modern for her time, Dahlgren nonetheless opposed suffrage for women.

DAICEY POND
DAICEY POND CAMPGROUND ME

There are a number of lumber dams bearing the name Daicey, giving rise to the conjecture that Daicey owned a timber operation. Or perhaps he owned land nearby, coming to hunt at Daicey's Clearing. The cabins around Daicey Pond are the remnants of the Yorks Twin Pine Camp. The name derives from the massive white pines that frame the camp entrance. From the 1930s until the late 1950s, it was possible to walk the entire AT in ME staying at "sporting camps" each night. Today, only two camps remain near the trail. Yorks Twin Pine Camp was the site of the 1939 AT Conference.

DALTON MA

Incorporated in 1784 and named for Tristram Dalton (1738–1817), who at the time of incorporation was the speaker of the MA House of Representatives. He later became speaker of the U.S. House of Representatives, treasurer of the U.S. Mint, director of the Bank of the U.S., and a personal friend of George Washington, but there is no indication he ever visited his namesake or had any connection with the area.

Zenas Crane (1777–1845), founder of the Crane Paper Company, is a much more notable figure in the town's past. He came to Dalton from eastern MA, where he had learned the paper-making business. In 1801, he built his first mill along the Housatonic River. In 1879, the Crane Company got the exclusive contract to manufacture paper for U.S. currency.

DAMASCUS VA

Henry Mock was on his way to settle in KY in 1821 when he happened onto the confluence of Laurel and Beaverdam creeks. He decided to stay, purchasing and building a home and a gristmill. The town that

Edward Talone

The Hiker's Hostel in Damascus has been an oasis for AT hikers and cross-country cyclists since the 1970s.

grew up around the mill was known as Mock's Mill. In 1886, Confederate general John D. Imboden purchased tracts of the Mock family acreage. Surveying the mountains, he believed they contained vast deposits of iron ore and other minerals, and so named the place Damascus—predicting that it would become as well known as the Syrian capital. Unfortunately, the iron Imboden found on the surface was all there was. After the mountain was logged of old growth, it was sold to the U.S. Forest Service.

The little town of Damascus is known to many hikers as the friendliest town on the AT, owing in part to its annual AT Days celebration. In 1997, it was designated Trail Town USA by the American Hiking Society.

DANA HILL VT

Named for a family from the town of Pomfret, 5 miles northeast of here.

Edward Talcne

A hiker partakes in the annual Damascus (VA) AT Days, in which the town's population grows by a few thousand for a week end of musical entertainment, a parade, and antics.

DANBY VT
Established in 1731, the town is thought to be named for either Basil Fielding, 6th earl of Denbigh, or Thomas Osborne, 4th earl of Danby. The first post office opened in the village of Danby in 1801.

DANIEL DOAN TRAIL NH
Formerly known as the Mousley Brook Trail, it was renamed in 1993 for Daniel Doan, a local writer.

DANIEL WEBSTER TRAIL NH
Named for the American orator and statesman Daniel Webster (1782–1852), who was born in Salisbury and attended Dartmouth College. He served in the House of Representatives for NH and MA, then later served in the Senate representing MA. He was secretary of state for three presidents, William Henry Harrison, John Tyler, and Millard Fillmore.

DANS PULPIT PA
Hiker Danny Hoch, who would later be known as U.S. representative Daniel Hoch, was the first legislator to push for AT creation in Congress. In 1948, he introduced a bill to create a "national system of foot trails," the precursor to the National Trails System Act of 1968, the legislation that provides protection for the AT and authorizes the creation of other national scenic trails. Hoch's "pulpit" is an outcropping of rock where he would sometimes lead Sunday services.

DARLINGTON SHELTER
DARLINGTON TRAIL PA
Named for Bishop Darlington of Harrisburg, PA, who maintained a trail in the 1950s along the crest of the same name. This trail was used for the original AT route in this area over to the Susquehanna River. There actually have been two Darlington shelters. The first was built in 1956 by Earl Shaffer, known as the first solo hiker to walk the length of the AT. It is now abandoned about a half mile east of the current AT. The second was built in 1977 by the Mountain Club of MD.

DARTMOUTH COLLEGE NH
Founded in 1790 with a single log hut built by the Rev. Eleazar Wheelock (1711–79), who had spent 15 years running Moor's Indian Charity School in Lebanon, CT. In 1769, Wheelock received a grant from King George III "for the establishment of a college for the education and instruction of youth of the Indian tribes." The Dartmouth Outing Club, founded in 1909, maintains numerous trails in VT and NH, including the AT.

DAUPHIN-POTTSVILLE
STAGECOACH ROAD PA
To connect local mining operations, a wagon road was constructed on Stony Mountain in 1840. Later, the road was improved for a stagecoach line from Dauphin to Pottsville. The town of Pottsville was named for John Pott, an iron maker and miller; he laid out the town in 1822. The town of Dauphin and Dauphin County were both named for the son of Louis XVI of France to honor French recognition of American independence. The title of dauphin was given to the eldest son of the king of France from 1349 to 1830. The origin of the title is the dolphin on the family's coat of arms, thought to be chosen by the family because the origin of the word "dolphin" is a Greek word for womb—the shape of the dolphin. The dolphin, or womb, would symbolize the son who would be king. Today the AT follows this stagecoach road for 7 miles.

DAVENPORT GAP NC/TN
In 1821, Col. William Davenport began his survey of the TN–NC border by marking a stone on the Cataloochee Turnpike. He is said to have promoted the use of the name

Bill O'Brien

The sign that once adorned the old Atwell Hilton on Atwell Hill Road in NH. It housed a Dartmouth Outing Club trail crew and hosted hikers during the 1980s and early 1990s. The house has since been razed by the National Park Service.

Smoky Mountains by lobbying politicians and others with influence, for no other reason than he thought it to be an appropriate name. His efforts succeeded.

DAVIS PATH NH
Named for Nathaniel Davis, who was married to Hannah Crawford, the daughter of Abel Crawford, hotel entrepreneur and trail-builder in the 19th century. *See* Crawford Path, NH.

DAVIS PATH SHELTER VA
James Davis first settled in the Middle Fork Holston River Valley in the mid-1700s. The Davis Path passed through a wind gap used by settlers. Some accounts of the pass describe it as a migration route; others say it was more likely used for local traffic.

DAVIS RIDGE NC/TN
Named for Ann Lovella Patrick Davis, who first conceived the idea of Great Smoky Mountains NP in 1923. She and her husband, influential businessman Willis Perkins Davis, worked to promote the idea. In 1925, Ann Davis was elected to the TN General Assembly, where she introduced a bill to purchase the first large parcel of land for the park. For this she is known as "The Mother of the Park."

DAWN HILL ROAD CT
More is known locally about the former name than the current, but "dawn" is thought to be derived from the road's location on the eastern, or morning, side of the hill. The road was once the turnpike that went from Swifts Bridge to Sharon and was originally called the Sharon-Goshen Turnpike. As an alternative to the

toll roads, there once were local "shunpikes" that bypassed the toll house. Dawn Hill Road connects Silver Hill with Guinea Road, used to transport iron from the Morgan Bros. Mine to a forge at the lower end of Guinea Brook.

DAY MOUNTAIN MA
Named for an early family of the area.

DEAD RIVER ME
Visible from the AT on Little Bigelow, the name refers to the "dead" flow and lack of current.

DEAD WOMANS HOLLOW PA
Still searching for this one, but anyone's guess is probably not far from the truth.

DEADENING NATURE TRAIL VA
A "deadening" was an area where settlers cut a ring through the bark around trees so they would die. The trees would remain standing for a long time, but because they no longer sprouted leaves, pasture grasses would grow in the newly created fields. In time, all the trees in the deadened area would be cleared for firewood.

DEER LICK VA
This damp, mossy area just off the AT near Keys Gap gets its name from locals who often see deer here looking for salt in the bog.

DEERFIELD RIVER VT
The name is possibly transferred from Deerfield, MA, because it was the hometown of Ebenezer Hinsdale, who had been granted land patents in VT. Hinsdale was educated at Harvard and ordained a minister, becoming a missionary in the cause to convert Indians to Christianity. He later became a trader and officer in the British Army, using his position to gain patents in several VT towns.

DELAWARE RIVER PA
Originally called the "Zuydt" or South River by the Dutch, the name Delaware was transferred from Cape Delaware, now known as Cape Henlopen. Cape Delaware was named for Thomas West, baron de la Warr, the colonial governor of VA in 1610–18. Like many colonial governors, he spent less than a year in the colony, assigning his duties to deputy governors. For four years, he enforced martial law in Jamestown, which was then the largest city in the New World. His title means "Lord of the Weir." The word "weir" itself is largely lost to contemporary use. Its modern usage generally refers to a fenced enclosure set in water for the purpose of catching fish. It can refer to a dam used to divert water or raise its level, or to all the land in the watershed of the weir—the likely origination of Delaware.

DELAWARE RIVER–LEHIGH GAP PA
Opened in 1926 and originally known as the Skyline Trail.

DELAWARE WATER GAP PA
The Delaware River breaks through the mountains at the site of the village. The Indian name was *Pahagualing,* meaning "a mountain with a hole in it." Formerly, it was known simply as Water Gap.

DELPS TRAIL PA
So named because it leads off the mountain to the village of Delps, which was founded in 1848 as Delph, after a German family that settled there. It was eventually altered to the more English-sounding "Delp."

DENNING HILL NY
William Denning was a wealthy New York City merchant who emigrated from Newfoundland. He bought considerable land holdings in Philipstown, NY, in 1784, later becoming a state senator. He died in 1819 at the age of 80.

DENNIS COVE ROAD TN

In the early 1800s, a man known now only as Mr. Dennis came from NC to hunt here. He went back home to tell others of the plentiful game to be found. Soon hunters were flocking to "Mr. Dennis's Cove." The name stuck. Dennis never actually lived in the area, but he apparently hunted here for many years. In this part of the country, a "cove" is a narrow valley leading into the mountain. A little farther north in WV, these are called "hollows." West of the Appalachians, they are called "shut-ins."

DENNYTOWN ROAD NY

Thought to be named for Richard Denny, who bought 207 acres here after the Revolutionary War. He stayed to operate the nearby Denny Mine, which produced iron ore from about 1800 until 1880.

DEPOT HILL
DEPOT HILL ROAD NY

The depot that lends its name was built by the New York and New England Railroad in 1912 at the base of the mountain. The road was formerly called Negro Hill Road. The area was called Freemanville, after Charles Freeman, a freed slave who lived there.

DERRICK KNOB SHELTER NC/TN

No natural feature now carries the name Derrick Knob, but the name is said to have derived either from a prominent early TN family, or from a man who owned a cabin in the area circa 1880. Famed naturalist Horace Kephart, in 1904, referred to the site as "Halls Cabin."

DEVILS MARBLEYARD VA

This 8-acre area of fractured Antietam quartzite is yet another Appalachian place strewn with boulders and rocks, making wagon travel so difficult that it was named for the Dark One.

DEVILS RACECOURSE MD

There are similar boulder fields with similar names throughout the Appalachians—remnants of the last ice age, when frost heaves caused rock to crack and separate. Longtime AT volunteer and pathfinder Thurston Griggs offers perhaps the best explanation for the name here. He recalls a gibe delivered years ago by a fellow hiker: "If the Devil were to construct a racecourse, this is the devilish kind that would result—impossible to race on."

DEVILS TATER PATCH NC/TN

The assignment of "devil" to this rugged ridge is not surprising, but the origin of "Tater Patch" remains elusive. One theory is that the many small stones sticking up out of the ground here resemble potatoes in a field.

DICKS DOME SHELTER VA

Named for Potomac AT Club member Dick George, who built this shelter on private land in 1990.

DISMAL KNOB GA

Not necessarily a gloomy place; the word "dismal" was often applied to areas that were unsuited for agriculture.

DOLLY COPP CAMPGROUND NH

Located at the end of Daniel Webster Trail, it is named for Dolly Emery of Jackson, NH, who married Hayes Copp in 1831. Dolly is credited with operating the first craft shop in the mountains, where she sold farm goods. The Copp family also ran an inn here. Only their name remains now. Dolly and Hayes separated in 1881 after 50 years of marriage and moved to separate towns in ME. The farm site became part of the White Mountain National Forest in 1915.

DOUBLE SPRING GAP NC/TN
Two springs, two states, two directions of flow. Only 50 feet separate the springs, nameless here, with one flowing north to the Little River and the other south to the Tuckaseegee. Both of these rivers drain into the Tennessee.

DOUGHTY HILL ME
Named for George Doughty, who settled here in 1816.

DOVER NY
The most likely theory is that it was named for the chalk cliffs of Dover in England in recognition of the large limestone and marble deposits in Dutchess County.

DOYLE RIVER TRAIL VA
Dennis Doyle settled along the river in 1741. The Doyle River was previously called Rivanna.

DRAGON'S TOOTH VA
The shape of this rock formation inspired Tom Campbell, an early member of the Roanoke AT Club, to bestow the name.

DRIPPING ROCK VA
Named for the spring that emerges below it.

DRY GULCH CT
This small ravine is scattered with boulders, known as glacial erratics, left by retreating glaciers 12,000 years ago. It is dry most of the year, except after heavy rains.

DRY SLUICE GAP NC/TN
The stream is a classic sink or subsurface channel. It flows aboveground for a time, then disappears into the ground. The aboveground bed channels high-water overflows, but is dry most of the year.

DUELL HOLLOW
DUELL HOLLOW BROOK NY
Named for a Quaker family that settled in the region in the 1730s.

DUNCAN RIDGE TRAIL GA
Duncan Ridge is thought to be the longest continuous ridge projecting from the main Blue Ridge; the trail along it was built in the 1970s by the GA AT Club and the forest service. The origin of the name remains elusive.

DUNCANNON PA
There is disagreement over whether the town was first founded as Petersburg in 1844, or as Clark's Ferry, after a ferry established there by the Clark family in 1788. Sometime in the early 20th century, however, people began calling the place Duncannon after Samuel Duncan, about whom little is known.

DUNN NOTCH ME
Named for the family of Henry Dunn, who lived here in the latter part of the 19th century.

DUTCHESS COUNTY NY
Named for the duchess of York, Mary Beatrice, who in 1671 married James Stuart, the duke of York. Stuart was the younger brother of King Charles II. After England took the colony from the Dutch, Charles gave it to James—calling it New York, after James's title. James became king when Charles died in 1685. Dutchess County was formed in 1683 as one of the first twelve counties in the new colony.

E

EAGLE ROCKS NC/TN

The name might typically be applied after a chance sighting of an uncommon number of eagles. In this instance, however, the name comes from a craggy collection of weathered rocks that to some resembles an eagle on a perch.

EAST BRANCH PISCATAQUIS RIVER ME

Piscataquis is an Abenaki word for "the river branch."

EAST MOMBASHA ROAD NY

Mombasha is thought to come from the Iroquois *mombaccus*, or "place of death." The area might have once been an Indian burial ground.

EASTMAN LEDGES NH

The ledges are along the Kodak Trail, which got its lighthearted name from trail-builders who declared, in reference to an advertising campaign of the 1980s, that the trail was so scenic it presented one "Kodak moment" after another. The ledges offer perhaps the pinnacle of visual delight along the trail—hence they are the Eastman ledges, named for the Eastman Kodak company. *See* Kodak Trail, NH.

EDMANDS COL NH

J. Raymer Edmands was a founder of the Appalachian Mountain Club in 1876. An influential path-builder, he believed that footpaths should follow landscape contours rather than simply head straight up a mountainside. Edmands boasted that his trails were so blended into the contour that "anyone's mother could walk to the summit of Mt. Washington." Although none of his trails actually approached this summit, he did build well-graded trails throughout the northern Presidentials. His ideas were at odds with those of another AMC founder, Eugene Cook, whose devotees believed that the straightest line between bottom and top created a rugged, wild experience most hikers would favor. These opposing philosophies influenced trail-building throughout the eastern U.S. To this day, footpaths in NY tend to be vertical, while those in the Blue Ridge make use of switchbacks and hug the terrain. One thing both Edmands and Cook agreed on was a kibosh on the word "trail," which to them evoked images of wagon trains. "Path" or "footpath" was the favored term.

Among Edmands' innovations are an early version of the backpack and the use of cairns—stacks of stones—to mark paths above the treeline.

Potomac AT Club

An AT hiker, circa 1930s. Location unknown.

EKANEETLEE GAP NC/TN

Ekaneetlee is an anglicized corruption of *egwanulti,* said to be a Cherokee term for "by the river," referring to the Cherokee route from valley villages to settlements on the other side of the mountain. Cades Cove, a white settlement along the route, had been a place of importance to the Cherokee also. They called it *tsiyahi,* or "otter place."

ELBOW POND ME

So named because of its distinctive shape.

ELEPHANT MOUNTAIN ME

A descriptive name, something of a Rorschach test of one's ability to see animals in the shapes of the mountains.

ELK PEN NY

Edward Harriman tried unsuccessfully in the 1920s and '30s to introduce elk to the region by bringing a herd of seventy-five to his estate. Many died en route, and others died before a herd was established. The survivors were sent out west to restore an elk herd that had been depleted by a very severe winter. A metal fence is all that remains of the attempt. *See* Bear Mountain–Harriman State Park, NY.

ELK RIDGE MD

To many people, Elk Ridge is the psychological northern terminus of the Blue Ridge, which actually continues well into PA. Most prominent in central VA, the Blue Ridge is a wide front of summits, ridges, and hollows. As it goes north, it diminishes to a single ridgeline that quietly disappears into the valley. Named for the abundant elk that once lived along the flat top of the ridge, Elk Valley Ridge was settled by Civil War deserters, weavers, and farmers in the late 19th century. By the early 20th century, illness from polluted water overwhelmed the community, and people abandoned the settlement.

ELLIS RIVER NH

Formed by the confluence of the New and Cutler rivers. The origin of the name is not known, but it appears on early maps as "Elise" or "Elis."

ENGINE GAP NC/TN

An engine that once pulled TN logs through the gap to NC sawmills had been abandoned here.

ENGLISH MOUNTAIN NC/TN

John English hunted on the west side of the Pigeon River with John Cosby in the late 18th century, when the Smokies were still a frontier. *See* Cosby Knob Shelter, NC/TN.

ENOLA PA

A popular myth was that Enola came from "alone" spelled backward and was named for the presence of a lonely telegraph tower here before the town was founded. Actually, the town took its name from the railroad station, which was named by Wesley Miller, a local farmer. He was approached by the Northern Central Railroad to sell 10 acres of land for a station. He sold the railroad the land, then donated 3 acres more. For this he was given the right to name the station. He choose Enola in 1888, for his daughter, who was 4 years old at the time. Enola Miller (1884–1962) was herself named after a character in the book *The Dangers of Darkness,* written by Isaac Kelso in 1850.

EPH'S LOOKOUT MA

Although confirmation whether the namesake ever visited the spot remains elusive, the vista is named for Col. Ephraim Williams (1715–55), for whom Williamstown, MA, and Williams College are also named. Williams was killed in the French and Indian War at the Battle of Lake George. He bequeathed money to found a "free school," the equivalent of a public high school today. There were two stipulations attached to the gift. First, the town of West Township had to be renamed Williamstown. This was done in 1765. Second, the school had to be in MA. This would take time, because NY and MA were fighting over which state held title to the land that included Williamstown. The dispute was resolved in 1784 in MA's favor. In 1785, the school was established; it became Williams College in 1793.

ETHAN POND TRAIL NH
Named in 1820 for Ethan Allen Crawford, one of the namers of the Presidential Range. *See* Crawford Path, NH.

ETHEL POND ME
Named for Ethel LaSalle, whose father owned the pond. The exact date of ownership is not known, but the name appears on maps dating to the late 19th century.

ETNA NH
Formerly known as Mill Village for the prevalence of mills in the town. When momentum built for a change to a more colorful name, resident Laura Camp suggested Aetna after the local life insurance company. She recommended dropping the silent *a*, however, thinking its pronunciation would be confusing. In 1884, the town of Mill Village became Etna.

EYEBROW TRAIL ME
The cliff that forms the west wall of Grafton Notch has the distinctive look of an eyebrow.

F

FAHNESTOCK STATE PARK NY
Maj. Clarence Fahnestock was a Manhattan physician who began buying abandoned farms here in about 1900. In 1915, he bought the property of the Pennsylvania and Reading Coal and Iron Company, which had ceased operations some 40 years earlier. Those operations had begun in 1756 when Col. Beverly Robinson gave two men permission to survey his land for minerals. An 8-mile iron vein was discovered. Much of that iron went to the West Point Foundry at Cold Spring, NY, where Robert Parker Parrott was superintendent. Parrott was the inventor of the Parrott gun, which gave the Union Army a superior weapon in the Civil War, and which was manufactured at the West Point Foundry.

Fahnestock died in 1918 while visiting France. In 1929, his brother Ernest donated 2,400 acres of Clarence's land to the Taconic State Park Commission. *See* Bear Mountain–Harriman State Park, NY.

FALLS VILLAGE CT
Located in the town of Canaan, this village was formerly called Canaan Falls and Housatonic Falls; both are references to the Great Falls of the Housatonic River, which are visible from the AT on the edge of town. Originally a settlement that grew up near the lumber, then iron, processing mills, Falls Village still contains remains of iron furnaces as well as luxurious homes built by the village's prosperous citizens during the heyday of iron in the 18th century.

At one time there was another Falls Village, on the west side of the Housatonic, in Salisbury. For a time, the village in

Canaan, on the east side, was called Falls Village in Canaan, to distinguish it from Salisbury's Falls Village. In the mid-19th century, planners had the idea to make the entire Falls Village area into a major industrial center. Locks and channels were built to bypass the falls and rapids in hopes of making the Housatonic navigable—to Pittsfield. There were also plans in place to connect the river to the Erie Canal in NY. Adequate financing for this project never materialized, however, and what was built was plagued by leaks. Salisbury's Falls Village eventually disappeared. In 1912, the Berkshire Power Plant was constructed, and the river was dammed just north of the falls in order to channel the water through generators.

FALSE GAP NC/TN

Travelers seeking a way over Laurel Top Mountain via Porters Gap sometimes became confused about the gap's precise location. Maps showed only one gap—Porters—but there seemed to be actually two. Travelers who made the trip up the mountain to the wrong gap, only to have to retreat and find Porters Gap, started referring to the wrong gap as False Gap. The name stuck. *See* Porters Gap, NC/TN.

FAWN TRAIL NY

The origin is unknown, but the name appears on the first trail map of Bear Mountain–Harriman State Park, printed in 1920.

FAYETTEVILLE PA

Named for Gen. Marquis de Lafayette (1757–1834), famed general of the Revolutionary War. After hearing about the revolution in America in 1777, he recruited French officers, bought a ship, and sailed to America. He was immediately appointed a major general by Congress, even though he was only 19. He served without payment and is said to have spent hundreds of thousands of dollars of his own money to outfit American troops.

FERNSIDE ROAD MA

The story goes that after the demise of a Shaker community in Tyringham, MA, Dr. Joseph Jones moved to the former settlement in 1874. He opened a hostelry and asked one of his visitors to suggest a name. The guest reportedly said, "You have ferns growing all over this mountainside. Why not call it Fernside?" Jones agreed and had the rooms decorated with a green fern design wallpaper. The road was named for this popular boardinghouse, which is still standing, although it's no longer a hostelry.

FIREWARDEN'S CABIN NH

The shelter got its name because it was used by the fire wardens who manned the tower on Smarts Mountain, beginning around 1920. It was opened to hikers in 1979.

FLAGSTAFF LAKE ME

Named for a flagstaff planted by Benedict Arnold during his famous march to Quebec in 1775. The lake was created in 1949 when the Dead River was dammed at Long Falls. The former town of Flagstaff and village of Dead River now lie at the bottom of the lake. The original route of the AT followed the Dead River where the lake is now. It was abandoned in 1939.

FODDER STACK NC/TN

This is the lower peak of the mountain called Charlies Bunion. Derivations of the Dutch word *fodderstack* dot the Appalachians in nearly as great a number as "sugar loaf." Fodder is livestock feed composed of whatever edible grains, grasses, and stalks are available. Loosely translated, fodder stack means "hay" or "haystack." So this mountain is one more known as Haystack, a descriptive name for its shape. *See* Charlies Bunion, NC/TN.

FONTANA DAM
FONTANA LAKE NC

When the sixth highest dam in the country was complete, its waters submerged the small lumber-company town of Fontana. According to Allen Coggins' *Place Names of the Smokies*, the name of the town was suggested by the wife of the lumber company's executive vice president. She called it Fontana for its waterfalls, which reminded her of leaping fountains, and the word had a romantic Italian sound to it. Coggins points out another Italian connection: Supposedly, an Italian naturalist named Felice Fontana visited the area in the 1700s.

Another explanation of the town's name is that Fontana is derived from an undetermined Indian word, said to mean "at the foot of the mountain." The Fontana Dam was built to supply power for the Oak Ridge nuclear plant, where plutonium was produced for atomic weapons. At the time of its construction, it was the fourth largest dam in the world.

FORK MOUNTAIN VA

So called because deep divisions in its slope give it a forked shape.

FORT MONTGOMERY NY

Built to defend the Hudson River in 1776. Richard Montgomery was born in Ireland in 1736 into a wealthy family; he joined the British Army in 1756. After the French and Indian War, and after being passed over for a promotion which he felt he deserved, he left Britain for NY. He arrived in 1772 and married into a landed family, the Livingstons. He was appointed to serve in the Provincial Congress in 1775. During the war, he recommended the famous fortification of the Hudson—a 1,500-foot chain stretched across the river to prevent British invasion. Montgomery was appointed to the rank of brigadier general in the Continental Army; after victories in Canada, including the siege of Montreal, he was killed trying to take Quebec City. His name is widely associated with place names in the eastern U.S.

FOSS & KNOWLTON BROOK ME

Located in Baxter State Park, the stream is named for Foss and Knowlton, a large lumber operation in this area that ceased operation in the 1920s.

FOUR PONDS MOUNTAIN ME

Named for four ponds that are nearby: Long, Round, Sabbath Day, and Moxie.

FOURTH MOUNTAIN ME

The fourth peak in the Barren Chairbacks, after Chairback, Columbus, and Third.

FOX GAP MD

Named for Johan Friederich Fuchs, who arrived in America in 1752 and whose name was anglicized to John Frederick Fox.

The route through Fox Gap is essentially unchanged since the 1700s. Some historians claim it was used by Braddock and Washington en route to Fort Cumberland in their attempt to protect English settlers during the French and Indian War. It was the site of heavy fighting during the Battle of South Mountain in the Civil War. Union major general Jesse Reno and Confederate brigadier general Samuel Garland were both killed here; future president Rutherford B. Hayes, then a lieutenant colonel, received a serious arm wound here. Prompt treatment by Hayes' brother-in-law saved the arm and his life. One month after the battle, he was promoted to the rank of colonel.

FOXVILLE ROAD (ROUTE 77) MD

George P. Fox, Sr., owned land near here in the Catoctin Mountains, close to the intersection of what are now MD Route 77 and Stottlemeyer Road. Foxville is a nearby village, which was officially named when assigned a post office in 1834.

FREEMAN TRAIL GA

Lawrence Freeman served as president of the GA AT Club in 1947–48, and again in 1953. He is credited with putting the AT on forest roads in places where it had become impassable during World War II. This strategy made the trail, in Freeman's words, "open for business."

FRENCH BROAD RIVER NC

One story names the river for a noted hunter named French, but others say it was named in the 1700s by Europeans because it flows south toward what was then the French territories.

FRONT ROYAL VA

The name origin is a matter of conjecture. In its earliest days, the place was known as "Hell Town" among the rivermen and packers who played here. It was also known as Luce and, later, Lehew, after Peter Lehew, who owned 200 acres here. Legend tells of a giant oak tree that stood in the public square. The oak was the "royal" tree of England. During the American Revolution, drill sergeants would holler for recruits to "front the royal oak," eventually, just "front royal."

FRYE NOTCH LEAN-TO ME

Built by the ME AT Club in 1983, the lean-to gets its name from Frye Brook, itself named for the Frye family that settled here.

FULL GOOSE SHELTER ME

One story tells of a migrating goose that spent the night and enjoyed a good meal here. Another likens AT thru-hikers to migrating birds; presumably they also leave well fed.

FULLER LAKE PA

The lake, in Pine Grove Furnace State Park, is named for Col. Jackson C. Fuller, who owned the property in 1877. The lake was formed when the water pumps failed on a 90-foot-deep mine here.

FULLHARDT KNOB SHELTER VA

Built by the Roanoke AT Club in 1962, it has the distinction of being the last shelter on the AT watered by a cistern.

FULLING MILL MOUNTAIN ME

Says the *American Heritage Dictionary,* fulling is "to increase the weight and bulk of cloth by shrinking and beating or pressing it." This would indicate the name might be derived from textile-making activity in the vicinity.

FUMITORY ROCKS PA

Named for the climbing fumitory, or "Allegheny vine," which grows here along Peters Mountain. A member of the poppy family, the vine can grow to 12 feet long; it usually blooms in July. Despite its range from Canada to NC, it is found nowhere else on the AT.

FURNACE BROOK NY

Typically, when a facility and a creek share a name, the building derives its name from the stream. Here, it's the other way around. The creek provided water to Queensboro Iron Furnace and so was called Furnace Brook.

G

GALEHEAD HUT NH
Refers to the hut's proximity to the headwaters of the Gale River.

GAPLAND ROAD MD
Formerly known as Clagett's Station (also Claggets Station) for a farming family that lived here, it was informally called Gapland for the "Gapland" estate of Civil War journalist George Alfred Townsend. The name was formally changed in 1890. The road was a Baltimore & Ohio Railroad branch-line stop, and later a toll road. *See* Gathland State Park, MD.

GARVEY SPRING NJ
Named for Edward B. Garvey (1914–99), an AT legend for his activism and writings. In an unsubstantiated but quintessentially Garveyesque story, he once wrote to the AT Conference to complain about the scarcity of water sources along the trail. So many springs were located too far from the trail, many with no signs to guide hikers to the water. NJ hikers soon blazed well-marked trails to the water so Garvey would have no trouble finding it. At this one, they made it even easier by painting a rock to make a sign at the side trail to the spring. The top line caught his attention: "Garvey." The bottom line pointed the way: "Spring."

Potomac AT Club

Natural and cultural history are preserved along the AT corridor. This sign at Gathland State Park in MD points the way to Civil War trenches.

GATHLAND STATE PARK MD
Although Civil War journalist George Alfred Townsend called his estate "Gapland," for its location at the top of Crampton Gap, the state of MD chose Townsend's nom de plume Gath as the name for the state park. On a buggy ride in 1884, Townsend was so smitten with Crampton Gap that he bought a huge parcel of land here with the proceeds from his novels and syndicated columns. He built a house for himself and one for his wife, a social hall, library, lodge, guest house, servants' houses, stables, and a tomb for his burial. It was a gathering place for the social elite of Washington DC and Baltimore. Mrs. Townsend's house, called "The Hall," contained 11 rooms. The library housed 5,000 books in 15 rooms. The 5-room guest house was called Mt. Gath; the 4-room guest house was called "The Lodge." Unfortunately, Townsend died penniless in New York City and was not interred in the estate's mausoleum. Only a wing of Gath Hall remains today, along with a memorial arch in Townsend built to honor war correspondents, the only such memorial in the world.

GENTIAN POND LEAN-TO NH

The name was transferred from nearby Gentian Pond, which derives its name from the plant with blue or purple flowers. The shelter was built in 1974.

GEORGE W. OUTERBRIDGE SHELTER PA

Named for a longtime AT maintainer from the Philadelphia Trail Club who finished "section hiking" the trail in 1939. He remained active with trail activities until his death in the 1970s.

GIANT'S THUMB CT

Once known as Tomsteen Rock, but the origin of that name has been lost. In fact, even that name was unknown by most. In the 1990s, inveterate AT place-namer Norman Sills figured it needed a new name. Apparently, he thought it looked like a thumb.

GIFFORD WOODS STATE PARK VT

Established in 1931 when three owners—Barrows, Kent, and Pierson—offered land for the park. Perry Merrill, the park commissioner at that time, recommended the name Barrows Woods. Barrows wouldn't have it. He said that the property had always been known as the Gifford Farm, for a local family of the 19th century, and so should be called Gifford Woods.

GLADE MOUNTAIN VA

Early settlers here drew their water from a clear spring in the glade, an open space in a forest. They referred to the place as Glade Spring. The town that grew up here was originally called Passawatomie Station for the rail station that opened in 1856. Passawatomie is thought by some to be a made-up word, but it may be a reference to the Pota Watomi nations, a name translated in the Chippewa to mean "people of the place of fire." The Pota Watomi, however, were native to the Great Lakes region.

GLASGOW VA

Founded in 1890 and named for ancestors of VA novelist Ellen Glasgow (1874–1945), who won the Pulitzer Prize in 1942 for *In This Our Life.*

GLASSMINE GAP NC

The gap and nearby Glassmine Falls were named for a former mica mine. Mica is a colored silicate used in making glass.

GLASTENBURY MOUNTAIN VT

The name is transferred from the nearby town of Glastenbury, which borrowed its name from Glastonbury in Somerset, England. The spelling change was made at a time when spelling in general was left to the discretion of the speller.

GLENCLIFF NH

Originally named Warren, after Sir Peter Warren of England (1701–51). In 1860, the name was changed to Warren Summit, shortly thereafter to Glenncliff Station, taking its name from the nearby Glencliff Sanatorium, named for its location on a bluff above the valley. When the train ceased operation, the town became simply Glencliff.

GLENN R. CAVENEY PLAQUE MD

Caveney maintained this section of the trail with his father until his death in an automobile accident in 1975. Soon after, Glenn's father established a fund that purchased 4 acres along the trail, providing permanent protection for the trail corridor and a memorial to his son. The parcel was dedicated on March 4, 1976.

GLENWOOD ESTATE VA

The name is transferred from the Glenwood Iron Furnace, which, along with about 20,000 acres, was owned by the Anderson family in the 1800s. Their holdings, which they named Glenwood Estate for its dense forest setting, became the core of the Glenwood District of the Jefferson National Forest.

GOLDEN ROAD ME
Built by the Great Northern Paper Company, it was likely named for the vast fortune in timber that rolled over it. It is now a private toll road owned by the Georgia-Pacific forest products company.

GOODLOE BYRON MEMORIAL FOOTBRIDGE MD
Rep. Goodloe Byron (1928–78) led a fight in the U.S. Congress to fund protection of the AT. He introduced a 1978 amendment to the National Trails System Act that authorized $90 million to purchase land for the AT corridor. When he died later that same year at the age of 50, his wife, Beverly, assumed his House seat and his commitment to trails. The bridge named for him opened in 1985.

GOOSE EYE PEAK ME
Possibly a corruption of "Goose High," referring to the height of the mountain—it is as high as a goose can fly. Another story is that someone thought a feature on the mountain looked like a goose's head.

GORHAM NH
Settled originally as Shelburnes Addition in 1771, it was incorporated in 1836 and named by Sylvester Davis, an early settler, for his hometown of Gorham, ME.

GOSHEN MOUNTAIN NY
An Old Testament word that means "promised land" or "land of plenty."

GOSHEN PRONG TRAIL NC
A prong is a fork or tributary. Goshen here, as elsewhere along the AT and the Appalachians, is a biblical reference to fertile ground. *See* Goshen Mountain, NY.

GOV. CLEMENT SHELTER VT
Built in 1929 by the family of William Field to honor Percival Clement, governor of VT, 1919–21.

Edward Talone

Gov. Clement Shelter in VT, built in 1929 by the Green Mountain Club, was named for Percival Clement, who served as the state's chief executive in 1919–21.

Bill O'Brien

Even the outhouse at the Gov. Clement Shelter in VT is a memorial. The structure is dedicated as the Lieut. Gov. Jarvis Snodgrass Memorial Gazebo.

Bill O'Brien

The homemade headstone for Eva Gragg, presumably carved by her husband, contains a homespun variation of the familiar "Gone but not forgotten." He may have meant to say that, but instead he wrote "Absent, Not Dead."

GRAFTON NOTCH ME
Named in 1852 by a woman named Hannah Brown. She is said to have chosen Grafton because Grafton, MA, is next to the town of Upton, MA, and this notch is just a few miles south of Upton, ME.

GRAGG GAP NC/TN
Named for George and Eva Gragg, who owned land here in the 1920s.

GRANDFATHER MOUNTAIN TN
Given by the Cherokees. When viewed from a distance the mountain looks like an old man peering toward the heavens.

GRASSY POND TRAIL ME
This was the route of the AT to Daicey Pond until about 1969. The name refers to the shallow, grassy character of the pond.

GRASSY RIDGE NC/TN
The only open natural bald above 6,000 feet close to the AT. Other balds have structures on top. A plaque at the top here honors Corneilius Rex Peake (1887–1964), who, with his wife, Winne Lee, operated what is said to have been the highest cultivated farm east of the Rockies. They also are remembered for their efforts to protect the Roan Highlands.

GRAVEL SPRINGS HUT VA
Built of stone by the Civilian Conservation Corps in 1940, the hut gets its name from the stream, which was called "Gravelly Springs" by local residents before the creation of Shenandoah NP.

GRAY KNOB CABIN NH
The knob receives its name from the gray rocky outcropping on Nowell Ridge, which is above the cabin site. The first cabin was built on this site in 1906 by Dr. E. J. Hincks on land he leased from a timber company. After the forest service acquired the land, Hincks was given a lease on the

condition that the cabin be open to the public. In 1989, a new cabin was built on the site.

GRAYMOOR MONASTERY NY

About 1830, a Rev. Gray built a mission in what is now Garrison, called St. John of the Wilderness. As the years went by, it fell into disuse and eventual ruin. In 1893, three ladies of the local Episcopal church decided to rebuild the mission. The largest contributor was a man named Moore, so the ladies decided to name the new church St. John of the Wilderness at Graymoor, after Rev. Gray and Mr. Moore. In 1899, a Catholic nun, Sister Lurana, laid the cornerstone of the convent of the Sisters of Atonement at the chapel of St. John in the Wilderness at Graymoor.

Later that year, Lewis T. Wattson, an Episcopalian minister, arrived and, with Sister Lurana, founded the Society of the Atonement. He believed that "Anglicanism should endeavor to repair the breach between the Church of England and Rome—by seeking to be . . . united—as the divinely constituted Center of Catholic Unity." Needless to say, the Episcopal Church did not embrace this idea, so Wattson became a Catholic priest in 1909, and the society became the home of Franciscan friars. In 1910, the friars erected St. Christopher's Inn to provide food and shelter for "homeless nomads of the highway, ill-in-spirit, discouraged, hungry, and penniless." For many years, the friars offered meals to AT hikers and allowed them to camp under a covered pavilion. The friary still is a neighbor to the AT.

GRAYSON HIGHLANDS STATE PARK VA

William Grayson was a VA delegate to the Continental Congress in 1784–89 and one of the first two U.S. senators from VA.

GREASY CREEK GAP NC/TN

In the 19th century, the practice of skinning and gutting bears at the creek in autumn left the stream ripe with fat peeled from the hides.

GREASY SPRING VA

This appetizing name was bestowed because cooks from a nearby lumber camp polluted the spring with dishwater.

GREAT FALLS CT

These are great indeed, the largest falls on the Housatonic and the largest between here and Niagara Falls in western NY. They are located just north of Falls Village. *See* Falls Village, CT.

GREAT GULF WILDERNESS NH

Reportedly named by Ethan Allen Crawford, one of the namers of the Presidential Mountains and, with his father, proprietor of the first hotel built on Mt. Washington. While leading a group on a trek here in the 1820s, Crawford became lost and found himself on the edge of a "Great Gulf"—in New England, "gulf" is a term for a gap or pass. Early descriptions referred to the area as the "Gulf of Mexico."

GREAT SMOKY MOUNTAINS NC/TN

The Cherokee called the mountains *Shacona-ga,* typically translated to mean "blue, like smoke," for the bluish haze that hangs above them. The haze comes from a combination of humidity from the many streams tumbling down the mountain, dense vegetation, and soil type. The mountains were previously called "The Great Iron Mountains." The Cherokee also called them *Unica,* meaning "white." From this word, Unaka and Unicoi were derived and used to name specific mountains in the area.

The first documentation of the mountains by settlers is a 1789 government decree about the border between NC and

Bill O'Brien

A thru-hiker puts on his gloves atop a rime-encrusted summit on Thunderhead in the Smokies after a 1992 storm. A previous passerby had etched "Hell" into the ice-covered sign.

TN. Great Smoky Mountains NP was the first to be created using private donations to purchase private land. Between 1925 and 1940, more than 6,000 parcels were strung together, totaling some 400,000 acres.

GREAT SWAMP NY

The swamp is great indeed; it forms the state's second largest freshwater wetland.

GREAT WALK PA

The name given to this trail near Fox Gap may refer to the Walkers Purchase, when Leni-Lenape Indians granted to a group of early settlers as much land as they could walk in a day. The settlers covered a roughly 20-square-mile area from the Delaware River to near Smith Gap. The Leni-Lenape felt they had been cheated, however, because the settlers had scattered themselves throughout the region, rather than all starting from the same place. This led to several battles here over a number of years.

GREEN POND MOUNTAIN NY

Hikers from the NY–NJ Trail Conference are said to have named this peak in 1947 after a small mountain lake, or tarn, south of the summit.

GREENBRIER LAKE
GREENBRIER STATE PARK MD

The park was named for the unincorporated hamlet nearby, which consists of a few remote houses. The story is that because of its location, the settlement was like a brier thicket: Once you got there, it was hard to get out. The dam was created in the 1960s to provide recreation in the Blue Ridge–Catoctin area.

GREENBRIER RIDGE TRAIL TN
Named for *Smilax rotundifolia,* a thorny vine that makes passage difficult.

GREENLEAF HUT NH
Built in 1929 with funds donated by Col. C. H. Greenleaf.

GREENWOOD LAKE NY/NJ
Originally known as Long Pond, it was dammed in the 1760s to provide water for the iron industry at Long Pond Iron Furnace, which operated between 1766 and 1882. The dam was enlarged in 1836 to provide water for the Morris Canal, which lifted coal-laden barges from the Delaware River and floated them through the highlands to the Atlantic. That same year, the name Greenwood Lake appeared. No one knows exactly why the name was chosen; it might have been a marketer's description of the beautiful green woods that surround the lake. Greenwood Lake became a popular resort in the mid-19th century.

GREER KNOB NC
In the late 19th century, Andy Greer of Cades Cove pastured oxen here in summer. One night Greer's oxen and some cattle huddled together on this knob during an intense electrical storm. Because the animals were in their high-elevation summer pasture, Greer, at home, was unable to reach his livestock before the storm hit. A lightning strike in the vicinity charged the land beneath the animals with ground current, killing them all.

GREGORY BALD TRAIL NC/TN
Russell Gregory came to Cades Cove sometime between 1820 and 1830 to farm. He tended cattle on this bald and built a stone cabin there. He was locally famous for his method of calling cattle to the top of the bald, then called Bald Spot Mountain; he would blow a large horn to summon his herd. Although Gregory spent much of his time in the mountains, he was involved in the civic life of Cades Cove. During the Civil War, he was pro-Union, but his son was a Confederate. In 1864, Russell Gregory led the residents of Cades Cove to turn back Confederate raiders who had been pillaging the area. No one was killed in this confrontation, but that night raiders returned and murdered Gregory. His son had been among the raiders in the earlier skirmish.

GREN ANDERSON SHELTER NJ
Named for a longtime member of the NY section of the Green Mountain Club and trail volunteer in the 1940s and '50s. The shelter was built in 1958.

GRIFFITH LAKE VT
Silas L. Griffith, known as the "Lumber King," cut millions of feet of lumber around here in the 1920s. The mansion he built in 1891 for his bride, Katherine, is now a bed and breakfast in the town of Danby, just outside the Green Mountain National Forest. Griffith was said to be the state's first millionaire.

GRIGGS MOUNTAIN VT
Named for a local family from Norwich.

GROVE CREEK MD
Grove Creek starts on South Mountain and ends in Smithsburg, where it empties into Little Antietam. Grove Creek is a recent name; its origin is unknown. The creek was formerly called Kinler Creek, after a potter named Kinler who lived along it, on East Water Street in Smithsburg.

Edward Talone

A long section of bog bridging near Griffith Lake, VT.

GUILDER POND MA
John Van Guilder, a Dutch settler, owned 50 acres adjacent to the pond. He was kidnapped by Indians, but rather than leading to his demise, the episode led to his marriage to the chief's daughter.

THE GUILLOTINE VA
This rock poised above the AT near Apple Orchard Mountain is reminiscent of the dreaded device. It was named in the early 1990s by Bill Foot, then president of the Natural Bridge AT Club, when the AT was relocated here.

GUINEA BROOK CT
The name is borrowed from another place name, the Guinea Coast, in Africa, the birthplace of Robert Starr, a slave who was freed following his service in the American Revolution. Starr claimed to have been a body-servant for George Washington.

GULF HAGAS RIM TRAIL ME
The 3.5-mile slate canyon here was cut by the west branch of the Pleasant River. Old trails here were reopened in 1934 by Walter Greene, a Broadway actor who built extensive sections of the AT in ME. The origin of the name Hagas is unknown, but the word "gulf" refers to a mountain pass or gap.

GULF STREAM VT
"Gulf" is a New England term for a pass or notch. This stream flows through Barnard Notch.

GULFSIDE TRAIL NH
So named because it circles the Great Gulf between Mt. Washington and the Madison Hut. *See* Great Gulf Wilderness, NH.

H

HAIRY ROOT SPRING NH
Capturing the essence of what it means to be a "trailee," a trail crew from the Dartmouth Outing Club bestowed the name in the 1970s because the spring emerges from the ground beneath the hairy roots of an old maple tree.

HALL MOUNTAIN LEAN-TO ME
Built by the ME AT Club in 1978, the shelter gets its name from Hall Mountain, which is named after a local family.

HAMLIN RIDGE ME
Visible from Katahdin, it is named for professor Charles Hamlin, who explored the Katahdin area in the 19th century.

HANG-GLIDER VIEW CT
Like many views from wooded mountains along the AT, this vista was "cut" by removing several trees so hikers could see a long distance. This view of the Taconics was first cut by hang glider devotees.

HANGING ROCK VA
The flat-topped cliff appears to hang over the valley.

HANOVER NH
Chartered by colonial governor Benning Wentworth on July 4, 1761 and first settled in 1765, the town was named in honor of the reigning house in Great Britain in that year.

HAPPY HILL SHELTER VT
Newly built in 1998, it replaced the historic Happy Hill Cabin, built in 1918, the oldest shelter on the AT. The name Happy Hill is likely transferred from nearby Happy Valley, a place that received its name, says Esther Munroe Swift in her *Vermont Place Names,* because people there "have found it a congenial place to live."

HARMON HILL VT
Named for a local 19th-century family.

HARMONY HOLLOW VA
Although the origin of the name is lost, the site is noteworthy as the first land placed under conservation easement for the AT in VA.

HAROLD ALLEN PLAQUE MD
Allen was a leader in the effort to establish the Shenandoah NP in 1924–26. He has long been credited with penning the words known by many AT hikers: "Remote for detachment; narrow for chosen company; winding for leisure; lonely for contemplation. The trail leads not merely north and south but upward to the body, mind, and soul of man." Recent research, however, has created doubt that the quote is Allen's. Not that he ever claimed it; it was originally attributed to Allen by AT icon Myron Avery in a tribute to Allen published in the *Potomac Appalachian* after Allen's death in 1939. But the words also appear in an article written by Avery and published in *American Forests* magazine in 1934. Why would Avery attribute words to Allen that appeared in an article Avery himself wrote? Avery was known as a hard-driving, tough-as-nails bulldog, and he might have attributed the quote to Allen because it was too flowery for his own taste. Or he might have been giving credit belatedly to his friend for helping him write the 1934 article.

HARPERS FERRY WV
Robert Harper purchased land here from Lord Fairfax in 1747 and secured a ferry charter from the colony in 1761. In the 19th century, the town became a bustling manufacturing center and the location of a federal arsenal. Its visually stunning location, at the confluence of the Potomac

and Shenandoah rivers, eventually was its undoing, as floods repeatedly destroyed the lower part of town. An act of Congress in 1944 enabled the creation of the Harpers Ferry National Historical Park, which is a blend of private business and national park buildings that preserve and interpret the past.

Harpers Ferry was the site of John Brown's ill-fated attempt to spark a slave revolt in 1859 and, later, the gathering place of African-American leaders who went on to found the NAACP. During the Civil War, the town changed hands so often some residents kept both Confederate and Union flags flying.

HARRIS TRAIL NH
Named for Fred Harris, founder and first president of the Dartmouth Outing Club in 1909.

HARRISBURG PA
Originally named Harris Ferry for its first settler, John Harris, it was founded in 1732 and became the state capital in 1812.

HARRISON GROUND VA
Originally, it was Harris's Ground, for George Harris, a hermit who built a cabin here in the 1860s. Some say he was avoiding a murder charge; others believe he was avoiding the draft during the Civil War. By the time the name took written form, it had been transformed to "Harrison."

HARRISON'S CAMPS ME
Just off the AT at Pierce Pond, these camps were built in 1933 by Ralph Sterling, who operated a hotel in Caratunk. The camps are now owned by the Harrison family. The pond may be named for the family of Peter Pierce, who settled in the area in the 18th century.

Edward Talone

Goodloe Byron Memorial Footbridge crosses the Potomac River from the Chesapeake and Ohio Canal into Harpers Ferry, WV. The bridge is named for the U.S. congressman who did much to protect the trail. The trestle the bridge crosses dates to the 1890s.

HATCH BROOK CT
Most people assume the name recognizes ichthyological activity taking place in the stream, but the name is borrowed from Hatch Pond, named for Capt. Ebenezer Hatch, who came to Sharon from Kent in 1768.

HAVERSTRAW BAY NY
Translated from the Dutch *haverstree,* it means "oak straw bay," thought to be connected to the technique for using straw to make bricks, which were made in nearby Haverstraw using a method developed by James Wood. Haverstraw was also the location of the Franklin Community, a utopian society founded in 1825 by followers of Robert Owen.

HAWK MOUNTAIN SANCTUARY PA
Established in 1934 as a sanctuary to protect the birds of prey that stream past here during fall migration. Before 1934, the peak was called North Mountain for its proximity to South Mountain on the other side of the Lehigh Valley.

HAWKSBILL MOUNTAIN VA
At 4,050 feet, it is the highest point in the Shenandoah NP. You'd have to hike to New Market Gap on Massanutten Mountain to get a good view of the "hawk's bill."

HAZELTOP VA
The area around the peak was called the "Hazel Wilderness" as early as 1763, but the origins of the name are unknown.

HEADFOREMOST MOUNTAIN VA
Visible from Apple Orchard Mountain, this mountain gets its name from the steepness of its slope: If you fell off, you would likely go down headfirst, or headforemost.

HELEN GA
Incorporated in 1913 and named for Helen Bagley, the daughter of lumber baron Henry Bagley. The town is nicknamed the "Star of the North."

HELL HOLLOW BROOK VT
Farming in the nearby hollow was more than difficult—with all the seasonal flooding, rocky soil, and short growing season, it was downright hell. The name dates to sometime in the late 18th century.

HEMLOCK HILL SHELTER MD
Although the shelter has been replaced (and renamed Cowall), the story of Hemlock Hill deserves a place in the annals of the AT. The area is named for its many hemlock trees. The AT runs through the property of the Henneberger family, which granted the state an easement for the trail. The Hennebergers had three sons (Alfred III, Mark, and Douglas) who were active Boy Scouts and who worked on the campsite for their Eagle Scout badges. The oldest son cut chestnut logs from an old restaurant near Gettysburg, PA, notched them, and assembled them into a lean-to. The second son built a latrine at the shelter. The third son made fire rings for each of the four designated camping spots. Unfortunately, the shelter they built closed in 1999; its proximity to the roadway made it a target for vandals.

HENRY LANUM TRAIL VA
Lanum served as supervisor of trails for the Natural Bridge AT Club in 1978–91.

HENSON GAP GA
Named for a man who was killed here in frontier days; his first name and the circumstances of his death are unknown.

Edward Talone

High Point Monument in NJ marks the state's highest point.

THE HERMITAGE ME
Campbell Young lived for years in an isolated cabin here beginning in 1890. This small remnant forest of white pines, some 130 feet tall, is now owned by the Nature Conservancy.

HESSIAN LAKE NY
One of only two natural ponds in Bear Mountain–Harriman State Park, it was formerly known as Bloody Pond because the bodies of dead Hessian mercenaries hired by the British were put into the pond after the British attack on Fort Clinton in October 1777 during the Revolutionary War. In remembrance of the soldiers, it became known as Hessian Lake early in the 1800s. It was also known informally as Highland Lake for a time in the 19th century, and, earlier, it was named *Sinnipink* by Indians. The lake is no longer completely natural; it was enlarged by the installation of three dams in 1914.

HEXACUBA SHELTER NH
Built in 1990 by Jim DeCarlo and a crew from the Dartmouth Outing Club, it gets its name from its hexagonal shape.

HIGH POINT
HIGH POINT SHELTER NJ
A stone shelter built in 1934, named for the state's highest point, with an elevation of 1,803 feet.

HIGH ROCK MD
A 2-story wooden observatory, 30 feet high, was built here circa 1883. It was said to accommodate 500 people. Admission was free for those who had a Western Maryland rail ticket, and 10 cents for those who didn't. The structure was removed sometime in the 1940s. The rock is now popular with hang gliders.

HIGHCOCK KNOB VA
The name is attributed to two roosters owned by hunter "Bear" Tolley, who once lived near Petites Gap. Apparently, the roosters would fly to the top of trees on the side of the mountain—they were high cocks.

HIGHTOP HUT VA
Built by the Civilian Conservation Corps in 1939 on the shoulder of Hightop Mountain, it is the highest point in this part of the Shenandoah NP.

HIGHTOWER BALD
HIGHTOWER GAP GA
Thought to be either a corruption of the Creek word *italwa,* meaning "town," or the Cherokee word *itawa,* or *etowah,* meaning "dead wood."

HOG CAMP GAP VA
Hogs were driven here throughout the early 1800s to be fattened before they were sold. More than 12 miles of stone "hog walls" were built; many of them can still be seen today. Various stories credit this work to slaves or Irish laborers.

HOGBACK GAP NC
This and countless other "hogbacks" are named for their shapes.

HOGPEN GAP GA
There are many hogpen and cowpen names in the Appalachians. Typically, these places are in higher elevations and were once used to herd animals together after summer grazing for their return to lower elevations.

HOLLY BROOK ME
Named after the Holly family, early settlers.

HOLSTON MOUNTAIN VA
The Holston Treaty, a treaty between VA and the Cherokee Nation, was signed in 1791, but the origin of the treaty's name is unknown.

HOMER STONE BROOK VT
Homer Stone was a highway surveyor, lumberman, and farmer from East Wallingford.

HOOSAC RANGE VT
Visible from the AT on Maple Hill, the range gets its name either from the Mahican word for "stony place" or the Natick word for "pinnacle."

HOOSIC RIVER MA
Although the spelling is different for the river, the mountain (Hoosac), and the town (Hoosick), the name is thought to come from either the Mahican term for "stony place" or the Natick word for "pinnacle." The Hoosic Patent was granted to Maria van Renssalaer in 1688. A map published in 1739 calls the river the Hoosuck. It originates near Dalton and empties into the Hudson.

HOP BROOK MA
As early as 1737, Tyringham was often referred to as Hop Lands because of the abundance of hops growing wild in the valley. Hops were also heavily cultivated in the region to make beer and ale, which, next to apple cider, were the most common beverages of the time. The area also was sometimes called "Hop Swamps."

THE HOPPER MA
A hopper is a cirque formed by small glaciers that preceded the main sheet of ice that covered the region during the last ice age and remained after the main sheet retreated. Snow pushed down these smaller glaciers, eroding topsoil and breaking off chunks of rock as it melted and sank, forming a deep, steep bowl where once there had been a mountain. The steep bowl in what is now Mt. Greylock Reservation resembles a grain hopper.

Hopper Road was constructed to ford Money Brook and go through the Hopper. The route was laid out by pioneer farmer Almond Harrison circa 1800. In 1830, Williams College students extended the road to the Greylock summit and built the first observation tower there. According to the Federal Writers Project, the Civilian Conservation Corps developed the road into the Hopper Trail.

THE HORN ME
Because it is a peak on Saddleback, it was likened to a saddle horn.

HORSESHOE TRAIL PA
This trail intersects the AT at its northern terminus; it stretches 137 miles south to Valley Forge, near Philadelphia. The trail, shaped like a horseshoe, was conceived in the 1930s by, among others, Myron Avery—an early leader of the AT effort. He and forty-one others founded the Horseshoe Trail Club.

HORTONTOWN ROAD NY
Hortontown is in the town of East Fishkill and is named for one of its founding families.

Edward Talone

A trail marker high on the Saddleback Range in ME.

HOSNER MOUNTAIN NY

The story that survives is that of James J. Thompkins, who bought the mountain from Indians in exchange for gunpowder, muskets, a blanket, and a dog. Its timber was harvested and, over the years, it was cultivated as a potato farm. The area surrounding the mountain was owned by the Dutch, and the mountain is presumed to have been named for a man named Hosner.

HOT SPRINGS NC

The place had been a tourist destination even for Native Americans. Two settlers discovered the area in 1778, and by 1782, people were traveling here to experience the health benefits of the springs. In the 1830s, the Warm Springs Hotel was built, a popular, 350-room affair that burned down in 1884. It was replaced by the Mountain Park Hotel, during the construction of which a hotter spring was discovered. Marketers changed the resort's name to Hot Springs. The new hotel had 200 rooms, a golf course, and marble pools. It was leased by the federal government as a prison camp during World War I. About 2,800 German servicemen spent their war years here in the lap of luxury, entertaining each other with music and games. When a rumor arose that they were to be transferred, the men poisoned their own water, hoping to make themselves too sick to travel. The scheme backfired, however, and a few of the troops died. The Mountain Park Hotel burned down in 1920. It lives on, though, on a website devoted to its history: hotspringsnc.org.

HOUSATONIC RIVER CT/MA

The conventional wisdom is that the word is derived from the Algonquian word *Wussi-adene-uk*, meaning "beyond the mountain place"—this is the river that flows from beyond the rocky place. There was at one time a Mohegan settlement near Great Barrington, MA, and some sources claim the name referred to this settlement and was then transferred to the river. Spellings by Europeans included "Westenhook," "Awoostenok," "Ansotunoog," and "Ousetonuck."

A competing theory is that the name is derived from Dutch and that it was the Mohegan's use of the Algonquian *twang* that led settlers to believe it was an Indian term. The Dutch derivation theory may be true. "Westenhook," which appears on early maps, translates to "west corner or nook"; the river is on the west side of the mountains.

HOWARD E. BASSETT MEMORIAL NC/TN
Howard E. Bassett of CT thru-hiked the AT in 1968 at the age of 63. He died in 1987, and his ashes were scattered here the following year.

HUBBARD BROOK MA
Named for the Rev. Jonathan Hubbard, the first minister of the Sheffield Congregational Church, who owned land near the brook in the early 18th century.

HUDSON RIVER NY
When Henry Hudson, sailing for the Dutch West Indian Company, looking for the northwest passage to Asia, reached what is now Albany in 1609, he knew he had not found the passage. He did, however, find a beautiful landscape, which he suspected was ripe for mineral exploration.

There is disagreement over the origin and meaning of the Indian name for the Hudson. Some say it was named *Muhheakunnuk* in Algonquian, meaning "great waters constantly in motion." Others say it was the Mahigans, who called it *Mahikannituk,* which means "tidal river of the Mahikans," that named it. As well, Portuguese sailor Estevan Gomez, in the early 17th century, dubbed it the San Antonio. The Hudson's steep cliffs and tides characterize the river as a fjord, the only one on the AT. *See* Anthony's Nose, NY.

HUGHES RIDGE NC/TN
Said to be named for Rafe and Lizzie Hughes, who settled here sometime before 1814. Their descendants lived at the foot of the ridge until the Great Smoky Mountains NP was established. Another Hughes couple, Sarah and Ralph, settled in the vicinity in the late 18th century. The Pecks Corner Shelter was called Hughes Ridge until sometime after 1942.

HUMPBACK ROCKS VA
Named for the shape of the formation when it is seen from the Blue Ridge Parkway. The rocks sit at the base of Humpback Mountain. In the early days of the AT, before the parkway, this formation and the one below it were jointly referred to as "The Rocks." Gradually, after the opening of the parkway, the upper overlook became "Humpback Rocks" and only the lower area was called "The Rocks."

HUNT SPUR ME
Irving Hunt cut a route from Kidney Pond to the summit of Mt. Katahdin in 1890. The Hunts owned a large farm in this area.

HUNTINGTON RAVINE NH
J. H. Huntington was one of the first scientists to conduct winter research on Mt. Washington. He first attempted to winter on the summit in 1858 but couldn't raise funds to finance the trip. Eleven years later, he finally secured funding for winter research, but still hadn't found adequate shelter. That same year, 1869, the famous cog railway to the top of Mt. Washington began operation. Because the buildings that housed the railway machinery were unused in winter, Huntington hoped to stay in them, but he couldn't get the approval of the railroad. So Huntington in-

stead spent the winter of 1869 doing research while camped on frozen Mt. Moosilauke. Newspaper accounts of the scientist's situation generated bad publicity for the railway; he was allowed to use the railway's Mt. Washington buildings the following year.

HURD BROOK LEAN-TO ME

The name of the brook is attributed to Josiah Hurd, a local farmer of the 18th century. The lean-to was built in 1959 by the ME AT Club.

HURRICANE TRAIL NH

Leads to Hurricane Mountain, which was named for the September 1938 hurricane that blew down many of the oldest trees in the area.

HURST MEMORIAL TRAIL NY

Blazed in November of 1922 by Haven J. Hurst, a member of the Green Mountain Club. After his drowning death seven months later on a camping trip, the path became known as the Hurst Memorial Trail.

I

IMP SHELTER NH

The name is transferred from "The Imp," a cliff profile on North Carter Mountain which has been described as "a grotesque, colossal sphinx." The shelter dates from the 1930s.

INADU KNOB NC/TN

Inadu means "snake" in Cherokee, referring to the numerous rattlesnake and copperhead dens still found in the area. *Inadu* is one of the few Indian names to survive after a park commission renamed features within the park boundary after its founding.

INDIAN GAP NC/TN

Likely derived from the use of Indian labor to reconstruct an existing road here in 1830. The gap was later used by Confederate colonel William Thomas during the Civil War to transport saltpeter from Alum Cave Bluff for the manufacture of gunpowder. *See* Newfound Gap, NC/TN.

INDIAN GRAVE GAP GA

The gap is visible from the trail, but you must descend on a side trail to see the rock cairn monument, a mound about 2 feet high that marks a lone grave.

IONA ISLAND NY

The Indians called the island *Manahawagh,* a variation of Manhattan, which means "Island of the Hills." Most of its 118 acres are rocky; only 40 are suitable for cultivation. After it was acquired by Stephanus Van Cortland in 1683, the island became known as Salisbury, then Shelby's. Later names included Weyant's Island and Beveridge's Island. It was named Iona by C. W. Grant of Newburgh, who bought it in 1849 and grew apples, pears, and grapes here. Grant had quite an operation; reportedly his company produced the majority of fruit grown commercially in the country at the time. The "Iona grape" was once grown here. Iona refers to Grant's Scottish heritage. Iona, in the Hebrides, is the "Cradle of Celtic Christianity" and burial place of Scottish kings.

In November 1864, Grant hosted a horticultural convention here, but getting people to the island turned into a fiasco. Their steamship never arrived at its Manhattan port, so guests went upstream by train and boarded a ferry. But the ferry ran aground, so they hiked to another spot to be rowed across the Hudson to the island. A speech given by Horace Greeley at the gathering advocated the establishment of an Adirondack preserve to save the NY forest, which was being logged out of existence.

Iona later became a private resort, then a public park. In 1899, the U.S. Navy bought it for munitions assembly and occupied the island until 1951. In the 1960s, Iona was acquired by the Palisades Interstate Park Commission, but because it is a winter sanctuary for bald eagles, plans for a recreational site here were abandoned.

IRON BRIDGE CT
Built to replace the wooden Burral's Bridge, which dated to the 18th century, the one-lane iron bridge was constructed by the Berlin Construction Company in 1903 (although some claim the actual construction date was 1870).

IRONMASTER'S MANSION PA
Once owned by the family that operated Pine Grove Furnace, where iron products were manufactured, it is now an American Youth Hostel. The mansion was originally constructed in 1827, later serving as a stop on the Underground Railroad.

ISLAND POND NY
Along with Hessian Lake, it is one of two natural ponds in Bear Mountain–Harriman State Park. It is named for the island within the lake.

ISLAND POND MOUNTAIN NY
This mountain really has two summits, and Echo Mountain was once the name of the whole. But people were often confused, thinking one summit was Echo and the other was something else. In 1947, the NY–NJ Trail Conference cleared up the confusion. The group decided that the northern summit, which overlooks Echo Lake, would be called Echo Mountain, and the southern summit, which overlooks Island Pond, would be named Island Pond Mountain.

ISRAEL CREEK MD
Israel Friend mined iron ore on both sides of the Potomac near the mouth of Antietam Creek in the late 1720s. In 1919, a fire at the Savage Distillery caused the creek to burn all the way to the river. More than 650 barrels of whiskey were destroyed.

ISRAEL RIDGE PATH NH
Israel Ridge was named by J. Rayner Edmands, a founder of the Appalachian Mountain Club, because it is close to the source of the Israel River. The river was named for Israel Glines, one of two brothers who hunted here sometime before 1750. *See* Edmands Col, NH.

IVY CREEK VA
The only creek crossed by the AT in the Shenandoah NP is named for the patches of ivy found along its banks.

J

JACOB'S LADDER MA

The origin of the name is nearly as colorful as that of the road's history. Most interesting is that the name was born when the automobile was coming into vogue. A favorite legend involves Deacon Daniel Camp, who lived east of the summit and sported a long gray beard. Because early cars couldn't make the steep and treacherous ascent under their own power, Camp would pull them up with oxen. According to *A Bicentennial History of Beckett,* when a motorist from Springfield was telling friends about his trip to Pittsfield, he described Camp's assistance in biblical terms: "The last pitch was as steep as a ladder but an old chap who looked like the prophet Jacob pulled me over with his oxen!" The route became known as Jacob's Ladder.

JACOB'S LADDER TRAIL NJ

In the Bible, Jacob was an ancestor of the twelve tribes of Israel. In a dream, he saw a ladder extending from earth to heaven. The reference here is to the difficult climb up to a heavenly view.

JAMES RIVER VA

Named for King James I of England, it was formerly named the Fluvanna River, or "River of Anne," for Queen Anne of England. It is the longest river entirely within VA, draining about 9,700 square miles. At 450 miles long, it also is the longest river that flows from the Allegheny Mountains to the Chesapeake Bay.

JAMES RIVER AND KANAWHA CANAL VA

Completed in 1850, this canal once climbed from the tidal waters near Richmond for 197 miles to Buchannan, VA. It passed here on the south side of the James River. It was intended to connect the Kanawha River, named for the Indian people who inhabited it, all the way to the James' confluence with the Ohio River, but was never completed west of Buchannan.

JAMES RIVER FACE WILDERNESS VA

Authorized by Congress in 1975, this wilderness area on the "face" of the James was one of the first designated wilderness areas in the eastern U.S.

JANE BALD NC/TN

The story of the name's origin tells of a woman who died tragically here in 1870. Two sisters, Jane and Harriet Cook, had traveled across the mountains to visit their other sisters. While visiting, Harriet came down with "milk sickness," an ailment contracted by drinking milk from cows poisoned by snakeroot. Awaiting Harriet's recovery, Jane delayed their return over the mountain. But as winter approached, they decided they had best start home. The trip over the rugged mountains in the cold autumn proved too much for Harriet. She collapsed, and Jane went in search of help, entreating local residents to bring a wagon up onto the mountain to retrieve Harriet. They did, but she never recovered; she died at the age of 24. Jane, whose valiant attempt to save her sister is memorialized in the bald's name, lived some 70 years more, dying in the 1940s.

JARMAN GAP VA

William Jarman bought land at the gap in 1800 and for a time owned half interest in "Brown's Turnpike" at Browns Gap. Jarman Gap was first known as Woods Gap after being settled by Michael Woods in 1734. It was the site of the early "Three Notched Road," named because sets of three notches on trees guided travelers.

JARRARD GAP GA
There are plenty of Jarrards on the headstones of the cemetery on Blood Mountain; which one gave his name to this gap is not known.

JEFFERSON NATIONAL FOREST VA
President Franklin Roosevelt established the Jefferson National Forest on April 21, 1936, from lands that had been included in the Unaka and Natural Bridge national forests. At the dedication, Undersec. of Agriculture M. W. Wilson said: "President Roosevelt has named it the Jefferson. This is fitting, for Thomas Jefferson was a practical conservationist, and this national forest embraces much of the country he knew and loved. He knew that man's welfare depended in large part on use of natural resources."

JEFFERSON ROCK VA
Thomas Jefferson was so impressed with the view of Harpers Ferry Gap that he once wrote it was worth a trip across the Atlantic to see.

JENKINS SHELTER VA
Named for Dr. David Jenkins, a Virginia Tech Outing Club leader in the 1950s.

JENNINGS CREEK VA
Previously known as Orrix Creek, then Yoen's Creek, then Jennings Creek in the late 19th century, after a local businessman who owned property along it. The Middle Creek–Jennings Creek area was home to as many as 19 tomato canneries from 1890 to 1920. In 1920, a blight known as *fusarium wilt* wiped out the crop, and the canneries shut down.

JEREMYS RUN TRAIL VA
Called Jeremiah Run Trail for many years, it is probably named for Jeremiah Matthews, who owned land here and fought with distinction in the Revolutionary War.

JEWELL TRAIL NH
Sgt. W. S. Jewell ran the Mt. Washington Observatory in 1878–80.

JIM & MOLLY DENTON SHELTER VA
The Dentons were both longtime trail activists. Jim led the effort for the largest relocation in AT history. Between 1948 and 1951, 155 miles of trail were moved west between Roanoke and Damascus. The relocation was necessary because of the construction of the Blue Ridge Parkway. Jim also scouted the route for the Potomac AT Club's Big Blue Trail in the 1960s. Molly's book *Wildflowers of the Potomac Appalachians* is considered a jewel of natural history literature.

JOBILDUNK RAVINE NH
According to legend, three loggers, Joe, Bill, and Duncan, worked this area in the 1880s.

APPALACHIAN TRAIL

You are hiking on the APPALACHIAN TRAIL which extends for 2000 miles from Maine to Georgia. Follow the white paint blazes! Trails in this area are maintained by volunteer overseers of the POTOMAC Appalachian Trail Club. The overseer for this miles of trail is

Guide books, maps, and other information material may be obtained by writing to or visiting the

POTOMAC
APPALACHIAN TRAIL CLUB
1916 SUNDERLAND PLACE, N. W.
WASHINGTON, D. C. 20036
Office hours 7 p. m. to 10 p. m.
Monday thru Friday

Potomac AT Club

These signs were erected by the Potomac AT Club in the 1950s to advertise the club and highlight volunteer efforts to maintain the trail.

JOE'S HOLE BROOK ME
At the south end of Moxie Pond was the proprietary fishing spot of a ME guide named Joe—it was his fishing hole, and he fished it regularly in the late 18th and early 19th centuries.

JOHN WASILIK MEMORIAL POPLAR NC
Wasilik was an early ranger in the forest service. The poplar here was said to be the second largest yellow poplar in the eastern U.S., measuring 135 feet high. A storm in 1998 knocked it down to half that size.

JOHNS HOLLOW SHELTER VA
A man named John Tyler, for whom the hollow is named, lived in the area, and was said to have been a hermit. He is not known to have been a relative of the more famous John Tylers of VA—Gov. Tyler (1808–11) or his son, the 10th president of the U.S. The shelter was built by the forest service in 1961.

JONES MOUNTAIN TRAIL VA
Jones Mountain, over which this trail leads, may have been named for Cadwaller Jones, who explored the central Shenandoah Valley in 1673.

JONES NOSE MA
Seth Jones was the recipient of an 18th-century land grant nearby. The name refers not to Jones's body part but to the geologic nomenclature used for ridgelines in the northeastern U.S.

JORDAN ROAD VA
Surveyed by Samuel Jordan in 1835 and built a few years later.

JOSEPH BARTHA PLAQUE NY
Joseph Bartha was a pioneer trail builder. Born in Vienna, Austria, in 1871, he immigrated to the U.S. and worked as a waiter in Manhattan. He is credited with keeping the AT open northwest and north of New York City during World War II. At age 95, he witnessed the dedication of the plaque placed in his honor. He died in 1969, after a life illustrating what it means to be a trail volunteer.

JUG END MA
German settlers from Rhineland-Pfalz (or Rhineland-Palatinate) migrated to the area from NY in the early 19th century. Jug End is an anglicization of *jugend,* which means "youth." Still a mystery is why the German word for youth would become a place name—perhaps it was thought to be a way to attract other settlers.

JUMPUP NC
One use of the term "jump up," and the likely one used here, is a steep incline. Other uses include the act of fleeing up a hill from a predator animal, or the place where such flight is known to have occurred.

JUNE MOUNTAIN MA
Benjamin June lived on the mountain in the 19th century.

JUNIATA RIVER PA
This is a variation on the word *oreida,* which has been spelled more than twenty different ways. It is an Iroquois word translated variously as "projecting rock," "standing stone people," or "people of the standing rock." According to the *Handbook of American Indians,* the word is a reference both to a standing stone in the river that was the object of reverence and to a tribe that lived near the mouth of the river. The tribe's small village located on Duncan Island in the Susquehanna River was also known as Juniata.

K

KANCAMAGUS HIGHWAY (U.S. 3) NH

Named for Penacook chief Kancamagus, "The Fearless One," who in 1686 led a raid on Dover, NH.

KAY WOOD LEAN-TO MA

Kay Wood hiked the AT over two summers in the late 1980s, beginning the feat at the age of 73. At this writing, she still lives in the Dalton area and helps maintain a section of the AT there.

KEEP TRYST ROAD MD

The early name of the land patent that would later become Sandy Hook. It was first called Keep Triest, then Triste. "Keep" is an archaic word for fortress; "triest" is evocative of the Italian city Trieste. The AT does not cross the road, but hikers detouring for provisions or a hot meal at Cindy Dee's know it well.

KEEWAYDIN TRAIL VT

A Chippewa word meaning "people of the north" or "north wind."

KENNEBEC RIVER ME

The name is Abenaki for "long level water without rapids." This is the only remaining spot on the AT where ferry service is offered. At various times in AT history, because of trail relocations and storm damage, twelve other water crossings required ferry service. The Kennebec was once a major source of block ice for cities along the east coast. Giant chunks of ice were carved from the frozen river, packed in sawdust, and shipped south by rail.

KENT CT

Incorporated in 1739 and named for the English county, Kent was renowned for its high-quality iron ore during the Civil War era; it was second only to Salisbury, CT in production.

KENT POND VT

The Kent name has a long tradition in VT, although which Kent gave name to the pond is not documented. Remembrance Kent settled Kents Corner in Washington Co. in 1798. The name in general comes from Edward Augustus, duke of Kent, the 4th son of King George III and the father of Queen Victoria. As is the case with most American place names associated with British royalty, the namesake never actually visited the colony. The naming was meant to win favor with the king. The Kent name would later be associated with Atwater Kent radios.

THE KESSEL PA

Southcentral PA and central MD were settled by German immigrants. *Kessel* is German for "kettle," which is what this area looks like when seen from near the summit of Round Head.

KEYS GAP WV

Formerly called Vestal's Gap, there was a ferry referred to as "Keys Ferry" nearby on the Shenandoah circa 1747. Later both Keys and Keyes were used. Keys was made official in 1964, but there are no records of who Keys (or Keyes) was.

KID GORE SHELTER VT

Built in 1971 by the Green Mountain Club and Camp Najerog alumni and named for Harold M. "Kid" Gore, owner of Najerog. While this "Gore" is a surname, the word is a peculiarly VT term of geography, describing land grants that fell between the boundaries of town grants. Gores tended to be triangular in shape because their boundaries typically ended at the top of a mountain. Two boundary lines were then extended until they reached either the next gore or the township line below. Connecting these points with a third boundary created a triangle.

KILLINGTON PEAK VT

At 4,235 feet, it is the second highest peak in the state. The name is transferred from the town now known as Sherburne. The town was probably named for Killington, in Northumberland, England.

KIMMEL LOOKOUT PA

Named for Dick Kimmel, an avid trail worker in the 1940s through the '60s.

KING RAVINE NH

The ravine and Starr King Mountain are named for Thomas Starr King, a Unitarian clergyman who explored this area and wrote about it extensively over several summers. In 1871, he published a collection of his work, *The White Hills, Their Legends, Landscapes & Poetry,* credited with bringing many visitors here. King's explorations in the American West also led to the naming of Mt. Starr King in Yosemite NP in CA.

KINGFIELD ME

William King was the first governor of ME, serving 1820–21. The name was chosen by his wife.

KIRKRIDGE LEAN-TO PA

This church retreat is named for the nearby Kirkridge Retreat House. *Kirk* is Celtic for "church," and the ridge was added because of its location on the Appalachian ridge. The shelter was built around 1948.

KITCHEN BROOK VALLEY MA

Likely derived from the surname Kitching, a family name in this area from as early as the 18th century. Probably originally called Kitching Brook.

KITES DEADENING VA

"Deadening" refers to an area where early settlers killed trees by cutting away a ring of bark. The dead trees remained standing, but because they grew no leaves, the sun could get through, enabling settlers to plant crops or pasture animals among the trees. The trees would later be cut for firewood. The original name here may have been Hites Deadening, after Joist Hite, the first settler of the Shenandoah Valley, in 1734. At the time, Lord Fairfax controlled some 5 million acres of VA, with claims west to the Ohio River, including the area settled by Hite. Fairfax filed suit against Hite (also known as Hans Jost Heydt) in 1736. This incident led Fairfax to hire a young surveyor named George Washington to map his holdings.

How the name was changed from Hites to Kites is a matter of conjecture, but Kites is a name that appears only in AT literature. A plausible explanation is that mountain people living in the Blue Ridge at the time the trail was built had transformed the name over the centuries. Or perhaps early AT trail builders made a transcribing error, mistaking the handwritten *H* for a *K.*

KITTATINNY MOUNTAINS NJ

The word means "great hills" in Leni-Lenape.

KLOIBER'S POND NY

According to an AT volunteer in NY, the Kloibers were a friendly couple with a small house on a field through which the AT traversed. The house was razed in 1990, shortly after the Kloibers left it, so the area could be restored to its natural state. The field is now preserved for butterfly study by a lepidopterist who created and manages the habitat. *See* Butterfly Meadow, NY.

KNOT MAUL BRANCH SHELTER VA

The area is named for the knotwood gathered here to make mauls—any of a variety of hammers with wedge-shaped heads used for driving wedges. The shelter was built in the 1980s by the forest service.

KODAK TRAIL NH
The trail is named for Eastman Kodak cameras—it provides many photographic opportunities, or "Kodak moments," along the way. *See* Eastman Ledges, NH.

KOKADJO–B POND ROAD ME
The AT crosses this gravel road, which leads to Kokadjo, a small community some 19 miles west. The name is Abenaki for "Kettle Mountain." According to legend, Glooskap, an Indian demon, was hunting at Moosehead Lake and killed a moose, which changed into Mount Kineo. Glooskap pursued the moose's calf and, in order to lighten his load, discarded his kettle. The kettle landed upside down and became Kokadjo Mountain, which lends its name to the community. The "B Pond" part of the name is directional; the road leads east to the village of B Pond.

L

LAKE BUEL MA
On the original Kings Grant Survey, the lake was called Six-Mile Pond. A tragedy here led to the name change. After a terrible boating accident, Samuel Buel managed to pluck a few survivors from the waters. A number of others died. Accounts about when this occurred and how many people were involved differ: in 1876, involving eight boaters, or in 1812, involving seven. All accounts agree that Buel displayed incredible courage and strength.

LAKE HEBRON ME
Named for the Hebron Academy in Monson, MA.

LAKE LENAPE PA
Named for the Lenape, also known as the Delaware Indians, who once lived throughout this region. Three meanings of the name are offered. The first two, as with many Indian nation names, relate to the nation being the "first people in the world." One is "genuine men," the other is "the original people." A third meaning relates to the Delaware Indians as a collection of smaller nations or "people of the same nation."

LAKE ONAWA ME
Visible from the AT at Barren Ledges. *Onawa* is Chippewa for "awaken," but this is an unlikely place for a Chippewa name. Legend says that an Indian girl named Onawa committed suicide at the lake and is buried there. Others say the name comes from Longfellow's poem "Hiawatha," which would explain the use of a Chippewa word in ME. The original name was Ship Pond, named for the lake's Schooner Island, which is shaped like ship masts.

LAKE TIORATI NY
The first dams here were constructed in 1767 by Peter Hasenclever to provide water for a mineral furnace, which never went into operation. In 1844, a new owner broke the dams and grew vegetables on the resulting mud flats. The current lake was created in 1915. *Tiorati* seems to be either an Algonquian name meaning "skylike" or a Mahican word meaning "blue like the sky." Near here, on October 7, 1923, the first section of the AT was officially opened.

LAKE TRAIL VT
Originally a carriage road from the lake to the Griffith Lake House, which gives the trail its name. *See* Griffith Lake, VT.

Bill O'Brien

Bridge over Laurel Creek in VA.

LAKES OF THE CLOUDS HUT NH
The hut is named for two glacial lakes formed during the last ice age, sources of the Ammonoosuc River. They are located high on the fog-shrouded slopes of Mt. Washington. The hut was built in 1915 and later expanded by the Appalachian Mountain Club.

LAKEVILLE CT
Formerly called "Salisbury Furnace" and "Furnace Village." Ethan Allen had a blast furnace here prior to his Revolutionary War activities at Fort Ticonderoga and in VT with the Green Mountain Boys. His furnace was a technological innovation that put smaller forges out of business. The name Lakeville, which achieved currency in 1846, comes from Lake Wononscopomus, also known as *Wonoskopomuc*, meaning "bend in the pond land."

LAKOTA LAKE VT
It is not known how this lake in Barnard got its name. The Lakota are a branch of the Sioux Indian nation, and the name is said to mean either "allies" or "land of plenty." (*Sioux* is said to be of French origin; it means "cut throat.")

LAMBS KNOLL MD
The second highest point on South Mountain, thought to be named for Milton Lamb, who married into the family that once owned the land. It is called "Lamb's Improvement" on a 1796 survey, then "Lamb's Old Field"; it acquired its present name after the Civil War.

LAUREL CREEK SHELTER VA
Formerly Big Pond Shelter, built in 1960 and moved here in 1988. The creek is named for the mountain laurel abundant here.

LEEMAN BROOK LEAN-TO ME
Built by the ME AT Club in 1987 and named for Thomas Leeman, a local resident.

LEHIGH CANAL PA
In the Lehigh Gap, the AT crosses the route of the old Lehigh Canal, which stretched 64 miles from White Haven to Easton. It operated from 1829 until about 1935 and is noteworthy for two significant events in canal history—a first and a last. Cement was developed as the canal was being built and was used here for the first time on canal locks. This also was the last U.S. canal to employ mule power, in use until 1933. *See* Lehigh River, PA.

LEHIGH RIVER PA
Flows 122 miles from Stoddardsville to Easton. The name is a corruption of the Delaware Indian word *Lechauwekink*, meaning "where there are forks." German settlers shortened this to "Lecha" and English settlers made it Lehigh, a word that has no meaning.

LEMON SQUEEZER NY
In 1922, trail blazers from the NY–NJ Trail Conference set out to find interesting geologic features along the trail corridor. This narrow passage between a split rock ledge was discovered and named by J. Ashton Allis. *See* Allis Trail, NY.

LEROY A. SMITH SHELTER PA
Built by the Appalachian Mountain Club in 1972, it was originally supposed to be named the Katellen Shelter (for Kate and Ellen, daughters of the farmer who laid out the side trail that leaves the AT here). When the shelter was dedicated, however, it was named for longtime trail volunteer Leroy Smith (1920–73).

LETTERROCK MOUNTAIN NY
Originally known as "Lettered Rock" for the symbols believed to have been painted on the rocks by Indians. Two colorful legends relate to the name. One tells of a Frenchman who went into the mountains with his slave and returned with silver coins. He is said to have told a few people about a load of silver stashed east of a "lettered" rock. The second tells of Spaniards who came to mine here and left a cache of hidden treasure behind.

In 1935, a Madison Avenue investor took both legends seriously enough to hire four Swedes with mining experience to find the treasure. After blasting and searching for some time, they were noticed by hikers, who reported the activity to authorities. The "gold diggers" were arrested. They were allegedly carrying a map dating from 1720 that showed where Spaniards had hidden silver. In 1985, a professional treasure salvage company from FL received a 5-day permit to look for clues to the treasure. They had no luck. Numerous searches for the hidden fortune here and on the neighboring Goshen and Flaggy Meadows mountains have yet to make anyone rich.

LEWIS MOUNTAIN VA
Probably named for John Lewis, the first settler in Staunton, circa 1740. In the 1930s, shortly after the opening of the Shenandoah NP, a picnic ground here was designated for "colored use"; when park officials noted that more than 4,000 African-Americans were visiting the park each year, Franklin Roosevelt's Interior Department had directed the creation of a "colored campground" to accommodate them. Even though it was segregated, the campground was seen by some to be an improvement of conditions: Most parks, including national parks, at that time were not open to nonwhites.

LIBERTY CORNER ROAD NJ
During the American Revolution, this was the place where local people gathered to hear news of the War for Independence.

LICKLOG CREEK
LICKLOG GAP NC
Refers to the notches farmers would cut into fallen trees that were used to hold salt for livestock.

LIME ROCK CT
Previously known as The Hollow and, later, Rocky Dell, the village is named for the lime deposits in the vicinity. The former site of a gristmill owned by Thomas Lamb, Lime Rock also provided iron used to make muskets for the U.S. armories at Harpers Ferry, WV, now national headquarters for the AT Conference. Lime Rock is perhaps better known to flatlanders for its auto racing, which about half of the locals despise for its noise and the other half applaud for the economic activity it generates. It's a place for nonracers to get into the game. Walter Cronkite, Dick Smothers, Paul Newman, Tom Cruise, and Walter Payton have all raced at Lime Rock.

LINDEN VA
Tradition says it was named for a linden tree that was used as a local landmark.

LINER FARM CT
Liner family members were the last tenant farmers on land owned by the Stanley Works tool company.

LIONS HEAD CT
Some say that when viewed from the east, this feature looks like the king of the beasts, but it may take a bit of squinting and head tilting to reveal this form. The preferred view is that of Twin Lakes from 1,738 feet, as offered from atop Lions Head itself.

LITTLE BIGELOW MOUNTAIN ME
The name was first transferred from Bigelow Mountain in Franklin County, which was named for Maj. Timothy Bigelow, one of Benedict Arnold's officers. During the ill-fated 1775 march to Quebec during the Revolutionary War, Bigelow climbed this mountain hoping to see his destination.

LITTLE BOARDMAN MOUNTAIN ME
Named for J. H. Boardman and his relatives, one of whom was the surveyor here in the 1800s.

LITTLE FORT HILL NY
After being routed by the British at Peekskill on October 9, 1777, as many as 2,000 Continental troops fled to this area and created temporary fortifications.

LITTLE HAYSTACK MOUNTAIN NH
At one time Lincoln, Lafayette, Liberty, and Garfield mountains all had the name "Haystack" because they resemble haystacks when seen from the town of Lincoln. This is the only peak to retain its original name.

LITTLE POND LOOKOUT VT
Named for nearby Little Pond, which is slightly smaller than Big Pond.

LITTLE RIDGEPOLE MOUNTAIN NC
Named for its proximity to Ridgepole Mountain, which gets its name from its long, level summit that is so narrow that it resembles a ridgepole on a house.

LITTLE ROCK POND SHELTER VT
Built by the U.S. Forest Service in 1962, the shelter once stood on the island—the little rock—in the pond, but overuse led to its removal. It was the only AT shelter ever located on an island.

LITTLE SWIFT RIVER POND CAMPSITE ME
The name was transferred from Swift River Pond, so named because it is the source of the Swift River.

LITTLE TENNESSEE RIVER NC
The Overhill Cherokee built their principal villages, including *Tanase* (or *Tenese*), on what we now call the Little Tennessee River, from which the state and the Tennessee River derive their names. One tradition claims that Tennessee means "the great bend," but whether this is derived from a single bend or the many major turns the river takes we do not know. Another story is that the word *Tennassee* was a Cherokee term for "spoon."

LOCKED ANTLERS CAMP PA
According to the late Ray Fadner, longtime member of the Potomac AT Club, this was the site of a hunting camp named for two fighting bucks who had locked antlers.

LOCUST COVE GAP NC
LOCUST CREEK VT
Because locust trees are a recovery species, these names likely were bestowed after the forest's rebirth following heavy logging in the 1920s. One of the downsides of naming places after tree species is that the trees may disappear, whether from human-induced or natural

causes. (Note the number of places with "chestnut" in the name, after a tree that disappeared in the 1930s.) Here, the locusts likely sprang up along the creek after the surrounding land was cleared for agriculture. Within a generation, the locusts gave way to either other species in the woods or riparian species along the streambank. If nature is allowed to run its course, and hardwoods such as oak, hickory, and tulip take over, the locust name will outlive the locust trees themselves.

LOGAN BROOK LEAN-TO ME

"Logan" is a peculiarly ME word that describes deadwater in a brook. The brook here forms a logan in the valley between Whitetop and Boardman mountains, hence the name. The lean-to, built in 1983 by the ME AT Club, was named by club member Dave Field, who is also a former chair of the AT Conference board of managers.

LONG FALLS DAM ROAD ME

Built in 1949 after Flagstaff Lake flooded the Dead River Valley and named for the dam at Long Falls. The falls, the name of which is descriptive, is about 6 miles north of where the AT crosses the road.

LONG HOUSE ROAD NJ

Early settlers to this region built long log dwellings, some say to reduce the number of cuts their blades would have to make. Rather than building three or four small outbuildings for storage, they would build the storage sheds onto the house. So instead of cutting an 80-foot log into, say, 40-foot lengths for the house and 10-foot lengths for sheds, they might just cut fewer 50-foot lengths to construct one building.

LONG PATH NY

In 1931, Vincent J. Schaefer of Schenectady proposed that NY develop a Long Path similar to the Long Trail in VT. He envisioned a meandering, unmarked route from New York City to Lake Placid. Development of the trail began in the 1930s, but then interest waned. It was revived in the 1960s, and the NY–NJ Trail Conference started work again. Although it hasn't made it to Lake Placid yet, the Long Path currently runs from the George Washington Bridge to John Bryan State Park, south of Albany. Plans are in place, though, to extend it. The trail's name comes from Walt Whitman's "Song of the Open Road," which says: "There lies before me a long brown path, leading wherever I choose."

LONG POND ME

One of the "Four Ponds," its name is descriptive.

LONG TRAIL VT

Predating the idea of the AT by more than a decade, the Long Trail traverses the Green Mountains from the MA line to the Canadian border. It was the brainchild of a VT schoolteacher named James Taylor, who came upon the idea while waiting out a storm on a camping trip. (Taylor is also credited with the idea of establishing a federal tax on gasoline to pay for road building.) The trail is maintained, and its protection advocated, by the Green Mountain Club. The AT follows the route of the Long Trail for more than a hundred miles in southern VT.

LOST POND SHELTER VT

The name is transferred from Lost Pond, which was given the moniker because it was so far from roads and trails that it was "lost" to the hunters and trappers who sought it each year. The shelter, a gift from Louis Stare, Jr., was built on Cape Cod in 1965, then dismantled and transferred to the site.

LOST RIVER NH
So named because it disappears into the side of Kinsman Mountain.

LOST SPECTACLES GAP VA
The pass was named by Roanoke AT Club member Tom Campbell in the 1930s after he lost his glasses on a work trip here.

LOTTERY ROAD VT
The trail crosses the road several miles west of Shrewsbury. While the precise origin of this name remains elusive, the origin of lotteries in this country offers a glimpse of life in colonial and federal America. Lotteries were a common way for businesses to raise capital, individuals to dispose of property, and governments to finance public works. In 1783, for example, Anthony Haswell and David Russell requested and received from the VT legislature (VT was still an independent republic at the time) permission to hold a lottery for the purpose of financing VT's first paper mill. It was built in what is today North Bennington.

In 1775, William West, a Revolutionary War patriot, held a lottery to sell his land so that he could repay debts incurred during the war—most of the war effort was financed from the pockets of patriots. As for Lottery Road, conjecture is that the road was built from the proceeds of a lottery. It may also mean that you were as likely to get through this road in winter as you were to win the lottery.

LOVERS LEAP RIDGE
LOVERS LEAP ROCK NC
The participants are different, but the story seems to always be the same. The legend here tells of a Cherokee maiden who threw herself off the mountain after her lover, Magwa, was killed by jealous rival Lone Wolf. This story may be true, or it may be the early Cherokee version of an urban legend.

LOW GAP NC/TN
Aptly named, it is one of the lowest gaps along the crest of the Smoky Mountains.

LOWER COBBLE ROAD CT
Don't look for cobbles here now; they were all removed and the road regraded. Upper Cobble Road, however, is lined with small, rounded cobblestones.

LOWER JO-MARY LAKE ME
Jo-Mary was a Penobscot Indian chief whose hunting grounds extended from Pemadumcook Lake to Potaywadjo and the Jo-Mary Mountains. He was renowned as a swimmer who would blow water from his mouth in a way that resembled a whale. His nickname was "Puffer," which is also the name these Indians gave to the whale. Jo-Mary Lake was probably named by the early Europeans in the area sometime in the 18th century; previous names are unknown.

LOWE'S BALD SPOT NH
This open rocky knob was probably named for Charles Lowe of Randolph, a well-known mountain guide in the 1870s. He and Dr. William Nowell built a toll road up the Presidential Range from Randolf, which today is known as Lowes Path. Lowe later owned a hotel in Randolf called the Mt. Crescent House.

LOWLY MARTYR GAP NC/TN
Although TN joined the Confederacy, the state had many northern sympathizers. During the Civil War, the Confederate Home Guard, a band of vigilantes, rounded up "recruits" and forced them to join the Southern army. Those that refused to serve were hanged or shot; they were called lowly martyrs by northern sympathizers. Conjecture is that the gap was a transportation route used to move these unwilling Confederates.

LOY WOLFE ROAD MD
One source says that Loy Wolfe was the great-grandson of David Wolfe, Sr., who supposedly founded Wolfsville in 1828. But other sources name Jacob Wolf as the founder. Records show Jacob as postmaster in 1834, but offer no mention of a David or a Loy—which may have been a nickname. The only safe bet is that Loy was indeed a Wolfe.

LUFTEE KNOB NC
From the last two syllables of *Oconaluftee,* a corruption of the Cherokee word *Egwanulti,* which means "all towns along the river." Also known as "The Pillar."

LULA TYE SHELTER VT
Built by the forest service in 1962, it is named in honor of the secretary of the Green Mountain Club in 1926–55.

LURAY VA
Seen from the AT in Shenandoah NP, it is the site of the famous Luray Caverns. There are several stories about the origin of its name. One is that it was named for early blacksmith Lewis Ray, whose establishment was popular among early travelers; they referred to the place as Lew Ray's. Another more plausible but less colorful explanation is that the name was bestowed by the family of William S. Massie, early settlers who hailed from Lurray, France.

LUTHER HASSINGER MEMORIAL BRIDGE VA
The span along the VA Creeper Trail is named for an early timber baron who harvested millions of board feet in this area. The history of the natural beauty in the Appalachians is one of irony. So much of this land was given up as valueless by the barons after they extracted its wealth and laid it to waste. They often disposed of it on the cheap to the federal government. Today, the landscape is treasured for its natural beauty, not just for the potential profit to be made from it. Yet, were it not for the enormous scale of exploitation by people such as Hassinger, the government would never have been able to assemble such huge parcels of public land.

LYE BROOK WILDERNESS VT
So named because potash was produced here, then leached to make lye for soap.

M

MACEDONIA BROOK CT
The nearby town of Macedonia might have been named by hikers of yore in search of sustenance. Its named is derived from the Bible's Book of Acts, in which the supplicants beg "come into Macedonia and help us."

MAD TOM NOTCH VT
The name was transferred from Mad Tom Brook, which derives its "madness" from the wild rush the stream makes tumbling down the mountain. The origin of "Tom" is unknown.

MADISON SPRINGS HUT NH
The oldest hut in the White Mountains, having opened in 1888. The original hut was expanded in 1906, 1922, and 1929. Fire destroyed it in 1940; it was rebuilt in 1941 under the direction of hut-master Joe Dodge, longtime manager of the Appalachian Mountain Club hut system—a post he held for 30 years.

MAHAR TOTE ROAD ME
Some say there was a Mahar family that lived nearby; others say the name is derived from the Abenaki word *mahican,*

meaning "one who gathers them together." A "tote" road, also known as a haul road, is used by loggers to tote logs to the sawmill.

MAHOOSUC NOTCH ME

Thought to be Abenaki for "home of hungry animals," which may refer to the Mohegan-Pequot refugees who fled from CT to ME after the Pequot War of 1637. Another theory is that the word is Natick for "a pinnacle."

MAHOOSUC TRAIL NH

Once the AT route into Gorham. *See* Mahoosuc Notch, ME.

MAINE

Phillip R. Rutherford, in his *Dictionary of Maine Place Names,* gives three possibilities, admitting all are uncertain. The name could refer to the land which lay beyond the hundreds of coastal islands, or the Maine Land, as it was called. It might be named for being the land on the ocean, or "on the Maine." Also, there is a province in France called Maine, and the transference is not impossible.

MAINE JUNCTION VT

Guidebooks to the AT name this point of reference because here the AT leaves the Long Trail, with which it has coaligned since the MA line, to head for ME. *The Guide to the Long Trail,* published by the Green Mountain Club, refers to the place as Canada Junction because the Long Trail heads north toward Canada. This local perspective once dictated the color of the trail blazes. From here east to Gifford Woods State Park, at the insistence of the GMC, the AT was blazed blue, instead of its customary white, until the early 1990s, when the GMC finally consented to white blazes. Before that, the GMC claimed priority in choosing white for the blazes of the Long Trail, the nation's oldest long-distance hiking trail.

Potomac AT Club

Rocky Run shelter in MD, built by the Civilian Conservation Corps in 1941.

MANASSAS GAP
MANASSAS GAP LEAN-TO VA

First named Calmes Gap after Marquis Calmes. The word Manassas is derived from a local surname, Manassa. As often occurs in place-naming, the apostrophe was dropped from the possessive. The shelter was built of chestnut logs by the Civilian Conservation Corps in 1939.

MANCHESTER CENTER VT

This Old World name is thought to be an Old English word for "a camp on the meadow." Although the name ultimately leads back to England, the town more directly borrowed the name from Manchester, MA. That town's English counterpart was named for Charles Montague, first duke of Manchester.

MANITOGA NATURE RESERVE NY

Furniture designer Russel Wright purchased the land in 1942 and restored it over three decades. The landscape had been deeply scarred by logging and quarrying. Wright named it Manitoga, after the Algonquian for "place of the Great Spirit," because he saw the Indians as supremely respectful of nature. Trained as a theatrical scene-designer and sculptor, Wright designed a restored landscape of native trees and plants. The property was opened to the public in 1975, a year before Wright's death. Manitoga currently offers programs in ecology, science, art, and design.

MANITOU ROAD NY

Connects with a village in Putnam County called Manitou, a French derivation for the Algonquian "guardian spirit."

MARBLE BROOK ME

Named for Eben and David Marble, who moved here about 1824.

MARYLAND HEIGHTS MD

The highest of the three pinnacles—Loudoun, Bolivar, and Maryland—around Harpers Ferry, and the one located on the MD side of the Potomac River. It changed hands three times during the Civil War.

MARYS ROCK VA

The popular legend is that it is named for the wife of Francis Thornton, one Mary Taliferro (pronounced Toliver). A wealthy 18th-century landowner, Thornton is said to have proposed to her here, and the couple returned each year afterward to camp on the "Great Pass Mountain." On one such trip, they climbed to the summit, and he named the rock there for her. When Francis died, Mary insisted that the land near the pass be included as part of her "dower" right to the estate—in those days a wife of a man of Thornton's means would not have automatic rights to the full estate. Many years later, Mary left her valley estate and moved close to the pass to live in a log house. From here she could look upon Marys Rock. The area was known as "Madame Thornton's Quarter" during the last third of the 18th century.

A second origin story says that the sculptor William Randolf Barbee (1818–68), who lived in Page County, named the rock for his wife Mary. When he died, William's son Herbert made a bust of his father and placed it in the cemetery at his father's grave, looking upward toward Marys Rock. It was Herbert's intention to make a sculpture of Mary, but he died before completing the task.

MASHIPACONG SHELTER NJ

The word is Algonquian for "great pond"; the stone shelter was built in 1936.

MASON-DIXON LINE MD/PA

Originally known as the Mason and Dixon Line, it is named for surveyors Charles Mason and Jeremiah Dixon, whose east-west line through the wilderness and mountains created the border between MD and PA. The pair were already famous before they began the survey; they were picked for the job because of their renown. Descendants of William Penn and George Calvert, the original grantees of, respectively, PA and MD, had disputed the border since 1681. After a century of squabbling, they agreed to commission a survey to determine the boundaries. Both agreed that their colonies would live by the findings.

Beginning in 1763, Mason and Dixon placed milestones and, every 5 miles, capstones to mark their transects. Anyone who has ever stumbled onto a Mason and Dixon stone in the rugged mountains can't help but be amazed by their efforts, especially given how remote the western sections of those colonies were at the time. To smooth the way, a road was built to transport the pair's provisions and equipment, and the two were accompanied by a battalion of local surveyors, lumberjacks, cooks, rodmen, and chainmen. Their boundary line long ago created an emotional dividing line between North and South. (While they were at it, Mason and Dixon also surveyed the north-south line that now divides MD and DE.)

MASSANUTTEN MOUNTAIN VA
Seen from many points on the AT in northern and central Shenandoah NP, the generally accepted origin of the name is an Indian word meaning "potato ground." Another claim is that the word means "The Basket" because the northern end is split into two ridges forming a basket-shaped valley. Local legend has it that Massanutten was so named because it was a "big mass of nothing"; it was too steep and rocky to farm. Its earlier name was Peaked Mountain because when seen from the southeast, many peaks are visible. This name is now reserved for the southern end of the range.

MATTAGAMON GATE ME
Abenaki word for "horse."

MATTHEWS ARM VA
This Shenandoah NP campground is named for Israel Matthews, who received a grant for this land from Lord Fairfax.

MAU-HAR TRAIL VA
The name of the connecting path between the Maupin Field Lean-to and the Harpers Creek Shelter is a made-up word. The trail was built in 1979.

MAUPIN FIELD SHELTER VA
The shelter, built in 1961, is named for the Maupin family, whose presence here dates to the late 18th century. The Maupins married into the Brown and Jarman families that settled in the area. The lean-to's presence leads to another story. In 1973, the superintendent of Shenandoah NP decided to remove all the existing lean-tos in order to make the park more primitive. Within a year, all the log lean-tos were gone. Ed Garvey, then president of the Potomac AT Club, which maintains trails in the park, intervened, contesting that the shelters were essential for long-distance hikers, whose packs were already too full of provisions to carry tents. His efforts saved the lean-tos that remain today. Between 1973 and 1983, the shelters were considered closed except in "severe" weather. Since 1983, however, the shelters are again open. *See* Browns Gap, VA, and Jarman Gap, VA.

MAURY RIVER VA
Visible from the AT near Sulfur Spring Trail, the river is named for Commander Matthew Fontaine Maury (1806–73), an instructor at the Virginia Military Institute known as the "Pathfinder of the Seas" for his work charting ocean currents. Maury's system of recording oceanographic data from naval vessels and merchant marine ships was adopted worldwide. In 1855, he published *The Physical Geography of the Sea*, which is now credited as the first textbook of modern oceanography. During the Civil War, Maury held the position of commander in the Confederate Navy. After the war, he lived for a time in England, then returned to Lexington in 1868 to accept a position at VMI. Upstream, the river is known as the Calfpasture River.

MAX PATCH MOUNTAIN NC
The name Max Patch, a farmer who owned land here, dates to the 19th century, but records are unclear as to the exact date.

MCCAMPBELL GAP
MCCAMPBELL KNOB NC/TN
Robert McCampbell went to Cades Cove circa 1850 to find gold. He struck out, but later found copper on the other side of the mountain.

MCCORMICK GAP VA
Probably named for Cyrus McCormick, inventor of the grain reaper, who was born a few miles from here at Steele's Tavern.

MCGEES BRIDGE NH
Named for the Dartmouth graduate who built the bridge.

MEADOW SPRING TRAIL VA
Departing the AT 2.3 miles south of Thornton Gap, it is named for a cabin in the meadow next to Skyline Drive—Meadow Spring Cabin, built in 1930 by the Potomac AT Club for $100. The club's second cabin, it burned on Thanksgiving Day 1946 and was never rebuilt.

MICHAUX STATE FOREST PA
Established in 1912 and named for Andre and Francois Michaux, French botanists who explored the area. Andre, the father of Francois, worked in the area in 1793, with the son following a decade later. The name was suggested by Gifford Pinchot in 1902, when he was chief of the U.S. Forest Service. Known as the father of American forestry, Pinchot would in the 1920s become governor of PA.

MIDDLE MOUNTAIN ME
So named because it is the middle peak between South and Pleasant Pond mountains.

MIKE MURPHY SPRING NH
Named for the last fire warden at Smarts Mountain.

MILESBURN CABIN PA
Built by the Civilian Conservation Corps, circa 1932, for Michaux State Forest fire wardens. Its location, in Miles Hollow, and its use as a fire warden's cabin provide the only clues to the origin of its name. It was leased to the Potomac AT Club in December 1936.

MILL RIDGE NC/TN
Probably a reference to the grist mill operated by William Marion Walker here in 1850–70. He lived at the base of the ridge.

MILLER HILL ROAD NY
Named for John Miller, a Revolutionary War veteran who received land as payment for his service. Miller Hill, in the town of East Fishkill, is the south peak of Hosner Mountain. The road is an extension of the old Dutchess and Westchester Turnpike, on which construction began in 1809.

MINERVA HINCHEY SHELTER VT
Built in 1969 by the Green Mountain Club and named in honor of Minerva Hinchey, club secretary in 1955–69.

MIRY RIDGE NC/TN
This is the rarely used adjectival form of the word *mire,* here describing one of those wet, mucky basins atop many an Appalachian ridge, always filled with soaked organic matter.

MIZPAH SPRING HUT NH
Mizpah is thought to be an archaic Hebrew word meaning "watch tower." The mountain location, 6 miles north of Crawford Notch, might be the reason for the name.

MOHAWK TRAIL CT
Many of the trails in the CT Blue Trail System are named for Indian nations. Although the area was never inhabited by Mohawks, they are known to have come here on hunting excursions from NY. But the name Mohawk here is meant to be more evocative of frontier days than a historical reference to the Mohawk tribe.

MOHAWK TRAIL (ROUTE 2) MA
The Mohawk Trail, designated a scenic route by the MA state legislature and opened on October 22, 1914, was the first scenic road in New England. It was originally a Mohawk footpath. Although the Mohawk, an Iroquois tribe, lived primarily in NY, they ventured into MA to hunt. The

Europeans used the route for travel between Boston, Deerfield, and the Dutch settlements of NY. During the Revolutionary War, Benedict Arnold used the trail to get from MA to Fort Ticonderoga, where he made his famous capture of a British cannon.

MOHHEKENNUCK FISHING AND HUNTING CLUB MA

Muh-he-ka-nuk is the pre-anglicized "Mahican," a tribe pushed northward from NY into what is now northwest MA by the Mohawks. Once established there, by 1628, they became known as the Stockbridge Indians. Originally, they hunted in the Berkshires but lived primarily in the Hudson River Valley. The Mohhekennuck Fishing and Hunting Club was founded in the early 1900s. In 1909, members acquired 13 acres on Upper Goose Pond, where they built a 2-story cabin. The National Park Service purchased the property in the 1980s.

MOLLIES RIDGE SHELTER NC/TN

According to an ancient Cherokee legend, Mollie was a young woman who died while searching for her lover, White Eagle, after he failed to return from a hunting trip. Her body was found on the ridge.

MOLLY STARK HIGHWAY VT

The name given to this stretch of VT Route 9 honors the wife of John Stark, a hero of the Battle of Bennington.

MONEY BROOK MA

In 1765–83, counterfeiters supposedly ran an operation in a cave near here, producing pine tree shillings—a coin minted in mid-18th-century Boston. The coin had a pine tree imprint. Another story has them working from a cabin near here and producing Spanish dollars.

MONT ALTO PA

Originally called Funkstown, the village took its new name from an iron furnace built in 1808 by Samuel and David Hughes and called Mont Alto—but no one knows why. Pig iron from here was transported across Sandy Ridge to the Old Forge on the East Branch of Little Antietam Creek.

MONTICELLO LAWN NH

Transferred from Thomas Jefferson's VA estate because it sits at the base of Mt. Jefferson. *See* Presidential Range, NH.

MONTVALE VA

First called Bufords Gap for Capt. Paschal Buford, who fought in the War of 1812 and owned land here. It was later called Bufordsville when Buford gave land to the railroad. In 1890, it became Montvale because it sits in a basin surrounded on three sides by the Blue Ridge Mountains.

MONUMENT CLIFF ME

Name given to the summit area of Third Mountain, where a plaque memorializes Walter D. Greene (1872–1941), a Broadway actor and ME guide who built a trail here.

MONUMENT KNOB MD

Previously known as Blue Rocks for the abundance of talus scattered on the slope, this peak of South Mountain was renamed after citizens from nearby Boonesboro built the nation's first monument to George Washington in 1827.

MONUMENT MOUNTAIN MA

According to Stockbridge Indian custom, anyone found to have violated tribal tradition hurled themselves from this mountaintop—or they had the favor done for them. Sources disagree as to whether one particular Indian maiden was pushed or threw herself from the mountain, but they agree it was her demise that is the source of the monument and the summit's name.

The most well-known story involves a maiden who broke custom by marrying into another tribe. Refusing to throw herself from the mountain, she was bound and pushed off. But that didn't do her in. She became stuck in a tree limb. Because her arms were tied, she was unable to free herself. After several days of hanging there, a storm kicked up, burned the tree, and lifted the maiden into the heavens. Another story, told in a poem by William Cullen Bryant, describes a maiden who lusted for her brother-in-law. Racked with guilt, she threw herself from the top.

The monument itself is a pile of rocks that Indians stacked for atonement for the maiden's death, adding to it each time they passed the spot. Nathaniel Hawthorne and Herman Melville are said to have met here during a picnic in 1850.

MOODY MOUNTAIN ME

Said to be named for a man named Moody who fell from a cliff to his death.

MOONEY GAP NC

James Mooney was a historian for the U.S. Bureau of American Ethnology who wrote *Myths of the Cherokee* in 1898. The gap is named in his honor, although no particular event associates him with the gap.

MOORMANS RIVER TRAIL VA

The river is named for Charles Moorman from the Isle of Wight, Great Britain. A prominent Quaker, he settled here in 1735. This trail to Jarman Gap is the original route of the AT.

MOOSELOOKMEGUNTIC LAKE ME

Visible from the AT crossing of ME Route 17; the name is Abenaki for "portage to moose-feeding place."

MORGAN MILL STREAM VA

Possibly named for Daniel Morgan, whose mill was on this creek. Morgan fought in the French and Indian War and, as a general in the Revolutionary War, defeated Burgoyne at Saratoga.

MORGAN STEWART SHELTER NY

Built by volunteers in 1984. Morgan Stewart arranged for IBM to donate construction funds.

MOSBY CAMPSITE VA

Named for Col. John Mosby (1833–1916), who led a series of successful raids against the North during the Civil War. His band of men was known as "Mosby's Raiders." Mosby himself was known as the "Gray Ghost" because of his band's surprise attacks on the unsuspecting enemy. He knew the northern Blue Ridge and his area of operations well, having grown up in Edgemont, 40 miles west of Richmond. Mosby Campsite borrows its name from the nearby community of Mosby (no longer in existence), which was so named because some of Mosby's men settled there. This was not entirely their choice. Mosby required his men to live within an area he demarcated, from Snickers Gap to Linden in the north, and east to The Plains and Aldie. The region would become known as "Mosby's Confederacy." This campsite was once the location of Mosby Shelter, but in an act of intrigue that Mosby himself would appreciate, the entire structure disappeared in 1980.

MT. ABRAHAM ME

The origin of the name is unknown, but it could be named for Abraham Reed, who settled in nearby Kingfield in 1871 and whose name is associated with Reed Brook (about 3 miles north), Reed Hill, and Reed Pond, all in the general vicinity of Kingfield.

Edward Talone

This sign in the White Mountains warns "many have died above treeline."

MT. ADAMS NH

Mt. Adams consists of three peaks named after famous Adamses. The highest peak is named for John Adams, the 2nd president of the U.S. The peak to the east is Mt. John Quincy Adams, the 6th president and son of John. The west peak is named for Samuel Adams, a cousin of John Adams and early leader in the American Revolution (for whom the brewery is named). A group called the Atherians believes Mt. Adams has special powers. They consider it holy and hold ceremonies here to send energy out into the world.

MT. ALGO CT

The name is believed to derive from Andrew Algur, who, with his brother Samuel, came to Kent circa 1740. Samuel Algur and his wife owned a farm, given to them by her father, at the foot of the mountain. Mt. Algo is known for rocky ledges and rattlesnake dens. At one time, rattlesnake hunters conducted annual spring trips here to collect rattlesnakes for the venom used in the manufacture of snakebite antidote.

MT. ANTHONY (MT. ANTONE) VT

Visible from the AT on Maple Hill, it was known as Mt. Antone as early as 1797, according to the 1897 determination of the U.S. Board of Geographic Names. The agency admitted, however, that there was not then, nor is there now, any record of the name's origin. The anglicization is a popular usage only; the official name is still Antone.

MT. ASCUTNEY VT

Abenaki for "a place at the end of the river fork."

MT. BUCKLEY NC/TN

Samuel Buckley (1809–84) was a member of Thomas Clingman's expedition to measure the mountain now called Clingmans Dome.

MT. BUSHNELL MA

Named for the Bushnell family that in the late 18th century occupied part of the northwest corner of Sheffield, near the Egremont line.

MT. CAMMERER NC/TN

Formerly known as White Rock by people on the TN side and High Tops by those in NC. It also has been called Sharp Top and, according to a 1937 oral history interview with Zilphi Sutton, Old Mother. It is named for Arno B. Cammerer, the 3rd director of the National Park Service (1933–40), who helped determine the boundaries of Great Smoky Mountains NP. But his most influential role was as a friend and advisor to John D. Rockefeller, Jr., who put up much of the money to purchase the park and went on to exemplify the idea of conservation philanthropy.

MT. CHAPMAN NC/TN

A native of TN and proprietor of Chapman Wholesale Drug Company in Knoxville, Col. David C. Chapman (1876–1938) is remembered as the father of Great Smoky Mountains NP. He was chairman of the Great Smoky Mountains Conservation Association, an organization that advocated the creation of the park, in 1931–44. Later, he served as chair of the TN Great Smoky Mountains Park Commission, which led efforts to purchase land for the park.

The mountain named for him had been called Mt. Alexander, Old Black, and The Black. It also had apparently been called "Lumadaha," from the first two letters of four men's names (Lucien, Marshall, David, and Harvey). They made up the word and passed it off as Cherokee. The name gained currency until a linguist exposed the hoax.

MT. CLAY LOOP NH

This loop trail gets its name from the mountain named by botanist William Oakes in 1848 for American statesman Henry Clay (1777–1852). Despite his reputation as one of the most popular and influential political figures in American history, Clay was an unsuccessful candidate for president three times, in 1824, 1832, and 1844. He was secretary of state under John Quincy Adams. Oakes is the author of *Scenery of the White Mountains*. *See* Presidential Range, NH.

MT. CLINTON NH

The mountain now known as Mt. Pierce Peak still appears in some guidebooks and maps as Mt. Clinton, originally named to honor De Witt Clinton, best known as the promoter of the Erie Canal. He was also a governor of NY and a U.S. senator. The name was officially changed by the NH legislature in 1903 to honor Franklin Pierce, the 14th president and the only one to hail from NH. *See* Mt. Pierce Peak, NH.

MT. COLLINS NC/TN

Robert Collins (1806–63) was a tollkeeper on the Oconaluftee Turnpike and guide for Arnold Guyot's explorations. Guyot, a scientist and explorer of the entire Appalachian chain, is remembered also as a prolific place-namer. He named this gap for Collins.

MT. EASTER CT

Part of the Easter-Mine-Sharon grouping, in which the names are more associated with separate peaks than they are with distinct mountains. No pre-Depression era references to the name Easter have been uncovered, leaving many to speculate that the name emerged during Civilian Conservation Corps activities in the 1930s. It's the kind of name that invites conjecture. One imagines a remote CCC work camp, men separated from their families, a binge of drinking and card-playing, then redemption at a memorable sunrise Easter church service on the summit.

MT. EISENHOWER NH

What's interesting about this name is not that it supplanted another through politics: Former governor and President Dwight Eisenhower aide Sherman Adams successfully lobbied the NH legislature to replace the all-too-common "Pleasant Mountain" in 1972. What's most notable is the toponymical debris the renaming left behind. There is still on the mountain a stream called Mt. Pleasant Brook. Although some have argued for changing the name of the stream to Eisenhower, such concern for consistency has never been held in high regard by people who enjoy the history of the mountain.

MT. EQUINOX VT

Visible from the summit of Stratton Mountain, Equinox consists of three peaks: Deer Knoll, Big Equinox, and Little Equinox. Two stories offer origins of the name. VT surveyor Gen. Colonel Partridge is said to have chosen it because he was on the mountain during an autumn equinox in the 1820s. Or perhaps Equinox is an adaptation of an Indian word *Ekwanok,* supposedly meaning "place of fog." Scholars, however, disagree on whether the word *Ekwanok* ever existed.

MT. FITCH MA
The Rev. Ebenezer Fitch was the first president of Williams College, in 1793–1815.

MT. FRANKLIN NH
Named for Benjamin Franklin in 1820 by a group who climbed Mt. Washington with the purpose of naming nearby mountains. They began by naming peaks for former presidents, but there had been only four presidents up to that time, so they named one for the revered Franklin, who had died in 1790, and one for Henry Clay, a dynamic statesman who at the time was assumed to be a future president. *See* Presidential Range, NH.

MT. GARFIELD NH
Formerly called Little Haystack, it was named for assassinated president James Garfield in 1901.

MT. GREYLOCK MA
An early-20th-century storybook promulgated the tale of Chief Greylock, a marauding warrior who would retreat to this mountain after his attacks on European settlers. But the supposedly Indian name seems rather English. One of the earliest uses of Greylock for this peak comes from the book *Scenery of Massachusetts*, published in 1824: "During that season the frost attaches itself to the trees, which thus decorated, it needs no great stretch of the imagination to regard as the gray locks of this venerable mountain." Greylock has inspired such noted writers as Thoreau, Hawthorne, and Melville—the view of Greylock from Melville's home in Pittsfield is said to have inspired his tale of the great white whale.

MT. GUYOT NC/TN
MT. GUYOT NH
Named for Arnold Guyot, a Swiss scientist and professor of geography at Princeton. He published a map of the White Mountains in 1860 and explored the geology and ecology of the entire length of the Appalachian range. Peaks in five states, plus a crater on the moon, bear his name, which is associated with nearly every early exploration and scientific measurement of the Smokies.

Guyot developed a system of measuring elevations using a fragile glass barometer, and his advances in the observation of meteorological events led to the formation of the U.S. Weather Bureau. He was also a voracious place-namer. In his travels, he named more than three dozen features along what would become the AT. He is credited with influencing the acceptance of the word Appalachian for the entire eastern mountain chain—chosen over Allegheny, now associated with a single range. Mt. Guyot in the Smokies was named by S. B. Buckley, a fellow Appalachian explorer.

MT. HAYES NH
Named for Mrs. Margaret Hayes, who owned the White Mountain Station House in Gorham, circa 1870.

MT. HIGHT NH
There are two stories about the origin of this name. In one, it is named for farmer James Hight from Jefferson. In another, two hunters—one named Carter and the other Hight—hunt together in this area. When they become separated, they each climb adjoining peaks. The one Carter climbs becomes known as Carter Dome. The one Hight climbs becomes Mt. Hight, a name it held until Arnold Guyot impetuously changed the name to Wildcat Mountain. Later, to preserve the Hight name, and the story, the peak north of Carter Dome was renamed Mt. Hight. *See* Carter Mountain, NH.

MT. JACKSON NH

Often mistaken for one of the Presidentials, this mountain was named by William Oakes, author of *Scenery of White Mountain,* not for Andrew Jackson, but in honor of Charles Thomas Jackson, who was named NH's state geologist in 1838 and who studied the White Mountains extensively.

MT. JEFFERSON NH

Named in honor of Thomas Jefferson, the 3rd U.S. president. *See* Presidential Range, NH.

MT. KATAHDIN ME

At 5,267 feet, the northern terminus of the AT is also the highest point in ME. The name comes from the Abenaki word *Kette-Adene,* meaning "The Greatest Mountain." The first recorded ascent was by Charles Turner in 1804. AT history begins here on August 19, 1933, when Shauler Philbrick, Albert Juckman, and Frank Schairer followed Myron Avery and his trusty measuring wheel to the summit and officially established the trail by placing a mileage marker. Avery's words to commemorate this event: "Nail it up."

MT. KEPHART NC/TN

Along with Bartram and Boone, Horace Kephart (1862–1931) is one of the most remembered southern Appalachian explorers. Horace Soners Kephart was working as a librarian in St. Louis, MO, when his wife moved with their six children to New York City because of her husband's drinking. Kephart moved to the wilds of the Smokies and spent countless days exploring the mountains. Unlike most other explorers, he immersed himself in mountain culture. His books *Our Southern Highlands* and *Camping and Woodcraft* are still highly regarded, as are the articles he wrote for *Field & Stream* and *Sports Afield.* He was a passionate advocate for wilderness but ambivalent about the establishment of the Great Smoky Mountains NP. He knew the park would save the forests from logging, but he lamented that it would bring roads, hotels, and millions of visitors to the wilderness.

Pecks Peak, also known as Laurel Top, was renamed by the U.S. Geographic Board for Kephart in 1931. It was a highly unusual honor because it came while Kephart was still living. Two months after the peak was named for him, he died in a car crash in NC.

MT. KINSMAN NH

Named for Asa Kinsman, who came to this area in the 1780s.

MT. LAFAYETTE NH

Formerly called Great Haystack Mountain, it was renamed for Revolutionary War hero General Lafayette about 1825.

Ken Isaac

Summit sign on Mt. Katahdin, ME. It was the site of the first AT trail register, placed in the mid-1930s in an effort to prevent vandalism of the summit sign. The AT Club placed a painted board here bearing the legend, "If you must write something, then write it here." The practice of hikers sharing thoughts on the approach to Katahdin was so popular that a mailbox was installed containing a notebook, which could accommodated the musings of many. A tradition was born, leading to the placement of trail registers in every AT shelter.

MT. LECONTE NC/TN

Called *Walasiyi,* or "frog place," by the Cherokee; there is disagreement over which LeConte gives the mountain its official name. Tradition has it that the peak is named for Joseph LeConte, noted geologist and friend of inveterate Smokies place-namer Arnold Guyot. He assisted Guyot in developing the barometric instruments that were used to chart the elevation of numerous peaks. Guyot is the peak's apparent namer. Joseph's brother John, a physician and college professor, was a friend of another famous southern Appalachian explorer and place-namer, Samuel Buckley. According to some sources, it was Buckley who named the summit for John after John assisted him in measuring its height. *See* Mt. Guyot, NC/TN and NH.

MT. LINCOLN NH

Although the nearby town of Lincoln was named in 1764 for the earl of Lincoln, a cousin of a NH colonial governor, this mountain is named for the 16th president, Abraham Lincoln.

MT. LOVE NC/TN

Named for Dr. S. L. Love (1828–87), who accompanied Thomas Clingman and Samuel Buckley on the expedition to measure Clingmans Dome in 1858.

MT. MADISON NH

One of the original Presidentials, it was named for the 4th U.S. president, James Madison. *See* Presidential Range, NH.

MT. MINGUS NC/TN

Dr. John Jacob Mingus settled in the area in the 1790s and ran a mill near the present-day site of the Oconaluftee ranger station.

MT. MINSI PA

The Minsi were a division of the Munsee Indians, who lived primarily in the area surrounding the Delaware River headwaters in NY and adjacent PA. The Munsee's principal village, Minisink, however, was in present-day Sussex County, NJ, near the river. Some sources translate the name for the Minsi as "the people of the stony country," a name consistent with the topography of this region.

MT. MITCHELL NC

Elisha Mitchell, a Yale-educated mathematician, arrived in Chapel Hill to teach math and philosophy at the University of North Carolina in 1818. His interest in the geology of the state led to his appointment as head of the NC Geologic Survey. In 1835, he hiked to the summit of this mountain, which he believed was the tallest in the east. He measured it, returning in 1844 to confirm his measurements. In 1855, however, Thomas Clingman, a former student of Mitchell's, contested his mentor's findings, claiming another summit held the status of the highest mountain east of the Mississippi. At age 64, Mitchell set out on the arduous journey to measure this mountain once again, but the attempt proved too much for him. His body was found in a pool at the base of a waterfall on the slope. He was later proven right, however; at 6,684 feet, Mitchell is the tallest summit of the east. The mountain was named in his honor, and he is buried atop it. *See* Clingmans Dome, NC/TN.

MT. MONADNOCK VT

Seen from Stratton Mountain, this mountain gets its name from the Abenaki word for "mountain which sticks up like an island." Monadnock, in various spellings, has become the term for any mountain or hill rising singularly from the surrounding plain.

MT. MONROE NH
Named for James Monroe of VA, the 5th president.

MT. MOOSILAUKE NH
With an elevation of 4,810 feet, this peak presents the first climb above treeline on the AT for northbound hikers. The name is Abenaki for "bald place." Early maps alternately refer to it as Mt. Moosehillock.

MT. MORIAH NH
Named by an early settler for Moriah Hill in Jerusalem.

MT. PETER NY
Transferred from an inn named for Peter Conklin, who owned land on which Michael Batz operated the establishment, circa 1890. Batz named his operation Mount Peter Inn; the mountain was later called by the same name.

MT. PIERCE PEAK NH
Originally named to honor De Witt Clinton, promoter of the Erie Canal, governor of NY, and a U.S. senator. The name was officially changed by the NH legislature in 1903 to honor Franklin Pierce, the 14th president and the only one to hail from NH. Both names still appear on most maps, with one or the other in parentheses. *See* Mt. Clinton, NH.

MT. RACE MA
Named for William Race, killed in a 1755 Dutch-English skirmish in the town now known as Mt. Washington.

MT. RIGA CT
The origination of Riga is unclear. Some say it is from the Swiss peak Mt. Righi. Others say it was named by Latvian and Russian immigrants who came to this area to work as charcoal burners. But there are no Swiss, Latvian, or Russian names in the Riga village cemetery or in the surrounding area.

Another theory is that Mt. Riga is named for "Raggies," woodsmen who once inhabited the area and around whom a lot of folklore exists. According to the Federal Writers' Project, Raggies apparently lived on the lower slopes of Mt. Riga and may have been ancestors of Hessian Revolutionary War deserters who worked the woodland iron forges atop Mt. Riga. Or they may have been early woodsmen of various ancestries who remained in the area after the forges closed in 1856. Raggies, named for their ragged dress, apparently lived primitively in the mountains, with large families crowded together in 2-room shacks. Lowlanders seem to have always been derisive toward Raggies, who claimed that their mountain ways were misunderstood. At the turn of the 21st century, a kind of Raggie pride emerged that still exists today. A car with the vanity license plate RAGGIE has been spotted. Perhaps this is the modern equivalent of an inscription on a tombstone atop Mt. Riga: "Raggie I be."

MT. ROGERS VA
Formerly called Balsam Mountain, for the existence here of the southernmost stand of balsam fir, it is now named for William Barton Rogers (1804–82), who served as the first president of the Massachusetts Institute of Technology in Cambridge, a position he held in 1862–70 and again in 1879–81. Rogers was also the first state geologist of VA. A native of Philadelphia, a city just barely above sea level, Rogers has a mountain named for him that at 5,729 feet is the tallest in VA.

MT. SEQUOYAH NC/TN
Named for Cherokee chief Sequoyah, or *Sikwayi* (1760–1843), who was born of a Cherokee mother and a German-immigrant father, a lieutenant colonel in George Washington's Indian Auxiliaries. A silversmith and painter, Sequoyah developed a written Cherokee language com-

pletely on his own, despite having no formal schooling and no ability to read English. Within 7 years, enough Cherokee people had learned to read the language that the newspaper *The Cherokee Phoenix* was published. The sequoia tree also is named for Chief Sequoyah.

MT. SNOW (MT. PISGAH) VT

Misidentified as Mt. Pisgah on many hiking maps, Mt. Snow is visible from the summit of Glastenbury Mountain. For a time, it was indeed known officially as Pisgah, after being changed from its original name: Somerset. Many believe the change to Snow was an attempt to promote the area's skiing.

MT. SQUIRES NC/TN

Formerly called Little Bald, it is named for Mark Squires (1878–1938), a NC state senator in the 1920s and leader of the state's commission to establish the Great Smoky Mountains NP.

MT. STERLING NC/TN

Thought to be named for a logger and woodcutter from Sterling, KY.

MT. TAMMANY NJ

Named for Tamenend, chief of the Delaware Indians, who in 1653 signed one of the first treaties with the English, represented by William Penn. Under it the two sides promised to "live in love as long as the sun gives light." After Penn's death, however, his son Thomas was not so honorable. A series of unscrupulous deals he masterminded robbed the Delaware of their land.

MT. UNDINE MA

Toponymist George R. Stewart speculates that the name is a literary connection of the flowing streams of the mountain and the main character in the book *Undine,* written by German author Friedrich Fouque in 1811. In the book, the character Undine is a water sprite who marries a knight to acquire a soul but later loses him to treachery. Fouque, who fought against Napoleon, gained fame as an author who provoked a sense of nationalism and German pride. After 1820, though, his popularity faded and he ended up dying in poverty. The name Undine has subsequently been applied to other watery features in MA.

MT. WASHINGTON MA

The smallest town in MA was known originally as Taghconic Mountain, the mountains here being part of the Taconic Range. Its earliest inhabitants were Mahicans who had been forced from the Hudson Valley by the Mohawks and, later, the Dutch. The first whites to settle here were Dutch traders from NY, who began to make permanent homes here in the 1690s. The lord of the manor at the time was Robert Livingston, Dutch by birth, but the son of a Scottish Presbyterian minister who had been exiled to Holland. When, in 1755, he sent an armed party to collect the rent owed him by English settlers, a skirmish erupted in which William Race was killed. Later, Livingston's henchmen burned six English houses. After the Revolutionary War, the town was incorporated as Mt. Washington, one of the first place names to honor the victorious war general. *See* Mt. Race, MA.

MT. WASHINGTON NH
Originally called *Agiocochook,* an Algonquian word meaning "place of the Great Spirit of the Forest," it was named for George Washington. At 6,288 feet, it is the highest point in the northeast U.S. Weather systems collide here, and in April 1934, they produced a wind speed of 231 mph, the highest ever recorded on land and a record that stood until 1999. Wind speeds here reach 100 mph on more than 100 days each year (75 mph is considered hurricane force). A temperature of minus 41 degrees F and a wind speed of 110 mph were recorded here on February 12, 1967. The first trail to the summit was cut by Abel and Ethan Allen Crawford in 1819. *See* Crawford Path, NH.

MT. WASHINGTON "AUTO ROAD" NH
Originally called the "Carriage Road" and constructed in 1851–61, it provides an 8-mile route to the summit of Mt. Washington at grades of up to 12 percent. There really is no official name for the road; "Carriage Road" was merely a description of its use, just as "Auto Road" is today. As late as the 1960s, people still called it the "Carriage Road," even though only cars used it.

MT. WEATHER VA
A weather station was established here in 1901 by professor Willis Moore, chief of the U.S. Weather Bureau. In 1907, the station crew flew a kite to a height of 5 miles above the earth, a record at the time.

MT. WILLIAMS MA
Situated near Williamstown, the mountain is the second of two named for Col. Ephraim Williams, a benefactor of the school that would become Williams College. He was killed on September 8, 1755, at the Battle of French Mountain, near Lake George.

MOUSETOWN MD
Likely an anglicized version of Maus (or Mause), a family of German settlers who lived nearby.

MOXIE BALD LEAN-TO
MOXIE POND ME
Until recently, Bald Mountain was known as Moxie Bald and still appears as such on some maps. Moxie is said to be Abenaki (or another Indian language) for "dark water." After lending its name to the uniquely New England beverage of the same name in the 1890s, moxie has come to mean "spunk," or "smarts." The current lean-to was built by the ME AT Club in 1958. It replaces one built in 1938, which was destroyed by fire in 1946.

MOYERS CAMPGROUND PA
Named for a Mr. Moyers, who owned it. In the 1970s and early '80s, the AT passed through his campground, which is now owned by the National Park Service.

Potomac AT Club

Myron H. Avery (1899–1952), the driving force behind early efforts to build the AT and its network of supporting clubs.

Edward Talone

A watchtower on Avery Peak in ME.

MYRON AVERY LEAN-TO
MYRON H. AVERY PEAK ME

The ME legislature named the peak in 1953 for Myron H. Avery of Lubec, who is generally credited with doing more than anyone else to establish the AT and its volunteer culture. His accomplishments on behalf of the trail are staggering. Between 1927 and 1935, he covered the entire length of the AT, almost always pushing a measuring wheel. He served as president of the Potomac AT Club in 1927–41 and chairman of the AT Conference in 1931–52 and organized numerous clubs along the AT to carry out the work of routing, building, blazing, and maintaining the trail. In 1935, he founded the ME AT Club and was its supervisor of trails until 1949, despite living in Washington DC at the time.

ME is the state in which Avery's will manifested itself most clearly. Shortly after his death, ME guidebook editor Jean Stephenson wrote of Avery, "He . . . would not give up the plan of making Katahdin the northern terminus. . . . Each person did the various things which resulted in the AT in Maine, [but] it was Myron H. Avery, of Lubec, Maine, and Washington DC who interested them in it, and usually it was he who initiated the specific action. He personally measured the entire then 269 miles, wrote the trail data, arranged for the CCC work, and later for the campsites, and each year did personally much toward the maintenance of the Trail. . . . Had it not been for Myron H. Avery, there would probably have been no AT in Maine." Many would assert that the same could be said for Avery's role over much of the trail, and certainly of the AT Conference's success as an affiliation of trail-maintaining clubs.

A lean-to here was constructed in Avery's honor by the ME AT Club in 1953, shortly after Avery's death, but it is now gone. It is ironic that the man who did more to get AT shelters built than anybody no longer has his name on one.

MYRON GLASER CABIN VA

This Potomac AT Club cabin is named for the member who in 1977 donated the land on which the cabin was built.

N

NAHMAKANTA LAKE
NAHMAKANTA STREAM CAMPSITE ME

The word is Abenaki for "plenty of fish." The campsite was opened by the ME AT Club in 1996.

NANTAHALA RIVER NC

In Cherokee, the name means "middle sun," or midday sun. Steep gorges here block the sunshine until noon.

THE NARROWS NC/TN

A slim rocky ridgeline here separates NC and TN.

NATURAL BRIDGE VA

This natural rock bridge is visible from the top of Bluff Mountain. Once owned by Thomas Jefferson, it is still privately owned. The bridge gave its name to Rockbridge County and the Natural Bridge National Forest, the original name of the Washington and Jefferson National Forest.

NED ANDERSON MEMORIAL BRIDGE CT

When planning the AT's route through the northeast, some people wanted to bypass CT altogether. In 1929, Judge Arthur Perkins of Hartford, who had been trails chairman of the Appalachian Mountain Club and was then a leader in the AT Conference, encountered Ned Anderson in the woods and described the trail project to him. Anderson was eager to help out, so Perkins handed him maps of the area and told him to have at it. By the summer of 1930, Anderson had blazed a trail from Macedonia Brook State Park to Flanders Bridge (North Kent Bridge), north of Kent; he also blazed the Undermountain Trail. By 1933, Anderson had blazed the entire CT portion of the trail. To many hikers, Ned Anderson left a legacy far grander than the bridge that bears his name.

NEELS GAP GA

Formerly known as *Walasiyi,* a Cherokee word meaning "Place of the Great Frog." The name was changed in 1924 to honor W. R. Neel, surveyor of the American Scenic Highway through the gap.

NELSON CRAG TRAIL NH

S. A. Nelson, of Georgetown, MA, was one of a group of men who spent the winter of 1870–71 with J. H. Huntington on the summit of Mt. Washington conducting scientific research. *See* Huntington Ravine, NH.

NESOWADNEHUNK STREAM ME

The name is an Abenaki word meaning "swift stream between the mountains." It was revised from "Sowdnahunk" by order of the U.S. Geographic Board in 1929 to clarify an error of earlier scholarship—the board added the prefix and exchanged some vowels. It is known locally as Sowdy Hunk. Stretching across Nesowadnehunk Stream are the ruins of a lumberman's dam once used to store water which would be released to form freshets that carried logs downstream. Before 1956, the AT crossed here. That year, a cable bridge collapsed where the Abol Bridge is today, leading to the development of the current route.

Since about 1840, timber had been the dominant industry in ME. It evolved through three phases. First, the state's massive pine trees were harvested for shipmasts and other products up until about the Civil War. From about 1860 until 1890, spruce logs were harvested. Since 1890, the wood was cut into 4-foot lengths, much easier for hauling. Smaller pulp trees, or popple, are now harvested and made into paper products. Early tote roads, or "haul roads," used to transport timber were primitive affairs on which logs were skidded, usually to a stream or river for further transport. After a prohibition on river transport went into effect in 1976, larger and longer haul roads were built.

NESUNTABUNT MOUNTAIN ME

Abenaki for "three heads"; so called because the mountain has three distinct peaks.

NEW JERSEY

Named for the island of Jersey in the English Channel.

NEW RIVER VA

Once called Wood's River, after Abraham Wood, who explored the area in 1654. This ancient river is said to be the second oldest on earth; only the Nile is older. It is an unusual river for such a major drainage in that it flows northwest on its way to the Mississippi. Legend says that people thought its northward flow must make it a *new* sort of river. Some claim that the river was named by Dr. Thomas Walker in 1750 for a man named New who operated a ferry here. *See* Big Walker Mountain, VA.

NEWFOUND GAP NC/TN

Indian Gap was once thought to be the lowest pass through the Smokies. When Arnold Guyot measured this gap in 1872, he declared it the "new" lowest. This was the site of President Roosevelt's dedication of the park in 1940 and the site of a modest monument to John D. Rockefeller, whose $5 million donation helped establish Great Smoky Mountains NP. *See* Indian Gap, NC/TN.

NEWTON LANE VT

Thought to be named for John and David Newton, brothers from MA who built mills along the Connecticut River in the 1890s.

NICHOLSON HOLLOW VA

Visible from the AT about 3 miles south of Skyland, it is named for Harvey Nicholson and his family, who lived here in the days before the Shenandoah NP was established. It was once called "Free State Hollow" because three counties joined here and residents could conveniently claim that none had jurisdiction over them. Whenever a sheriff arrived to take someone in, the resident would claim jurisdictional immunity, claiming to be in one of the counties other than the one the sheriff was from.

NICK GRINDSTAFF GRAVE & MONUMENT TN

Orphaned at age 3, Nick Grindstaff (1851–1923) developed self-reliance and ingenuity. On a trip to the West in 1876, he was robbed and beaten. Bad choices of business associates led to further financial losses. Grindstaff decided he was better off alone. He became a hermit, spending 45 years alone on Iron Mountain. Sometime in 1923, after neighbors noted that he had not been seen for some time, they went to check on him and found his body. His dog was so protective that they had to destroy it to reach Nick. The trailside monument that marks his grave was built from brick taken from Nick's cabin fireplace. The inscription says "lived alone, suffered alone, and died alone."

NO BUSINESS KNOB TN

The name is used for various features throughout the Appalachians, and the story is always similar. In this version, a severe fire here once burned the vegetation down to rock. Soon after, a man tried to climb the knob, but it had become overgrown with thick brush, making it nearly impassable. After his unsuccessful attempt, the man declared that he had absolutely "no business" climbing the knob.

NOLICHUCKY RIVER TN
Likely a corruption of *Na'natlugun'yi,* the name of a Cherokee settlement in what is now Washington County. The name means "spruce tree place": *na'na* means "spruce," *tluguni* means "tree," *yi* means "place."

NOONTOOTLA CREEK GA
Probably Cherokee for "land of the shining water," but the name might be a corruption of *Nantahala,* meaning "midday sun."

NORTH AND SOUTH CROCKER MOUNTAINS ME
The name recognizes the Crockers, a 19th-century family that for a number of years was the only family living in the area.

NORTH CLARENDON VT
Thought to be named for one of the earls of Clarendon.

NORTH MARSHALL, SOUTH MARSHALL VA
According to conventional wisdom, these mountains are named for John Marshall, chief justice of the U.S. Supreme Court in 1801–35, whose family once owned these lands. But the mountains may actually take their names from the chief justice's father, Thomas, a surveyor who worked with George Washington and was granted the land that included both peaks. North Marshall was the site of a lookout tower that blew down in the early days of the AT.

NORTH WOODSTOCK NH
After choosing Fairfield, then Peeling, residents of this town wanted a name more evocative of the forest landscape (anything was better than Peeling). They settled on Woodstock in 1840, which is Old English for a "place in the wood."

NORTHEAST UTILITIES DAM CT
The origin of the name is self-evident, but the dam is notable as the oldest power plant on the Housatonic, built in 1904. At the time, it was the largest power plant in the country; it had a 780-kilowatt capacity.

NORWICH VT
Originally named Norwhich in 1761 by residents who had migrated from Norwich, CT. The extra *h* was dropped soon after.

NUCLEAR LAKE NY
Before it was dammed, the swamp was known as Pawling Pond. The land was purchased by the United Nuclear Corporation, which dammed the swamp and used the area as a nuclear-fuels-processing research facility until 1972. During the 1960s, the waters became known as Nuclear Lake. When the surrounding land was purchased in 1979 by the National Park Service for the AT corridor, stories told of 55-gallon drums containing nuclear waste dumped into the lake. After extensive testing, the lake was declared safe.

NUMERAL ROCK CT
Each year, the numerals change when students from the Kent School in nearby Kent paint the year for the next graduating class.

OCONALUFTEE RIVER GORGE NC/TN
A corruption of the Cherokee word *Egwanulti,* or "river," and *Nulati,* meaning "near or beside." Together, it means "by the river." There was once a Cherokee town called Oconaluftee here, mentioned by William Bartram in about 1775.

OCTOBER MOUNTAIN STATE FOREST MA
October Mountain is said to have been named by Herman Melville, who wrote: "One fine morning I sallied forth upon the errand. I had much ado finding the best road to the shanty. No one seemed to know where it was exactly. It lay in a very lonely part of the country, a densely-wooded mountain on one side (which I call October Mountain, on account of its bannered aspect in that month), and a thicketed swamp on the other." The state's largest forest is comprised of two estates—one belonged to William C. Whitney, secretary of the navy under Grover Cleveland.

OGLESBY BRANCH NC
Named for the founder of the TN Eastman Hiking Club, who had the distinction of being the first member to fall into these waters, which he did shortly after the club was formed in 1946.

OJI MOUNTAIN ME
Visible from the AT near Tracy Pond, the summit is named for the letters which at one time were formed by three talus rockslides on the southwest face. Later slides obscured the letters.

OLD ALBANY POST ROAD NY
In the Publick Highways Act of 1703, the NY provincial legislature designated a highway from Westchester to Albany. The road, which followed a former Indian trail, was called Queen's Road during the reign of Queen Anne. It was widened during the French and Indian War so military supplies could be transported. It later became known as the Albany Post Road because of the mileposts along its sides. It was the main route between New York City and Albany during the Revolutionary War.

OLD CHEESE FACTORY GA
Maj. Edward Williams came to the Nacoochee Valley by way of New England in 1828. Some 20 years later, after he became acquainted with transplanted VT dairyman Joseph E. Hubbard, he set up a dairy operation high on the mountain. Making butter and cheese, Williams' operation is described in publications of the day as the only commercial operation of its kind in GA. Here is a colorful account: "We have a dairy on the top of a mountain, distant from the first farmhouse some fifteen miles, and inaccessible by any conveyance but that of a mule or well-trained horse. The bells of more than half a hundred cows are echoing along the mountainside; and instead of clover, they are feeding upon the luxuriant weed of the wilderness."

OLD FINCASTLE ROAD (USFS 186) VA
This 18th-century turnpike was the road to Fincastle, named for Lord George Fincastle, son of John Nurray, who was the 4th earl of Dunmore and the last royal governor of VA. The town was founded in 1772 and served as one of the last trading posts for westbound settlers. Fincastle County was also created in 1772 but it became extinct 4 years later when it was divided into Washington, Montgomery, and Kentucky counties.

Kentucky, itself named for a Wyandot word for "broad plains," was part of the vast VA claim of all lands from ocean to ocean—although Spain and France recognized the claim only as far as the Mississippi River; this western boundary was codified by the 1783 Treaty of Paris. VA also claimed much of the land from the western border of NC north to the Great Lakes. In 1780, Kentucky County was divided into three and renamed the Kentucky District. It held that name until 1792, when KY was granted statehood.

OLD FORGE PICNIC GROUNDS PA
"Old Forge" on Little Antietam Creek used pig iron from the Mont Alto Furnace to manufacture "Fen-plate" stoves, much prized in the area.

OLD HIGHLAND TURNPIKE NY
Private road developers once created toll roads to connect the remote villages in the Highlands region, among them North Highland and South Highland. They hoped to make a profit from these transportation links, but most lost money because fees collected from travelers through the mountains could not defray road maintenance and operating costs.

OLD HOTEL TRAIL VA
Never really a hotel, the building was built by Zacharias Drummond between 1820 and 1830 and was known as the Old Mansion House, then the Higginbotham House, for a later owner, George Higginbotham. Herders often used the place while tending hogs or cattle in the summer. A wounded Union soldier whose name has been lost was cared for and died here. His grave is said to be along the trail, but its location is now unknown.

OLD HOUGHTON FIRE ROAD ME
Probably named for James Houghton, a settler here in the early 1800s. Six miles of this fire road served as the original route of the AT in the 1930s.

OLD JACKSON ROAD NH
The name was transferred from Jackson, near Pinkham Notch, first named New Madbury. In 1800, the name was changed to Adams to honor President John Adams. After the 1828 presidential election, in which all but one of the townspeople voted for Andrew Jackson over John Quincy Adams, the name was changed to Jackson.

OLD JOB TRAIL NH
The route of the AT before 1964. The name comes from lumbering days: An "old job" refers to a site where lumbering had taken place in the past. Old Job Shelter was built in 1935 by the Civilian Conservation Corps on the site of a former lumber camp.

OLD MINE RAILROAD TRAIL NY
Narrow gauge rail lines were the preferred method of moving minerals from the mountains throughout the Appalachians. The one here was used to haul iron to a foundry at Cold Spring.

OLD ORCHARD SHELTER VA
Yes, it does sit among the remnants of an old apple orchard.

OLD RAG MOUNTAIN VA
"Old Raggedy" may have been named for its craggy summit. Or it may have been named by the mountaineers who grazed cattle and hogs in the hills—to them, the steep-sided mountain was of "no more use than an old rag."

OLD ROOTVILLE ROAD VT
Rootville was a 19th-century village that stood nearby. It was named for a local family whose best-known member was Henry Root, credited with raising funds for the Bennington Battle Monument and a member of the College of Electors when Abraham Lincoln was elected president.

OLD SOUTH MOUNTAIN INN MD
The original structure is thought to have been built by Robert Turner sometime around 1750 or 1760. It had 22 rooms to rent and blacksmiths on staff to shoe horses and repair wagons. Abraham Lincoln spent a night here on his way to be seated in Congress in January 1847. It was reportedly a favorite hangout of Daniel Webster and Henry Clay. During the Civil War, Clara Barton, founder of the Red Cross, came here on September 15, 1862, to attend the wounded from the Battle of South Mountain; she then went on to Antietam.

OLD SPECK MOUNTAIN AND SPECK POND SHELTER ME
The wide variety of tree species that cover the mountain here presents a speckled appearance, especially in autumn. The pond gives its name to the shelter, built in 1978 by the ME AT Club to replace an older structure.

Edward Talone

Keith and Pat Shaw outside Shaw's Boarding House in Monson, ME.

OLD STAGE ROAD ME
This stage road, which ran from Monson to Greenville, dates to at least 1824, when the village of Savage's Mills was settled along it. The town, and the road, were abandoned in 1858.

ONION MOUNTAIN VA
Visible from Apple Orchard Mountain, it gets its name from the abundance of ramps, or wild onions, that grew there in the 1830s. It had previously been known as Big Onion, Ingin, and Big Indian.

OQUOSSOC ME
An Abenaki word meaning "slender blue trout."

ORANGE COUNTY NY
Established in 1683 as one of the original provincial counties, it is named for King William, known as the Prince of the House of Orange.

ORBETON STREAM ME
Named for the Orbeton family.

ORE HILL TRAIL NH
Named for the iron ore mine once located nearby.

OSBORN LOOP TRAIL NY
William Henry Osborn was once president of the Illinois Central Railroad. In 1974, his son, William Henry Osborn II, donated the land for the Osborn Preserve, which is reached by this trail. The younger Osborn served as president of the Hudson River Conservation Society.

OSGOOD TRAIL NH
Opened in 1878 and the oldest trail to the summit of Mt. Madison, the trail was cleared by, and named for, Ben Osgood, a famous guide at the Glen House.

OTTAUQUECHEE RIVER VT
A Natick Indian word for a "swift mountain stream."

OTTIE CLINE POWELL MEMORIAL VA
Several AT shelters commemorate young hikers who died before their time, but this is the only one known to be named for a child. Late in 1890, 4-year-old Ottie Cline Powell wandered away from his classmates who were out collecting firewood for their school's stove. A massive search party followed his tracks to no avail. In the spring, little Ottie's body was found where this shelter now stands, miles from his school.

OVERALL RUN VA
Named for Col. Isaac Overall, who owned 28,000 acres in what is now Shenandoah NP.

OVERMOUNTAIN SHELTER
OVERMOUNTAIN VICTORY TRAIL NC/TN
The Overmountain Men were colonists who had defied King George's 1763 proclamation that settlers stay east of the mountains. On September 7, 1780, John Sevier led a group through the Yellow Mountain Gap en route to King's Mountain, SC. There they defeated the British, freeing the south from British control and allowing George Washington to focus on the north.

OWL TRAIL ME
Formerly known as the Abol Mountain Trail, its name is descriptive of the shape of a nearby mountain. *See* Abol Bridge and Abol Pond, ME.

OXBOW LAKE ME
Descriptive of the shape of this lake, and otherwise used to refer to a U-shaped body of water, often a cut-off bend in a river that has changed course.

P

PAGE VALLEY VA
This name, applied to the valley of the South Branch of the Shenandoah River, was transferred from Page County, named for John Page, VA governor in 1802–05.

PAINTER BRANCH NC
"Painter" is a local term for panther, or mountain lion, common in the southern Appalachians until hunting and trapping led to its demise.

PALISADES INTERSTATE PARKWAY NY
"Palisades" refers to vertical cracks that break riverside cliffs into columns that resemble the pole, or palisade, construction techniques of early military forts. Efforts to preserve the Palisades along here from quarrying began early in the 20th century, but it took a land donation from John D. Rockefeller in 1935 to make the attempts succeed. The 38-mile parkway connecting the George Washington and Bear Mountain bridges was completed in 1958 at a cost of $47 million.

PALMERTON PA
A company town laid out in 1898 by the NJ Zinc Company and named for Stephen Palmer of NY, the firm's first president. The zinc mine is closed now, but its devastation lives on. Described by hikers as a "moonscape," this area features stunted or dead trees and little else. Once applauded for promoting the "health and well-being" of its people, the company left behind a disaster that caused the Environmental Protection Agency to name the land here a Superfund site.

PAMOLA MOUNTAIN ME
To the Abenaki, the spirit *Bahmolai Pamola* was the god of Katahdin. In 1866, a Catholic missionary translated *Pamola* to mean "he curses on the mountain." The spirit is traditionally pictured as having the head of a moose, the body of a man, and the wings and feet of a bird.

PANTHER FORD VA
Legend says that a woman and child were killed by a mountain lion here while crossing the creek.

PARAPET BROOK NH
Possibly named for the steep bank, or parapet, on one side of the brook.

PARIS VA
Founded by a Revolutionary War veteran who served under Lafayette. The soldier might have named the village for the French city, or Lafayette himself might have named it. One story says that while traveling past the village, Lafayette had asked that it be named Paris.

PARKERS GAP VA
Named for the several families of Parkers that lived here. One member, Calahil Parker, was a Confederate sharpshooter.

PASS MOUNTAIN VA
During the 18th century, Thornton Gap was known as the "Great Pass" through the mountain. The ridge on which Marys Rock is located was known as "Great Pass Mountain." The name now refers only to the segment of the ridge north of Thornton Gap.

PASTURE FENCE MOUNTAIN VA
Visible west of the AT in the vicinity of Blackrock, in the 19th century it was cultivated with grass, then fenced and leased for summer cattle-grazing.

PAUL C. WOLFE SHELTER VA
Paul Wolfe was a longtime trail worker for the Old Dominion AT Club. Following a tradition that has led to the construction of many shelters along the AT, the family of Paul Wolfe financed the shelter in 1991, after Paul's death.

PAWLING NY
Settled in 1740 by English Quakers and incorporated in 1788, the town is named for a colonial family.

PEABODY BROOK TRAIL NH
Probably transferred from Peabody River in Gorham. Legend tells of a Mr. Peabody from Andover, MA, who saw the river born when a torrent of water from Mt. Washington swept away the cabin in which he had just been sleeping.

PEAKS OF OTTER VA
Seen from the AT in Bedford County, the two peaks are Sharp Top and Flat Top mountains. Sharp Top originally was known as Sharp Knob or Sharp Peak; it was finally shown as Sharp Top on a 1917 map. The name may come from a ridge in Scotland that it resembles. (There are many people of Scottish descent living here.) At one time it was thought to be the highest peak in the eastern U.S., then merely the highest peak in VA. By 1859, its official elevation had been whittled down to 4,600 feet. Today, its official height is listed at 3,870 feet. Stone from Sharp Top was used in the construction of the Washington Monument.

Flat Top (a descriptive name) rises 4,004 feet. The name Otter may derive from *Otteri*, Cherokee for "mountain or high hill."

PEARISBURG VA
Capt. George Pearis, an officer in the Revolutionary War and one of the first settlers of this region, started a ferry service here

across the New River in 1782. The town was named for him in 1808 when he donated land for the courthouse.

PECKS CORNER NC/TN
The Peck family received an early land grant in the area. "Corner" refers to a marker tree at the corner of two large state grants—one to Moses and Henry Peck, the other grant to Benjamin and Elliott Peck.

PEDLAR DAM VA
Transferred from the Pedlar River, which is identified as such in a 1792 land grant.

PEMADUMCOOK LAKE ME
A Molicite word for "extended sandbar place."

PEMIGEWASSET WILDERNESS NH
Abenaki for "rapidly moving," referring to the stream of the same name. In 1969, this area was established as the Lincoln Woods Scenic Area. It obtained wilderness status in 1986.

PEN MAR COUNTY PARK MD
Situated on the Blue Ridge near MD's border with PA (hence Pen Mar), the old park was opened by the Western Maryland Railroad in 1878 to create demand for rail service from Baltimore. It worked. By the beginning of the 20th century, there were a half dozen hotels and several dozen boarding houses here. Known as the Coney Island of the Blue Ridge, the park featured a dance pavilion, dining hall, pony and goat cart and miniature train rides, and a Ferris wheel, as well as a swimming pool, bowling alley, movie theater, carousel, penny arcade, rollercoaster, and roller-skating rink. Wives and children would stay for the summer; husbands could take the train out for weekends. In the 1920s, when the majority of visitors arrived by car, the railroad leased the park to private operators. It fell into disrepair during World War II and was demolished by railroad employees. The new park here was dedicated in 1977.

PENNSYLVANIA
Named by William Penn to whom the land was granted, the name is Latin for "Penn's Woods."

PENNSYLVANIA MAINLINE CANAL PA
Between 1834 and 1913 the canal carried goods 395 miles between Pittsburgh and Philadelphia. The line consisted of two railroad sections, totaling 118 miles, and 277 miles of canal. Very little of it remains today.

PENOBSCOT RIVER ME
The name refers to an Indian nation in the area and has been assigned various meanings; among them are "descending ledge place," "rocky river," and "at the descending rocks."

PERHAM STREAM ME
Lemuel and Silas Perham settled here sometime before 1788.

PERIMETER ROAD ME
So named because it surrounds three sides of Baxter State Park.

PERKINS DRIVE
PERKINS MEMORIAL TOWER NY
Both honor George W. Perkins, Sr., the first chairman of the Palisades Interstate Park Commission, who served from 1900 until his death in 1920. The tower was dedicated in 1934 as a fire and weather lookout and refurbished in the 1990s for public displays.

PERU VT
Originally called Brumley, then Bromley. Early townspeople were dismayed at the town's inability to attract residents and investment; they thought that the town's

Edward Talone

Mt. Wilcox fire tower, MA, was built by the Civilian Conservation Corps. Fire towers were once a common sight along the AT, but most have disappeared. This photo was taken in 1983, shortly before the tower was replaced by a relay tower.

name was partly to blame. "Bromley," they said, was too boring (of course, the town was known as a home for clergymen's widows). In 1804, the town was renamed to evoke South America's rich resources.

PETER BUCK PLAQUE NY
Peter Buck (1894–1962), a native of Vienna, Austria, worked with Joseph Bartha's patrol during World War II to keep the AT open. His ashes were spread at this spot.

PETERS MOUNTAIN VA
Peter Wright was an early settler from the Covington area. Once when crossing this mountain, he was trapped by several days of bad weather and presumed lost.

PETITES GAP VA
The original name was Poteet's Gap, after John Poteet, who settled here in 1740. It evolved into Petites Gap.

PHILIPSTOWN NY
The town lies within the original Philipse Patent, granted in 1788 to Adolph Philipse.

PHILLIPS ME
Jonathan Phillips of Boston was an early settler here.

PICKENS NOSE NC
Resembles a nose when seen from the valley. The nose honored by the name is probably that of Revolutionary War colonel Andrew Pickens.

PICO CAMP VT
This cabin, now closed, was built in 1959 by the Green Mountain Club. The name was transferred from Pico Peak. *Pico* is thought to be Abenaki for "the pass or opening."

PIGEON RIVER NC/TN
Once home to flocks of carrier pigeons, which were hunted out of existence in TN by 1893. The last sighting in NC was in 1894.

PINE COBBLE MA
A cobble is an area with an abundance of small stones. Pitch pines are present here.

PINE GROVE FURNACE PA
A charcoal furnace built here circa 1770 operated until 1895. The charcoal, made by piling wood in squares and burning it for many days, was used to fire iron furnaces. There is evidence of other industrial activity in this vicinity, including pits used to burn pine for the manufacture of pitch and tar for ships. Pine Grove Furnace Park was established in 1913 by the Cumberland Valley Railroad to create de-

mand for its passenger railroad, as was done at Pen Mar Park, MD. It became a state park in the 1930s.

PINE GROVE FURNACE CABIN SITE PA
Situated near the crossing of Toms Run, just south of where the trail crosses PA Route 233, and originally called the Bunker Hill Farm. Later, the Rupp House was built here, dating to the early 19th century. The Potomac AT Club leased the house during the 1930s from Michaux State Forest. Despite being made of durable chestnut, the cabin had to be razed about 1990 after an unfortunate mistake by a well-meaning volunteer. Sometime in the 1940s, a sealant had been applied to the logs inside the cabin. Unable to breathe, the logs rotted from their cores.

PINEFIELD HUT VA
This stone hut was built in 1940 by the Civilian Conservation Corps and named for the area's dense pine woods. The pines were likely planted by farmers to create a fast-growing source of wood for construction and fuel.

PINKHAM NOTCH NH
Previously called "Eastern Pass" or "The Glen" in early literature and renamed Evans Notch after Capt. John Evans cut a road here in 1774. In 1824, the state contracted with Daniel Pinkham to expand the existing road. Pinkham was a farmer, dentist, blacksmith, mason, carpenter, and Baptist preacher, as well as a road builder.

PINNACLE LEAD TN
"Lead" is a term for a smaller mountain or spur "leading" off a larger mountain. "Pinnacle" refers to a subordinate peak or ridge of a mountain.

PISGAH NATIONAL FOREST NC
The Rev. James Hall, a Presbyterian chaplain who accompanied Gen. Griffith Rutherford's troops here in 1776, is thought to be the namer of this region in western NC which became a 495,000-acre national forest. In the Bible, Mt. Pisgah was the peak from which Moses viewed the Promised Land, and where he died.

PITTSFIELD MA
Named for William Pitt, an English statesman whose birthday in April was the same day that Berkshire County split from Hampshire County. Pitt, a loyalist, would later seek reconciliation between the colonies and the crown. The original name of the town was Pontoosuck, the Mohegan name for "winter deer."

PLATEAU CAMPSITE CT
Built by the Appalachian Mountain Club in the 1980s, the shelter is located on a plateau above the road.

POCHUCK MOUNTAIN NJ
From the Leni-Lenape word *putschek*, or "out-of-the-way place."

POCONO MOUNTAINS PA
The word is a corruption of *Pocohanne*, or "a stream between two mountains," a reference to the Lehigh River, which flows into the Delaware River. *See* Lehigh River, PA.

POCOSIN CABIN VA
Built by the Potomac AT Club in 1937 from chestnut timber, it lies just off the trail at Pocosin Fire Road. Although there are several theories about the name's origin, the most cited is from the Bureau of American Ethnology's *Handbook of American Indians*, which says that *Pocosin* is a "name applied in eastern MD, VA, and NC, to a low

wooded ground or swamp, which is covered with shallow water in winter and remains in a miry condition in summer."

PODUNK BROOK VT
May have been named by settlers from CT, based on a derivation of a Natick Indian word for "a boggy place." Another possibility is its more common usage meaning a small, out-of-the-way, rural place.

POGO MEMORIAL CAMPSITE MD
Established by the Mountain Club of MD and named for Walter "Pogo" Rheinheimer, Jr. (1958–74), who drowned in a canoe accident on the Potomac River near Harpers Ferry. It is built on the former site of the Black Rock Hotel. *See* Black Rock, MD.

POLLOCK KNOB VA
Named for Skyland founder and booster for the creation of Shenandoah NP George Freeman Pollock (1869–1949). *See* Skyland, VA.

Potomac AT Club

A hiker enjoys the view from Black Rock in MD, circa 1930.

POLLYWOG STREAM ME
"Pollywog" is another name for tadpole.

POND MOUNTAIN WILDERNESS TN
Designated a wilderness in 1986 and currently covering 6,890 acres. At 4,329 feet, Pond Mountain is the highest point in the area.

PONTOOSUC LAKE MA
Pontoosuc is Mahican for "place of winter deer," but this name was given by white settlers. The Mahicans called the lake *Shoon-keek-moon-keek* after two young lovers who were also cousins, Shoon-keek (the boy) and Moon-keek. According to legend, the cousins were forbidden by their fathers to see each other, but they arranged for a secret night meeting at the lake. On his way there by canoe, Shoon-keek was ambushed and shot with an arrow by a jealous suitor who also sought Moon-keek's affections. Moon-keek looked all around the dark lake for Shoon-keek; when his empty canoe floated past, she threw herself into the water and drowned. An empty canoe is said to be seen floating on the lake at night, as the ghostly calls of the lovers echo: "Shoon-keek" and "Moon-keek."

POOR VALLEY VA
Beneath the topsoil here is a bed of shale, causing bad drainage and poor, acidic soil. *See* Rich Valley, VA.

PORT CLINTON PA
Founded in 1829 as a transfer point for the canal boats on the Schuylkill Navigation, it is likely named for De Witt Clinton, the first governor of NY, serving in 1817–23 and again in 1825–28. He may be better known as a booster for the Erie Canal, which was completed in 1825.

PORTERS GAP
PORTERS MOUNTAIN NC/TN
Named for James P. H. Porter, a lawyer and politician. On one occasion, as the Democratic candidate for the state legislature, he was defeated by a single vote. He lived in Sevierville, TN, in a place called Porters Flat for most of his life. He died May 1, 1846.

POTATO TOP TN
Said to look like a hill of potatoes, but no source indicates whether that means a pile of whole spuds or mashed.

POTAYWADJO MOUNTAIN
POTAYWADJO SPRING LEAN-TO ME
Visible from the AT, the mountain probably gets its name from an Indian word meaning "whale mountain." In the legend of Penobscot chief Jo-Mary, the Indian would blow air and water out of his mouth in the manner of a whale, causing wind to blow over the mountain. The lean-to was originally built in 1957, then rebuilt in 1995 at the site of one of the largest springs in ME, 20 feet in diameter. *See* Lower Jo-Mary Lake, ME.

POTOMAC RIVER MD
Said to be a Powhaten word, but there is no agreement on its meaning. Variations include Patowmeck and Patomack Creek. The south branch has been called Wappacomma or Wappacomo, with *wapi* meaning "white" and *ahkamiku* meaning "ground." The north branch was known as Cohongorooto, or "goose river."

POWELL GAP VA
The legend is that the gap got its name from a man named Ambrose Powell who once carved his name on a tree that grew here. That's all it took! The tree and its trace of Powell are now gone.

POWELL KNOB NC/TN
George Powell settled with his family in Cades Cove in the mid-1800s.

POWELLS FORT VALLEY VA
Visible from the AT west of Shenandoah NP and named for a counterfeiter who in the mid-19th century hid there to avoid authorities—which led to the valley's moniker "The Fort." Legend says Powell buried a cache of gold and silver on Signal Knob, on Massanutten Mountain.

PRESIDENTIAL RANGE NH
The name originally referred to four peaks named for the first four U.S. presidents: Washington, 6,288 feet; Adams, 5,798 feet; Jefferson, 5,715 feet; and Madison, 5,363 feet. A fifth peak was named for Benjamin Franklin. NH state historian Jeremy Belknap named Mt. Washington on an expedition in 1784. The others retained lyrical Indians names such as Agiocochook until 1820, when a party from Lancaster, NH, ascended Washington to name the surrounding peaks. Mt. Clay was named a little later—although Henry Clay was never a president, the namers assumed that such an ambitious leader certainly would become president one day. Other mountains in NH named for presidents—Lincoln, Garfield, and Cleveland—are not typically considered part of the Presidential Range, but as years go by, they are often lumped together with the others.

THE PRIEST VA
Either a lone priest or a man named Priest, DuPriest, or DePriest once lived nearby, according to most sources. Some say the name came from Pastor Robert Rose, who once led a congregation nearby—and apparently did quite well; he owned 33,000 acres. *See* Religious Range, VA.

PROSPECT MOUNTAIN CT
At one time, most of this mountain had been cleared for pasture land. As such, it offered long views, or prospects. Today, views from the mountain are cut by hand. *See* Rand's View, CT.

PROVINCE ROAD NH
Now a dirt road, this path was cut in 1772 by order of Sir John Wentworth, the last royal governor of NH. The name refers to the "province" of NH. Today Clark Pond Loop follows the road.

PUGWASH POND ME
Thought to be Abenaki for "pond at the end."

PUNCHBOWL SHELTER VA
The name comes from the man-made lake near the shelter shaped like a punch bowl. The shelter was built by the forest service in 1961.

PURGATORY CREEK VA
Nineteenth-century wagoneers found themselves in a never-ending battle to keep horses and wagons free from the deep mud at the stream crossing near Buchanan. They likened getting stuck to being in purgatory. It would end sooner or later, but it was hell while you were in it.

PUTNAM COUNTY NY
Gen. Putnam was commander-in-chief of continental forces east of the Hudson River during the Revolutionary War. Putnam County was created out of Dutchess County in 1812.

Q

QUARRY GAP SHELTERS PA
Originally built by the Civilian Conservation Corps in 1934 and refurbished by the Potomac AT Club in 1993, it is named for its proximity to an old quarry.

QUIMLEY MOUNTAIN VT
James Quimley was an early settler who raised sheep and ran a sawmill.

QUINTTOWN NH
Situated at the end of Doan Trail, now a ghost town. It was named for Benjamin Quint, who settled here after serving with John Paul Jones in the American Revolution.

QUIRAUK MOUNTAIN MD
Formerly called Mt. Misery, it was given its Algonquian name, said to mean "blue mountain," by executives of the Western Maryland Railroad. They rightly surmised that the Indian name would be more appealing to tourists than "Misery."

R

RAINBOW LAKE
RAINBOW LAKE DEADWATERS
RAINBOW LAKE LEDGES
RAINBOW STREAM LEAN-TO ME

Named for the arching rainbow shape of the lake. Deadwaters are swampy areas cut off from the main body of a lake. The Rainbow Stream Lean-to was constructed by the ME AT Club in 1971.

RAMAPO-DUNDERBERG TRAIL NY

The route was suggested by Maj. William Welch, superintendent of Bear Mountain–Harriman Park. It was blazed in November 1920 by NY–NJ Trail Conference volunteers. Ramapo is said to be an Algonquian word for "many ponds." It also has been described as meaning "a river into which empties a number of ponds." Other spellings include "Ramspook" and "Ramapogh."

Dunderberg Mountain, a Dutch name, is alternately called by its English translation, Thunder Mountain. According to an early-20th-century travel guide, *New York: A Guide to the Empire State,* Dunderberg in Dutch legend is the home of *Heer,* a goblin of the imagination who touches off summer storms. His "belches of fire split the heavens; barrages of thunder from unseen batteries ricochet off Dunderberg up the river." During storms, the sound of thunder rolls over this mountain. The trail was first known as the Tuxedo–Tom Jones Trail. It is the oldest maintained and marked trail in Harriman Park, dating to 1920 and running for 25 miles from Tuxedo to Jones Point on the Hudson River. *See* Tuxedo, NY.

RANDOLPH PATH NH

Built between 1893 and 1899 by J. R. Edmands, a founder of the Appalachian Mountain Club, the trail goes from Edmands Col to the town of East Randolph, which is named for statesman John Randolph of VA (1773–1833). He is remembered for his uncompromising defense of state sovereignty. Among other things, he opposed national banks, federal tariffs, any internal improvements, and interference with slavery. He even opposed Thomas Jefferson's attempts to buy FL because it was a federal purchase. Randolph capped off his political career during the election of 1824 by loudly denouncing Henry Clay's support of John Quincy Adams, who believed in strong central government. This led to a duel with Clay, but neither man was a marksman—both emerged unhurt. *See* Edmands Col, NH.

RAND'S VIEW CT

Situated on a slope of Prospect Mountain, this view of Mt. Greylock was the summer home of artist Ellen Emmet Rand and her husband William. They owned Hamlet Hill Farm here for about 50 years, until Ellen's death in 1941. Born in 1876 in San Francisco, Rand moved with her family to NY in 1884 after the death of her father. After studying art in Boston, she had successful one-person shows while still in her early 20s, including one at Boston's Copley Hall, where only James Whistler, John Singer Sargent, and Claude Monet had had such exhibits. She returned to NY, operating a portrait studio on Washington Square. Her portraits were in high demand; she completed about 800 during her career. She married William Rand and raised three sons, living and painting primarily in NY, but spending summers at Rand's View.

RANGE VIEW CABIN VA

Named for its views of the Blue Ridge Mountains. Construction was begun by Charlie Sisk, a stone mason from Free State Hollow in what is now Shenandoah NP. Despite threats from displaced moun-

Edward Talone

Many of today's trails were once main roads. This one led to Jackson, NH.

tain families, Charlie persisted until the park service took over and finished the cabin about 1933. These early cabins were built to house trail-building crews, which until then had found shelter in caves and under ledges.

RANGELEY ME

Named for Squire Rangeley of Yorkshire, England, who bought the land here in 1825 and tried to establish "a semi-feudal system in the wilderness." Rangeley has a measure of fame for being located exactly halfway between the equator and the North Pole.

RAPIDAN FIRE ROAD VA

The Rapidan River flows east from Shenandoah NP. It was originally named the Anne, honoring Queen Anne of England. Later, the swift movement of the water evoked the name "Rapid Ann," shortened to "Rapidan" through use.

RATTLESNAKE DEN CT

The story goes that in the early days of the AT, a bottle of snake venom hung from a tree here, to be used by hikers bitten by the local timber rattlesnakes. Stories also tell of early hikers eating rattlesnakes as camp food. There are scarcely enough snakes here now for hors d'oeuvres; most were killed by hunters awarded a bounty for every rattle they brought to local authorities.

RAVEN ROCK MD

European settlers apparently encountered gaggle upon gaggle of the birds here. Perhaps a more fitting name would be Harrison Rock, however. In 1841 work began on a monument here to honor President William Henry Harrison. But, like Harrison's presidency, the effort sputtered. Harrison is remembered as the president whose inaugural speech was longer than his presidency. After speaking for more than 2 hours in a cold rain, he fell ill with pneumonia and died a month into his term. The rock is still a fine place to watch a raven ride a thermal.

RAYMOND PATH NH

Named for Maj. Curtis B. Raymond of Boston, who re-cleared this trail in the 1870s while a guest at the Glen House.

RED GATE FIRE ROAD VA

Thought to be named for Redgate Farm in the valley north of Front Royal, this old road was the Gordonsville Turnpike before the Shenandoah NP was created. If this is true, it may be that the road was used to take cattle to summer grazing land on the mountain.

REDINGTON ME

Named for a local family, the town was abandoned in the late 1950s to make way for a naval training operations center. Redington Base had a brief moment of notoriety when a navy pilot accidentally dropped a bomb into nearby Rangeley Lake, a popular summer recreation spot. No one was injured, and training at the base continues today.

RELIGIOUS RANGE VA

Pastor Robert Rose is said to have named the peaks in the range: Cardinal, the Friar, Bald Friar (now known as Bald Knob), the Priest, and Little Priest.

RENO MONUMENT
RENO MONUMENT ROAD MD

Thought be the earliest road over South Mountain and the route taken by Maj. Gen. Edward Braddock during the French and Indian War, the road dates to the 1730s. It was previously known as Middletown-Sharpsburg Road. The monument was erected to honor Maj. Gen. Jesse L. Reno, a Union officer who surrounded Confederates in a battle at Fox Gap on September 5, 1862. He and his Confederate counterpart, Brig. Gen. Samuel Garland, were killed a few days later during the Battle of South Mountain. The monument was dedicated on September 14, 1889, by veterans of the 9th U.S. Army Corps. *See* Fox Gap, MD.

RENTSCHLER MARKER PA

Dr. H. F. Rentschler, an early member of the Blue Mountain Eagle Climbing Club, was instrumental in finding the first route for the AT along Blue Mountain; he pioneered the first route between the Susquehanna and Lehigh rivers, circa 1926. His effort resulted in scrapping the original idea for the route, which had been to follow Tuscarora Mountain from Sterrets Gap to Hancock, MD, on the C&O Canal.

REX PULFORD MEMORIAL NC/TN

This stone memorial honors Pulford, who died of a heart attack here during a thru-hike in April 1983.

REYNOLD'S ROCK MA

Named for C. J. Reynolds, who owned property here in the 19th century.

RICH KNOB TN

Like other "rich" locations in the Appalachians, this one is probably named for the quality of its soil.

RICH VALLEY VA

This descriptive title is associated with dozens of place names in the Appalachians. It refers to the fertile soil and good drainage, which makes it prime agricultural land. *See* Poor Valley, VA.

RICHARD B. RUSSELL SCENIC HIGHWAY (GA 348) GA

Constructed in 1966 through Hogpen Gap and named for Richard B. Russell (1897–1971), a senator from GA.

RICHARDSON LAKE ME

Visible from the AT on Old Blue Mountain and named for the Richardson family, one of the first to settle in the area.

RIDGE ROAD PA

This route through Michaux State Forest was constructed as a fire break by the state bureau of forests in 1934. The AT followed sections of this road in the early 1930s. Today, the trail crosses it a number of times but does not follow it.

RIPSHIN RIDGE TN

Another lyrical name describing the consequences of venturing into the wilds. Here the rhododendron is so dense that you would rip your shins if you tried to scramble through it.

RITCHIE ROAD MD

Albert C. Ritchie (1876–1936) was the 49th governor of MD. A Democrat, he served 4 terms, from 1920 until 1935. Fulfilling the dream of many a politician, he is known for improving state roads. He also reorganized the state public school system. He vied for the party nomination for president in 1932 but was defeated by Franklin D. Roosevelt. He declined Roosevelt's invitation to join the ticket as vice president and was later defeated in his run for a 5th term as governor.

Camp Ritchie opened as a National Guard training site in 1927, then was used by the War Department for field training during World War II. The military created a faux German village here, where GIs practiced raiding and street fighting. The camp was renamed Fort Ritchie by the federal government, which bought it in 1948 to develop the Alternate Joint Communications Center, an underground facility capable of handling communications for the government in emergencies. The AJCC was built 6 miles northeast of Fort Ritchie in PA.

ROAN MOUNTAIN NC/TN

English and Scottish settlers likened the mountain ash trees in the area to their rowan trees back home. The spelling transformation was likely caused by the clipped-vowel pronunciation of Scots—hence "Roan."

ROANOKE VALLEY VA

Roanoke is an Indian word meaning "white shells," or money.

ROARING FORK VALLEY NC

Stand by Roaring Fork Creek during a spring freshet and you'll think you're standing next to a speeding train. This valley was briefly the route of the AT in the mid-1930s.

ROBINSON BROOK VT

Thought to be named for a local family from the Shrewsbury area.

ROBINSON POINT VISTA MA

Named either for Judge Arthur M. Robinson of Williamstown for his 13 years of service on the Mt. Greylock State Reservation Commission, or for George D. Robinson, who represented MA in Congress in 1877–84 and served as governor in 1884–87.

Photo by Steve Wilson, courtesy Tennessee Eastman Hiking and Canoeing Club

The Roan High Knob shelter, built by the CCC in 1934 as a fire warden's cabin. At an elevation of 6,285 feet above sea level, it is the highest elevation shelter on the entire AT. It became an AT shelter in 1980.

ROCK REDOUBTS VA

Redoubt is a little-used word for a protected or defended place. Redoubts on Loudoun Heights were used by northern troops during the Civil War. They were abandoned in September 1862 after Stonewall Jackson took Harpers Ferry.

ROCKFISH GAP VA

The original spelling was "Rochefish," which suggests a surname. Most likely, it was corrupted by a scribe (and now sounds like the Chesapeake-area term for striped bass). The land near the gap and the river was called Rockfish in a 1728 land grant. The site is famous for a meeting that took place here in 1818 at the Mountaintop Tavern, which no longer exists. Twenty-eight people, including former presidents Madison, Monroe, and Jefferson and chief justice John Marshall, gathered to decide whether the University of Virginia should be located in Lexington, Staunton, or Charlottesville.

ROCKWELL ROAD MA

Born in 1844 in Pittsfield, Francis W. Rockwell was appointed to fill the unexpired term of Rep. George D. Robinson, who resigned when elected governor in 1884. Rockwell was re-elected to Congress three times. The road was named for him to honor his service as a member of the Greylock Reservation Commission in 1898–1926.

ROGER'S RAMP CT

Roger Moore worked for the Appalachian Mountain Club in the 1970s and went on to become a "professor of trails." He earned a Ph.D. and attained a university position teaching recreation and tourism and conducting significant research on trails. The ramp was named by Norman Sills, with whom Moore blazed this section of the AT. They were trying to find a way up this rocky area when Moore found a way through two huge boulders, which themselves are noteworthy; they are two pieces of glacial erratic.

ROSS KNOB NC/TN

Probably refers to former Great Smoky Mountains NP superintendent Blair A. Ross, who served in 1945–49.

RPH SHELTER NY

Named for Ralph's Peak Hikers, a walking group led by Ralph Ferrusi. It is constructed of cinderblock and has glass windows—a rarity for usually primitive AT shelters. It contains church pews, a rocking chair, and three bunks.

RUMFORD ME

Sir Benjamin Thompson, the count of Rumford, was one of the original owners of the land.

RUSSELL FIELD NC/TN

Russell Gregory had a hunting cabin and grazed cattle on this bald in the 1880s.

RYE VALLEY VA

Wild rye still grows along creeks and glades here.

S

SABBATH DAY POND LEAN-TO ME

The name was transferred from nearby Sabbath Day Pond. The lean-to was built by the ME AT Club in 1993, replacing a lean-to built in 1935 by the Civilian Conservation Corps. The origin of the pond's name is not known, but it may have been named on a Sunday. It is one of the so-called "Four Ponds."

SABLE MOUNTAIN ME

Visible from the AT near Hall and Wyman mountains. "Sable" is the local name for the marten.

SADDLE BALL RIDGE MA

The Mt. Greylock region is itself a study in toponymy. Greylock had been called Saddle Mountain and Saddle Ball by some. Even now, there is disagreement on exactly which peaks make up Saddle Ball. Depending on the viewer's vantage point, different peaks appear to be the "ball" of the saddle formed by Mt. Prospect, Mt. Fitch, and Mt. Williams. Some people have given the name Saddle Ball to a southern peak slightly lower than Greylock, a peak sometimes called Mt. Griffin, named for Edward D. Griffin, Williams College president in the early 19th century.

SAGES RAVINE MA/CT

Simeon Sage founded the Sage Iron Company on the CT side of the border here in the 19th century. When an iron forge opened nearby, the settlement became known as Sage's Forge, even though the Sages did not operate the forge. When the forge was purchased by John D. Joyce, the settlement was called Joyce's Forge. The ravine, however, is still known as Sages Ravine. Nineteenth-century abolitionist clergyman Henry Ward Beecher wrote that a visit to the ravine was worth a trip from NY every month of the year.

SALISBURY CT

Conventional wisdom holds that the village was named for the cathedral city in Wiltshire, England. The name dates to 1738. Although the Dutch settled the area in 1719, English settlers surveyed the village in 1732. According to one story, one of the settlers was the son of a man from the English city. A colorful alternate theory claims that it is named after a Mr. Salisbury, sentenced to be hanged at age 100 for dragging his servant girl by a horse (he was given a reprieve).

The Dutch called it "Wigwam Place," or "Wootawk" (variant spellings include "Wiatiak," "Wetaug," and "Wesatogue"). The name refers to an Indian settlement of 70 wigwams in the northeast corner of the town, which was there as late as 1740. The township was formally chartered by the British in 1741. It includes Amesville, Lakeville, Lime Rock, and Taconic, as well as Salisbury.

SALMON KILL VALLEY CT

Kill is the Dutch word for "river." The stream now known as Salmon Creek, which runs through the valley, was first known to settlers as Salmon Fell Kill or Salmon Falls River. Earliest usage of the names dates to 1732 land records.

SALT LOG GAP VA

A "salt log" had notches cut in it to hold handfuls of salt for livestock. Today salt blocks are used.

SALT POND MOUNTAIN VA

Early settlers took cattle here to feed on the salt contained in a natural depression. The continuous trampling closed off a water outlet, and Mountain Lake was formed. In 1958, the 14th AT Conference was held at nearby Mountain Lake Hotel.

SAM MOORE SHELTER VA
Built in 1993 and named for Sam Moore, a member of the Potomac AT Club in 1938–98.

SAMS GAP NC/TN
Sam Cook was an early settler here.

SANDY HOOK BRIDGE MD
Sandy Hook is the name of a village that grew up along the Baltimore and Ohio Railroad line. The village was originally called by its land patent, "Keep Triste." Sandy Hook illustrates how a single event in the lives of isolated, rural people can create a name that lives for generations. In the 1840s, a teamster en route to Frederick got stuck in a stretch of quicksand here, losing his horses. It's been called Sandy Hook ever since.

In the summer of 1859, abolitionist John Brown boarded here for a short time, and Union generals used Sandy Hook as a headquarters during the Civil War. When B&O freight yards moved to Brunswick in the 1880s, Sandy Hook residents went with them—there is still a neighborhood in Brunswick called Sandy Hook. Other stories of South Mountain history are described in *The Blue Hills of Maryland* by Paula Strain. *See* Keep Tryst Road, MD.

SANDY RIVER ME
The river is shallow and sandy.

SANDY RIVER & RANGELEY LAKES RAILROAD ME
A narrow-gauge railroad operated here until July 1935, and this spur ran from Phillips to Rangeley. *See* Rangeley, ME.

SARGENT BROOK VT
The stream supposedly gets its name from Leonard Sargent, who once had a blacksmith shop in the area, or from one of his family members.

SASSAFRAS BALD NC
The sassafras tree, commonly used for tea, and in these parts to thicken stew, is abundant here.

SATULAH MOUNTAIN NC
According to James Mooney, a researcher for the U.S. Bureau of American Ethnology in the 1890s, the word derives from *Sutalidihi,* a Cherokee phrase meaning "six killer." But Mooney is silent on why the name was given.

SAUNDERS SHELTER VA
Built in 1987 as a memorial to Walter Saunders, an avid outdoorsman.

THE SAWTEETH NC/TN
Nearly 2 miles long, the ridge is a succession of sharp knobs and broken peaks, in places only a foot wide and rarely much more than 10. Its jagged teeth are all that stand between hikers and a long tumble.

SAWYER MOUNTAIN ME
Named for a local family.

THE SCALES VA
A summer grazing area in the high elevations until the 1920s; cattle were loaded and weighed here each autumn.

SCARE ROCK VA
According to legend, Jess Richeson once came to this remote valley to visit his land holdings. Along the way, he beat one of his slaves mercilessly. As he headed home on his horse, traveling down Brown Mountain Creek, he went by a large creekside boulder, and something—an apparition, a ghost—jumped off and grabbed him around the waist. Richeson couldn't see the attacker, but both he and his horse sensed it. The horse bolted, taking Richeson on a wild ride through rugged terrain and over steep, narrow pathways. Back

home, Richeson claimed that the ghost held him tight all the way. Shaken, he went straight to bed; by morning, both he and his horse were dead. Since then, the boulder from which the spirit jumped has been called Scare Rock.

SCHAGHTICOKE INDIAN RESERVATION CT

Schaghticoke is a Dutch variation of the Mohegan word *Pishhgachtigok,* which means the "confluence of two streams." During the Revolutionary War, the Schaghticoke Indians were said to have sent 100 braves to help the colonial cause. They used a drum, fire, and smoke signals to send messages in a code that was never cracked by the British. The original English translation for the name of the tribe was "Scatacook."

SCHUNEMUNK MOUNTAIN NY

Alternate spellings include Skoonnenoghky, Skonnemoghky, Skonemugh, and Schunamock. The name means "fire place," from the Algonquian *sko,* or "fire." A principal Indian village was once located on the north spur of the range. As early as 1684, this area was referred to as Skoonnenoghky Hill. In the 18th century, it was called Skonemugh or Schunamock.

SCORCHED EARTH GAP VA

Possibly named for the practice of clearing land for planting by setting it afire.

SEELEY-WOODWORTH SHELTER VA

Built in 1984 as a memorial to Harold Seeley and Jack Woodworth of the Natural Bridge AT Club.

SENTINEL MOUNTAIN TRAIL ME

The mountain stands like a sentinel over the Penobscot River Valley.

SETH WARNER SHELTER VT

Seth Warner was a Green Mountain Boy who led the VT militia against the British at the Battle of Bennington in 1777. The shelter was built in 1965 by Manpower, Inc.

SEVEN LAKES DRIVE NY

The road alignment dates from 1809 and was improved in 1913, when it acquired its current name. Originally, it passed seven lakes; it now passes nine.

1777 TRAIL AND 1779 TRAIL NY

The 1777 Trail follows the route of British troops under Sir Henry Clinton on their October 6, 1777, march from Stony Point to attack American forces at forts Clinton and Montgomery. The 1779 Trail follows the route of Mad Anthony Wayne's troops in their effort to recapture Stony Point from the British. Wayne started north of Fort Montgomery and headed south around Bear Mountain and through a valley called Beechy Bottom.

Both trails were blazed in 1974–75 by the Rockland County Boy Scout and Girl Scout councils, the Palisades Interstate Park, the Cooperative Extension Association of Rockland County, and the NY–NJ Trail Conference on routes determined by Jack Mead, director of the Trailside Museum in Bear Mountain–Harriman State Park. He used information gathered from military records in London and maps from the American army of 1778–79.

SHADY VALLEY ROAD TN

The original road across Holston Mountain, between Shady Valley and Bristol. The name comes from a time when the entire valley was covered with tall trees that shut out the sunlight. Yuchi, Shawnee, and Cherokee Indians hunted there. The valley is ecologically significant for keeping the cranberry species alive during the last ice age. Before then, beavers had dammed up the valley, creating a boggy habitat that suited the cranberries delivered by the advancing ice sheet, which paused only 150 miles north of here.

SHANAMAN MARKER PA

William F. Shanaman was once mayor of Reading, an early trail worker, and president of the Blue Mountain Eagle Climbing Club in 1916–39.

SHANNONDALE ROAD VA

This old mountain road connecting Hillsboro, VA, and Shannondale Springs, WV, is named for the Shannondale Springs Resort. Little is known about the origin of the Shannondale name, other than that on May 17, 1739, Lord Fairfax conveyed by deed to John Covil 29,129 acres referred to as Shannondale. George Washington visited the area in 1760, on an invitation to explore a potential site for an iron foundry at Shannondale Springs. The iron works were later constructed and supplied iron to the arsenal at Harpers Ferry, about 8 miles north, a site chosen by then-President Washington.

In 1821, an article describing the curative waters of the spring attracted wide attention, and Shannondale Springs was launched into sudden fame. A 4-story hotel and ballroom were constructed there, followed by cottages and recreation buildings, a casino, bowling green, stables, and bridle paths. Presidents James Monroe, Andrew Jackson, and Martin Van Buren were all visitors. In 1858, the hotel was destroyed by fire. It was rebuilt but burned again in 1909. In 1955, the first road was cut into the western slope of the Blue Ridge to create a new resort. Today, Shannondale is more a suburban-style subdivision than a resort; it has a population larger than any other town in Jefferson County.

SHARON
SHARON MOUNTAIN CT

New Sharon, as the town was first known, alludes to the biblical fertile plain. The name was chosen to attract land buyers.

SHAWANGUNK MOUNTAINS NY

One of those classic Indian names that has been assigned a half dozen or more meanings by toponymical experts, including "white stone," "white salt rocks," and "at or on the hillside," for a fortified Waranawonkong village that was destroyed by the Dutch in 1663. Another meaning could be "the place of the south water," dissected as follows: *shawan*, meaning "south"; *guma*, meaning "water"; *ink*, meaning "place." Hence, the name refers not to the mountains or streams but to the entire region.

SHAYS' REBELLION MONUMENT MA

Daniel Shays served in the Continental Army during the American Revolution but quit when soldiers were not paid. In 1786, as a Berkshire County farmer during a severe economic depression, he led a local revolt demanding lower state taxes and the end of debtors' prisons. A group of some 800 protesters descended on the county courthouse, causing enough disruption to stop judges from issuing foreclosure orders. Shays then led an attempt to seize the arsenal at Springfield, but a state militia paid for by businessmen and landowners put the rebellion down in a battle at Sheffield Plain, site of the monument. Shays and others were tried, but Shays was pardoned in 1788. The episode highlighted the need for a stronger central government, and led in part to the Constitutional Convention of 1787.

The monument was made of granite from Goodale Quarries in Sheffield and engraved by James Tully of Rutland, quarry superintendent at the time.

SHELBURNE NH
Hikers pass through here when they take the Austin Brook Trail "short route" into Gorham. It was named for the earl of Shelburne, William Petty Fitzmaurice, in 1769.

SHELTON GRAVES NC/TN
A single grave marked by military tombstones honors William Shelton and his uncle David, who enlisted in the Union army during the Civil War, leaving their fields behind. On a furlough, they returned home to check in on farm and family and were shot by Confederate soldiers. A lookout who accompanied them was also killed.

SHENANDOAH MOUNTAIN (LOOKING MOUNTAIN) NY
SHENANDOAH RIVER AND MOUNTAINS VA/WV
This mountain in NY and river and mountains in the Virginias provide an interesting glimpse into the toponymy of the AT. One northern source says that Shenandoah is an Iroquois word meaning "Great Plains" and was used to refer to a hamlet in Fishkill, NY. Another claims that *ononda* means "hill" and *goa* means "great"—combining to mean "stream flowing by a great mountain." Still another says that the word may derive from *schind-han-dowi*, meaning "the sprucy stream" or "stream passing through spruce pines."

Southern sources, by and large, cite an undocumented legend that Shenandoah means "daughter of the stars." Still others claim that the name comes from Sherando, an Iroquois chief who camped on the river. And others say it derives from the Senedoe Indians. Even though it was christened the Euphrates by VA governor Spotswood in 1716, the river was called Shannandore by locals as early as 1764.

Potomac AT Club

A view of then nearly treeless Shenandoah NP at the time of the park's dedication in 1936. The chestnut blight, agriculture, and charcoal industry had left the Blue Ridge more field than forest.

SHERANDO RECREATION AREA VA
Visible from the AT and named for a mighty Iroquois chief who once lived here.

SHERBURNE VT
Named on November 4, 1800, to honor Benjamin Sherburne, one of the town's grantees. Other grantees included Ezra Stiles, a founder of Brown University and president of Yale University in 1778–95.

SHERMAN CT
Settled in 1737 and originally part of New Fairfield, it is named for Roger Sherman, a signer of the Declaration of Independence. The town was incorporated in 1802.

SHIKELLIMY ROCKS PA
The Oneida chief Shikellamy was appointed head of the Six Nations in 1728. Various place names nearby use Shikellamy and Shikellimy—sometimes interchangeably.

SHIPPENSBURG PA
Settled in 1730; title to the town was obtained in 1737 by Edward Shippen, whose grandfather, also Edward Shippen, was the first mayor of Philadelphia.

SHIRLEY-BLANCHARD ROAD ME
Shirley was named for Shirley, MA, by Joseph Kelsey of the ME legislature after his hometown. Blanchard was named for Charles Blanchard of Portland, one of the first owners of the township.

SHOOTING CREEK VALLEY NC
The Cherokee name *Du'stayalun'yi,* means the place "where it made a noise as of thunder or shooting."

SHOWERS STEPS PA
A 500-step rock stairway down to the base of "Round Head" was built in the late 1920s and early '30s by Lloyd Showers.

SHREWSBURY PEAK VT
Transferred from nearby Shrewsbury, which was named for the earldom of Shrewsbury, but there is no evidence that the name was given in honor of a specific earl.

SHUCKSTACK MOUNTAIN NC
Seen from Thunderhead Mountain, this peak resembles a standing bundle of corn stalks, called a shuckstack.

SIDNEY TAPPAN CAMPSITE ME
Opened in 1975 by the ME AT Club, whose overseer for eastern ME in 1952–71 was Sidney Tappan. At the time, two overseers covered the entire state. In August 1963, Tappan, Jean Stephenson of the ME and Potomac AT clubs and AT Conference chairman Stan Munay met to discuss the need for a protected corridor for the AT. They decided that only the federal government could do it. Thus began the campaign which culminated in the National Scenic Trails Act of October 1968.

SIGNAL KNOB (G. RICHARD THOMPSON WILDLIFE MANAGEMENT AREA)
SIGNAL KNOB (MASSANUTTEN) VA
The knob on Massanutten is visible from many points on the AT in VA; the other is on the AT in northern VA. Both were important Civil War signal stations. From Massanutten, signals were relayed to Fort Mountain, then onto Stony Man, and on toward Richmond. The two Signal Knobs are in direct line of sight of each other.

SILAS KNOB VA
Sometimes it's hard to live down a foible. This hill is named for a local surveyor who got lost here in the 18th century.

SILER BALD NC
Named for an early settler, William Siler, great-grandfather of the Rev. Dr. A. Rufus Morgan, who helped establish and maintain the AT in NC. *See* A. Rufus Morgan Shelter, NC.

SILERS BALD NC/TN
Called Big Stone by Arnold Guyot, it is officially named for Jesse Siler, who grazed cattle here in the mid-19th century.

SILVERMINE LAKE NY
Created in 1934 when a dam was built here by the Civilian Conservation Corps. It was first called Menomine Lake, an Algonquian word meaning "wild rice," for the swamp grasses that grew here prior to the damming. The swamp was also known as Bockey Swamp; a "bockey" was a wide-splinted woven basket used by charcoal burners and made by mountain people who were sometimes called Bockeys themselves. It comes from the Dutch *bockaal,* meaning "cup" or "bowl." In 1936, a ski slope was built on a hill next to the lake and christened Old Silvermine Ski Area because of its proximity to a legendary silver mine at Black Mountain. In 1951, the lake itself was renamed. *See* Black Mountain, NY.

SIMMONS GAP VA
George Simmons was an early settler here.

SINCKLER'S VALLEY VA
West of Petites Gap, it is named for Charles Sinckler, who bought this land from John Poteet circa 1750. *See* Petites Gap, VA.

SINKING CREEK VA
A nearby creek which goes underground near Hogues Chapel. The area was first settled in 1757.

SIX HUSBANDS TRAIL NH
Legendary Penacook Indian Queen Weetamoo had six husbands.

SKIFF MOUNTAIN ROAD CT
In 1761, Nathan Skiff settled in the Kent area and purchased land that included the mountain.

SKYLAND VA
When it became clear that efforts to produce a profitable copper-mining operation on Stony Man Mountain were futile, young George Freeman Pollock of Washington DC convinced his father (and his father's partner in the mining company) to give him a chance with tourism. On Stony Man, Pollock created a summer camp for wealthy early-20th-century urbanites who would stay for weeks on end in rustic summer quarters. In the evenings, there was entertainment, ranging from costume balls to bluegrass music. Pollock also became the first booster of efforts to establish Shenandoah NP, working tirelessly to gather political support. His book, *Skyland,* is a charming, outlandish tale of life on the mountain at the beginning of the century.

Today, Skyland lives on as a family resort within the national park. Pollock originally called the place Stony Man Camp, but was forced to change the name when he applied for a post office up on the mountain—there was already a Stony Man post office in the Shenandoah Valley.

SKYLINE DRIVE VA
Conceived to be the first leg of a parkway project that would stretch from ME to FL, as proposed by President Franklin Roosevelt. In the face of fierce opposition from the North, it eventually was shortened to 575 miles and combined with the Blue Ridge Parkway. The 105-mile drive opened in three sections: the central district in 1934, the northern district in 1936, and the southern district in 1939. It runs along the crest of the Blue Ridge.

SLAUGHTER GAP GA
A pass between Slaughter and Blood mountains, named for a fierce battle between Cherokee and encroaching Creeks. The Cherokee were said to have been victorious, and the battle created the boundary lines between the tribes that were in place when the Europeans arrived.

SMITHSBURG MD
Named for Christopher Smith (1750–1821), who founded the town around 1815.

SMITHSONIAN RESEARCH CENTER VA
A 4,000-acre wildlife preserve and research facility, the Smithsonian's Wildlife Conservation Research Center was once a U.S. Department of Agriculture research station for livestock study. Before that, it was a cavalry station. Still in operation, the wildlife research operation narrowly escaped closing in 2001, when a new head administrator of the Smithsonian Institution tried to shut it down in a budget-trimming measure. He changed his mind in the face of public opposition. The name Smithsonian comes from Robert Smithson, an Englishman who donated money to construct the original Smithsonian Institution. He never visited the museum he founded. During World War II, a prisoner of war camp sat on the ridge above this area.

SNICKERS GAP VA
Edward Snicker established a ferry at the foot of the Blue Ridge sometime before 1764.

SNOWDEN PEAK VT
Thought to be named to commemorate the highest peak in Wales.

SNOWY MOUNTAIN PA
Snow falls earliest and stays the longest on this highest mountain in the region.

SNYDER BROOK NH
Said to have been named by Dr. William Nowell for a dog named Snyder that belonged to Charles Lowe, a White Mountain guide and owner of the Mt. Crescent House in Randolph, circa 1880.

SOUTH BOURN POND SHELTER VT
Bourn Pond takes its name from a family best known for its involvement in a sensational murder trial. In 1819, seven years after the disappearance of Manchester resident Russell Colvin, two brothers, Jesse and Stephen Bourn, Colvin's brothers-in-law, were convicted of his murder and sentenced to be hanged. They maintained their innocence throughout the trial, but the jury convicted them even though no body had ever been recovered. Apparently, evidence of an argument between Colvin and the suspects was all the jury needed. But as the convicted men awaited their fate, a very-much-alive Russell Colvin appeared in VT, and the brothers were cleared. Colvin had been living quietly in NJ. The shelter here was built in 1966 by the forest service.

SOUTH MOUNTAIN MD
There is no hard evidence about this name's origin other than the mountain's proximity to North Mountain to the west. Ironically, both mountains trend south to north, which means that if they were named as companions, they should be known as West and East mountains. South Mountain, which separates the Monocacy River Valley from the Cumberland Valley, was formerly known as Shenandoah Mountain, and there are colloquial references to it as "Little Blue Mountain." The northern part of South Mountain, near Edgemont, has been known as Blue Mountain. South Mountain has also been called Shenandore Mountain, Shanandore, Shandore, and Shanon Dor.

In the Civil War, the mountain saw heavy fighting; the battle here is known as the engagement that could have ended the war. It led to Union general George McClellan's discovery of Robert E. Lee's plans to invade the North. McClellan's men had found the written plans wrapped around cigars. But McClellan did nothing. Three days later, the Battle of Antietam in nearby Sharpsburg would be the bloodiest battle of the war.

SOUTH POMFRET VT
Established as part of the Pomfret grant in 1761, it received its own post office in 1836. It was named by NH governor Benning Wentworth in honor of Thomas Fermor, the first earl of Pomfret.

SOUTH POND ME
A descriptive name; it's also called Pine Tree Pond because it sits in a pine forest.

SPENCE FIELD NC/TN
James Robert Spence moved from VA to White Oak Cove in the 1820s. In the '30s, he burned and cleared this field to create 100 acres of pasture. He and his wife spent the warm months in a cabin here and wintered down in Cades Cove.

SPERRYVILLE VA
Located east of Shenandoah NP and Thornton Gap and named for a man who settled here in the latter half of the 18th century.

Bill O'Brien

White blazes mark the route of the AT. This engraved blaze is found near Standing Indian Mountain, NC.

SPRINGER MOUNTAIN GA
Previously called Penitentiary Mountain, it is thought to be named for John Springer, the first Presbyterian minister to be ordained in GA (July 1790). Springer Mountain became the southern terminus of the AT in 1960. From 1930 until 1959, the trail ended at Mt. Oglethorpe, named after British general James Oglethorpe, who founded the colony of GA in 1733 as a debtors' colony, and as a buffer between SC and Spanish-held FL. The trail's southern terminus was moved because of the expansion of chicken farming in Oglethorpe.

SPRUCE PEAK SHELTER VT
Built in 1983 by the Green Mountain Club, the shelter takes its name from nearby Spruce Peak, so named because it was once covered with spruce trees. The spruce forest ecosystem, with its swamps, dense undergrowth, and deep moss, was once the dominant high-elevation system in the northeastern U.S. Spruce Peak is now better known for its autumn colors than for the few spruce trees that still grow here.

ST. ANTHONY'S WILDERNESS PA
Named not for a saint, but for a man who perhaps aspired to sainthood. In 1742, Conrad Weiser, officer of Indian affairs for PA, asked the leader of the Moravian Church, Ludwig Von Zinzendorf, to lead his followers on a peace mission to ease tensions with the local Indian tribes of the Kittatinny and Blue mountains, an area of deep, wooded wilderness with few roads and fewer provisions. Anthony Seyfert, one of Zinzendorf's fellow missionaries, was so taken with the beauty of Blue Mountain that Zinzendorf named this area St. Anthony's Wilderness—a name that appears on a map published in 1749.

ST. JOHNS LEDGES CT
The St. John family owned a farm that included these ledges, also known as Seneca Ledges. Everett St. John purchased the property in 1763. His son served in the U.S. House of Representatives in 1813–15.

STAFFORD BROOK TRAIL ME
The Stafford family were early settlers here. The trail is a section of the "Dead River" route that was the original AT, in use until 1939.

STAN MURRAY MEMORIAL PLAQUE AND SHELTER NC/TN
Murray was founder of the Southern Appalachians Highlands Conservancy, former chair of the AT Conference (1961–75), and a longtime member of the TN Eastman Hiking Club. His ashes are scattered on Hump Mountain.

STANDING INDIAN MOUNTAIN NC
A rock formation visible from the AT near the summit gives the mountain its name. The Cherokee called it *Yunwitsule-nunyi*, meaning "where the man stood." In their legend, a monster came from the sky and stole children, terrorizing the Indians for their practice of clearing mountaintops for signal stations and lookouts. The Indians trapped the beast on the south slope of this mountain and implored the Great Spirit to send thunder and lightning to destroy it. When the storm came, an Indian warrior fled the mountain instead of remaining at his post. He was turned to stone for his cowardice and remains there still.

STATE LINE TRAIL NJ
So named because it runs along the NY–NJ state line.

STECOAH GAP NC
Said to be from the Cherokee *stika'yi*, meaning "lean," because hunters in this area always went home empty-handed.

STERLING FOREST NY
STERLING RIDGE NJ
Named for William Alexander, a Revolutionary War general of Scottish origin who fought in the Battle of Long Island. Although he claimed the title of earl of Stirling, Scotland, no such title was officially bestowed upon him. His father, James Alexander, had purchased and surveyed the land in this area. The Stirling (later, Sterling) Furnace supplied the chain that colonists stretched across the Hudson River during the American Revolution. William Alexander died in Albany before the end of the war.

The origin of the name is much easier to trace than the turn of events that led to protection of much of Sterling Forest. A hundred years after Alexander's death, the Sterling Iron and Railway Company sold 20,000 acres of this land to Edward Harriman. The Harrimans later offered the land to NY, but the state declined, claiming it owned enough park land already. The Harrimans sold to private purchasers, who in the mid-1980s announced plans to develop the property, jeopardizing the AT here and the entire ecology of New York City's water supply. A quiet effort begun by a NY couple, JoAnn and Paul Dolan, at their kitchen table grew into a national movement to preserve the land. In February 1998, for $17.5 million in federal funds and more from state and private sources, 15,000 acres of what the Harrimans had offered to give to the state were sold to the Palisades Interstate Park Commission.

STEWART HOLLOW BROOK SHELTER CT
The stream, also known as Little Stony Brook, was named for James Stuart, who was granted mill rights here in 1756. The spelling change occurred on early-19th-century maps.

STILLHOUSE BRANCH ROAD VA
Most likely, a whiskey still hidden in a shack, sometimes called a "stillhouse," was once located here. The mountains of VA have known moonshining for centuries—many would say for justifiable reasons. In the 1930s, mountain residents had to deal with the loss of the American chestnut, which had been a major cash crop until a blight wiped out the species. Then came the loss of native game due to overhunting and bad overtimbering. As the Great Depression worsened, people got desperate. Although fruit trees offered a cash crop, primitive mountain roads made it impossible to get perishables to market before spoilage. Distilling fruit into liquor raised its value and increased its shelf life. But when a constitutional amendment prohibited the manufacture of alcohol, the government in effect took away the region's only cash crop. Many

mountain people felt they had no choice but to circumvent the law.

The term moonshiner comes from "moonlighter," used in England prior to the 19th century to describe nighttime brandy smugglers working the border between Holland and France. The dictionary *Classical Vulgar Tongue*, published in 1785, referred to the smugglers' product as "moonshine." In America, trade in illegal spirits became common with the imposition of the first excise tax, in 1792. Smugglers hid flasks of whiskey in the tops of their boots, a practice called "bootlegging."

STOKES STATE FOREST NJ

Edward C. Stokes was governor of NJ in 1905–08.

STONY MAN MOUNTAIN VA

At 4,031 feet, this is the second highest peak in Shenandoah NP (Hawksbill is highest at 4,050 feet). The cliffs here are the weathered remnants of lava beds, or greenstone outcrops, which form the Stony Man's profile.

STORER COLLEGE, WV

John Storer, of Sanford, ME, proposed to open a college for Negro youth in Harpers Ferry in 1867. He put up $10,000, which was matched by the president of ME's Bates College. The only stipulation was that the college be open to all regardless of race, sex, or religion. The school opened in October 1867 in buildings donated by the federal government to the Freedmans Bureau. It remained in operation until 1955.

STORM KING MOUNTAIN NY

The Dutch first called it Boterberg (or Beutter) for Butter Hill, because they thought it looked like a big, round pat of butter. It was earlier known as Klinkenberg, Dutch for "sounds hill," because of the distinctive, frightening sound thunder makes when it echoes through these hills. Nineteenth-century poet Nathaniel Parker Willis successfully lobbied the NY legislature to change the name to Storm King because he thought it much nobler than a pat of butter.

STORMVILLE MOUNTAIN
STORMVILLE MOUNTAIN ROAD NY

Stormville was settled in 1730 by Garret George and Isaac Storm after Thomas Storm purchased the land. Originally, the village was called Snarlington. A snarling iron is a silversmith's tool; the Storms, like many other early settlers in this mineral-rich region, were silversmiths.

STORY SPRING SHELTER VT

Built in 1963 by the forest service and named for George Story, a longtime trail-worker with the Worcester section of the Green Mountain Club.

STRATTON ME

The Strattons were early settlers here.

STRATTON POND VT

Known alternately as North Pond and Jones Pond; the current name was transferred from the town of Stratton, probably named for Stratton in Cornwall, England.

STUARTS DRAFT VA

Thomas Stewart established a mill here in 1749. His father, Archibald, came here after fleeing Britain as a fugitive from religious persecution. He settled in what is now Waynesboro. Stuarts Draft might have been named Stewarts Draft if Mary Stewart, queen of Scots, had not married a French prince. The spelling of her name was changed to Stuart because the French alphabet has no equivalent to the letter *w*. Other Stewarts in Britain followed suit. The origin of the "Draft" part of the name is unclear. Some say the word describes the wide, flat plain adjacent to the South River; others say it refers to the narrow valley north of town.

STYLES PEAK VT
The Styles family of Peru owned land below the peak.

SUCCESS TRAIL NH
The name is transferred from Mt. Success, which itself is named after the township of Success. The name recognizes the colonists' successful repeal of the Stamp and Tea Act of 1773 and prevention of the importation of tea into Boston.

SUCK MOUNTAIN VA
Visible from Apple Orchard Mountain, its name, according to Bob Ellenwood of the Natural Bridge AT Club, may be descriptive of a spring there that makes a sucking sound.

SUGARLAND MOUNTAIN TRAIL TN
Southern sugar maples here once produced much of America's maple syrup, although the area is no longer known as a sugaring center.

SUGARLOAF KNOB NC/TN
SUGARLOAF MOUNTAIN NY
Sugar was once molded into a conical shape, from which pieces were broken off to be sold. "Sugarloaf" is a ubiquitous term used for mountains of a similar conical shape in the U.S. and elsewhere. The original term was the Dutch *snycker broodt*, a loaf hung by a string above the table.

SUGARLOAF MOUNTAIN TRAIL ME
The trail takes its name from Sugarloaf Mountain, which shares its name with more than a dozen mountains in the Appalachians—rivaled only by hay and haystack in various languages. This trail was part of the AT until about 1971, when the trail was moved to skirt development. At 4,237 feet, Sugarloaf is the second tallest mountain in ME.

SUNDAY RIVER ME
Visible from the AT on Goose Eye; so named because it was discovered on a Sunday.

SUNFISH POND NJ
The southernmost glacial pond on the AT. In the 1960s, Supreme Court justice William Douglas and others fought to save it from being turned into a power plant reservoir. Local activist Casey Keys continued the fight against other development projects here until 1980, when the pond obtained protection—ensuring that its sunnies will continue to thrive.

SUNK MINE ROAD NY
It wasn't the mine that was sunk, it was the land itself. There was a major depression here before mining activity began. In 1756, a mammoth 8-mile vein of iron ore discovered here would make NY the nation's largest iron producer, providing iron ore for Civil War cannon, steamship boilers, and the first locomotive built in the U.S.

SUNRISE MOUNTAIN NJ
This name, common in the Appalachians, makes one wonder why a nation so fixated on westward expansion was continually looking east. Perhaps here it was to get a view of the town below.

SUNSET FIELD VA
Striking sunsets are visible to the west behind the Allegheny Mountains.

SUNSET ROCKS TRAIL PA
Cut by Potomac AT Club cartographer Egbert Walker in 1935 and considered for the AT route in the 1980s. It is named for the open view looking west from Little Rocky Ridge.

Potomac AT Club

A view from the AT in VA, circa 1930. The AT in VA has many such scenic views, including Sunset Field.

SURDAN MOUNTAIN ROAD CT
Locals insist the name is Surdam and that the official name is a map-maker's mistake. Others insist there is no Surdan Mountain at all, that the peak of Sharon Mountain doesn't distinguish itself enough to warrant its own name. William Surdam did not express an opinion on the subject; he lived to age 84 on a farm at the end of the road in the bottom of the valley, at Carse Brook. He died in 1880.

SUSQUEHANNA RIVER PA
Conventional wisdom is that the word is derived from *Sosquenhanne,* from an unknown Indian language. The word is said to mean "how muddy the river is." Other sources disagree not only on the origin but also on the character of the river. One claims it means "the long crooked river"; another claims the name is derived from the word *saskwihanang,* meaning "the place of the straight river."

SWAMP RIVER NY
When you're standing here, you get the picture. The river drains swampland along much of its course.

SWANN BROOK MA
The Arthur W. Swann State Forest in Monterey was established in 1918 when Swann's widow sold 978 acres to the state for a dollar as a memorial to her husband.

SWAPPING CAMP CREEK VA
Early settlers swapped horses, liquor, and other goods here.

SWEAT HEIFER CREEK TRAIL NC
Cattle were once driven upstream to summer pastures high on the balds near here. The heifers apparently worked up a sweat as they moved up the steep slopes.

SWIFT RUN GAP VA
Gov. Alexander Spotswood and his Knights of the Golden Horseshoe crossed this spot in 1716. He signed over vast territories to fellow Virginians, causing disputes with holders of existing Lord Fairfax grants.

SWIFT'S BRIDGE SITE CT
Named for an early settler. The settlement and bridge were lost in the flood of 1936, but the abutments can still be seen.

SWIM BALD NC
Unfortunately, more is known about its former name than the current one. The Cherokee called it *Sehwate'yi,* meaning "hornet place." Legend tells of a monster hornet that had its nest here and sunned itself on the bald, chasing people away.

T

TABLE LAND ME

The plateaulike area surrounding Thoreau Spring was caused by glaciation some 15,000 years ago.

TABLE ROCK TRAIL ME

The table-shaped rock cliff forms one side of Grafton Notch.

TACONIC MOUNTAIN RANGE MA

Taconic is derived from the Algonquian *Taghkanak*, which means "The Forest Hills." *Taghkan* means "a wood"; *aki* means "place."

TAR JACKET RIDGE VA

Called Buck Mountain until about 1927, legend has it that Natural Bridge AT Club president Cecil DeMott gave the ridge its current name because brush on this ridge was so dense that when you walked through it, it was likely to t'ar yer jacket.

TARGET HILL VA

Visible from Bluff Mountain and said to be named for Stonewall Jackson's use of the peak to field test the Parrott rifle in the late 1850s. It is also known as Hunter Hill for Union general David Hunter (1802–86), who placed cannon here to fire on the Virginia Military Institute in 1864. Hunter and 18,000 Union troops entered Lexington unchallenged on June 11, 1864, and occupied it for four days. The occupation led to no casualties, but the troops burned buildings at VMI, including the library, laboratories, and faculty houses. They also destroyed scientific equipment and stole a statue of George Washington, which they then shipped by train to Wheeling, WV. Hunter's forces left on June 14, retreating over the hill. They paused at the top to set up cannons, planning to fire on the college, but Confederate troops alerted to the occupation chased them off.

TELEPHONE PIONEERS SHELTER NY

Built and paid for by a local chapter of the Telephone Pioneers of America, a volunteer organization of AT&T employees and retirees.

TELLICO GAP NC

Named for the Cherokee Overhill town of Great Tellico. Overhill refers to the Cherokee towns once situated on the western slopes of the Appalachians, "overhill" from the Carolina settlements.

TEN MILE HILL
TEN MILE RIVER CT

Ten Mile River drains the surrounding hillsides, starting at the junction of Webatuck and Wassaic creeks in NY. From here to its confluence with the Housatonic River is 10 miles. Locals who care about such things are concerned that some maps now label the Webatuck Creek as Ten Mile River. If you include the creek, the river is definitely longer than 10 miles.

TERRAPIN MOUNTAIN VA

Seen from the Big Rocky Row, it looks like a turtle.

TESNATEE GAP GA

Cherokee for "turkey." After years of declining populations, turkeys are once again abundant here.

THAYER BROOK CT

There is no record stating for which of the long line of Thayers the stream is named, but the family has been resident long enough to have fought in both the American Revolution and Civil War.

THELMA MARKS MEMORIAL SHELTER PA
Built in 1960 to honor a longtime volunteer for the Mountain Club of MD by Earl Shaffer, regarded as the first solo hiker to walk the entire AT. Shaffer's hike took place in 1948; he repeated the feat in 1999. The lean-to was demolished in 2000.

THIRD MOUNTAIN ME
It's the third peak in the Barren-Chairback Range, after Chairback and Columbus.

THISTLE HILL SHELTER VT
Built by the Dartmouth Outing Club in 1995, it takes its name from a hill where thistle once grew in profusion.

THOMAS KNOB SHELTER VA
Nerine and David Thomas, who founded the Mt. Rogers AT Club in 1960, are still doing trail work every weekday.

THOMAS RIDGE NC/TN
Col. William Holland Thomas (1805–93), a native of Haywood County, commanded the Cherokee troops who joined the Confederacy. He later purchased 50,000 acres on behalf of the Cherokee, land that became part of the Qualla Reservation. He was named chief after the death of Chief Yonaguska; he also served in the NC state senate—he was thought to be the only white man to serve as both Indian chief and legislator.

THOREAU SPRING ME
Formerly called Governor's Spring, it was renamed by ME governor Percival Baxter in 1932 for Henry David Thoreau, who climbed Katahdin in 1846.

THORNTON GAP VA
Separating the northern and central sections of Shenandoah NP, it is named for Col. Francis Thornton, who owned a large estate east of the ridge in the mid-18th century, and who was the devoted suitor in the legend of Marys Rock. The vast area east of here was known as "F. T. Valley" from the initials Thornton once carved on a tree at the corner of his property. The gap was known as "Madame Thornton's Quarter" in the late 18th century. *See* Marys Rock, VA.

THREE FORKS GA
Three large creeks—Stover, Chester, and Long—converge here to form Noontootla Creek.

THREE LAKES TRAIL NY
Named for a passage near Canopus Lake, Hidden Lake, and John Allen Pond.

THREE RIDGES VA
There are three parallel ridges here. Some called it "Three Ridged Mountain."

THUNDERBOLT SKI TRAIL MA
Thirty men from the Civilian Conservation Corps worked on the trail in August through December 1934, using 300 pounds of dynamite. Oran McCarthy, a member of the Greylock Ski Club, suggested the name because the trail reminded him of the rollercoaster ride at Revere Beach north of Boston. The trail was the site of the 1935–36 U.S. Eastern Amateur Ski Association championships.

THUNDERHEAD MOUNTAIN NC/TN
Rock formations atop the summit resemble thunderhead clouds.

THUNDERSTORM JUNCTION NH
Conjecture is that it is named for a fierce storm that surprised a party here in the shadow of Mt. Washington.

TIGERTOWN ROAD VT
Transferred from the nearby hamlet in West Hartford; thought to be descriptive of a tough part of town.

TIMP-TORNE TRAIL NY
The trail connects the two summits Timp and Torne. Literally translated from the Dutch, *timp* is a "pointed extremity," also used for a hill. (One source claims that Timp is a family name.) Torne is derived from *tor*, a Middle English word for "rocky peak." Opened in 1921, the trail was the second one built by the Palisades Interstate Park Trail Conference.

TINKER MOUNTAIN VA
Legend says that a number of deserters from the Revolutionary War hid here and became tinkers, making pots and pans that they sold in valley towns.

TOBES CREEK TN/NC
Tobias Phillips, also known as Uncle Tobes, ran the toll-gate on the Cataloochee Turnpike in the 1860s.

TOE RIVER VALLEY NC/TN
Cherokee legend tells of a woman named Estatoe, whose family disapproved of a love affair she was having and so killed her suitor. She then threw herself into the river and drowned.

TOGUE POND GATE ROAD ME
The togue is a freshwater fish that lives in the pond. The gate is the AT's eastern entrance to Baxter State Park. The road goes to the pond.

TOM FLOYD WAYSIDE SHELTER VA
Activist, trail-builder, and member of the Potomac AT Club, Floyd served in many capacities, including supervisor of trails between 1974 and 1981. He led the effort to build the last 66 miles of the Big Blue Trail (now called the Tuscarora Trail). He also proposed the "Big Orange" Trail, a route that would leave the Tuscarora Trail in Massanutten and extend deep into WV.

TOTTS GAP PA
The Leni-Lenape Indian chief Tatami's name was corrupted to Tott.

TOWN CREEK GORGE GA
There was once a Creek Indian town on the banks of the stream.

TRACY POND ME
Foster Tracy was a partner in the logging company Tracy and Love, circa 1883.

TRAIL BOSS TRAIL VA
This former AT route is named for Keith "Trail Boss" Smith, a leader for the AT Conference's Konnarock Crew in the 1970s.

TRAILSIDE MUSEUM AND ZOO NY
While there is nothing notable about the name, the museum itself is noteworthy. Benton MacKaye, whose article proposing the AT spawned the movement to establish it, dreamed of museums and cultural institutions all along the trail. This museum of local natural and cultural history is the only one ever built specifically for the AT. Hikers who fail in their efforts to see a black bear on the trail can get a close look at one in the zoo.

TRANSMOUNTAIN ROAD VA
Formerly known as the "Transmountain Trail," which crossed the ridge here for 5.4 miles and appeared on the U.S. Geological Survey map of 1884. Extending from Frogtown to Upperville, it was one of the earliest AT side trails in northern VA.

TRAPPER JOHN SHELTER NH
There are a few places in America, such as Truth or Consequences, NM, named for television shows. This shelter, built by the Dartmouth Outing Club, follows in that tradition. It was named for Trapper John McIntyre from the novel, film, and TV series *M*A*S*H*. Apparently, someone really liked the show and the character.

Edward Talone

This footbridge, constructed in 1966, crosses Interstate 70 in MD. It was built for just $64,000.

TRAY GAP
TRAY MOUNTAIN
TRAY MOUNTAIN ROAD GA
Believed to be a corruption of Trail Mountain, a name given by Cherokee because there were many trails leading to the summit and over the mountain.

TRICORNER KNOB NC/TN
Three counties, three crests, the Smoky Mountains ridgeline, and the Balsam Mountain transverse all converge here. As well, the knob is said to resemble the shape of an 18th-century tricorner hat.

TRI-COUNTY CORNER PA
A pile of rocks here signifies the convergence of three counties—Berks, Lebanon, and Schuylkill. It is also notable as the location on which the AT was first blazed in PA, in 1936.

TRIMPI SHELTER VA
Avid AT hiker Robert Trimpi passed away in the 1970s. His family contributed funds to build two shelters, Trimpi and Wapiti. *See* Wapiti Shelter, VA.

TRITT GAP GA
Tritt, a local family name, appears on numerous old headstones around here.

TROLLEY LINE GAP (I-70 CROSSING) MD
The road offers a terrible intrusion on the trail, but past names for the gap bear noting. Once known as Orr's Gap, a Confederate soldier renamed it Hamburg Pass after the Frederick County village. It was later known as Trolley Line Gap for the interurban trolley that ran from Hagerstown to Frederick from 1904 to 1938. It closed when U.S. Route 40 made it obsolete.

TROUT DALE VA
The town lies in a narrow valley, or "dale," near Fox Creek, known for excellent trout fishing.

TROUTVILLE VA
Named for a family, not the fish, but which member is unknown.

TUCKERMAN RAVINE NH
Dr. Edward Tuckerman was a professor of botany at Amherst College in 1858–86 who classified the vegetation of the Presidential Range into four categories: lower forest, upper forest, sub-alpine, and alpine.

TUMBLEDOWN DICK STREAM ME
Transferred from a mountain of the same name in Oxford County. There seem to be two stories about the name's origin. In one, a horse called Dick falls off the mountain; in the other, it's a shepherd named Dick who tumbles over the ledge while chasing a runaway sheep.

TURNERS GAP MD
In 1748, Robert Turner was appointed overseer for roads in the "Antietam Hundred," the area west of South Mountain in the newly formed Frederick County. The jurisdiction had been drawn from acreage in Prince George's County. In 1750, Turner

purchased property that included the gap and the present-day location of the Old South Mountain Inn.

Conventional wisdom is that this was the route of British general Edward Braddock's westward movement to protect Fort Cumberland during the Revolutionary War. In 1806, this route was designated the route of the National Road, which brought federal improvements. Stonewall Jackson and his troops used Turners Gap on September 10, 1862, en route to the Cumberland Valley, Harpers Ferry, and Martinsburg, VA (now in WV). Robert E. Lee also crossed that day to camp in Boonesboro, in the days before the Battle of Antietam. *See* Fox Gap, MD.

TUSCARORA TRAIL PA/VA

The name is a corruption of the Iroquois *skaruren*, or "hemp gatherers." The Tuscarora people broke from the Iroquois and migrated to what is now NC, but there they faced hostility and disease from white settlers, so they moved north. Over the course of 90 years, they eventually rejoined the Iroquois, and the Five Nations of the Iroquois became the Six Nations.

In the early 1960s there was concern as to whether the AT could remain viable between Shenandoah NP and PA. On numerous occasions, landowners had closed the trail in VA. More troubling were the military facilities at Mt. Weather in VA and Quirauk Mountain in MD. So AT advocates planned this alternate route, a 255-mile trail with a southern terminus at the AT in Shenandoah NP and a northern terminus at the AT in Deans Gap, near Harrisburg, PA.

Now that the AT is protected, the preservation of Tuscarora is the object of major efforts by the Potomac AT Club. Because much of the trail follows roads, the club is now working to relocate it. Until the late 1990s, it was known as the "Big Blue" south of PA, but it now carries the Tuscarora name over its entire length.

TUSQUITEE MOUNTAINS NC

Tusquittah is the Cherokee word for "rafters." Some might say that the mountains here look like the rafters of a dwelling. The Cherokee once had a settlement called Tusquitah near what is now Hayesville. Tusquitee Creek took its name from the village, and the mountains through which the creek flows took their name from the creek.

One source offers a more colorful alternate explanation of the name's origin. It claims that the word is derived from the Creek word *tsuwa'uniyetsun'yi*, said to mean "where the water dogs laughed." According to Creek legend, a hunter crossing the mountains in a dry season heard voices. He followed the sounds to find two water dogs, or salamanders (or perhaps mudpuppies), walking on their hind legs and talking. Their pond had dried up and they were going to the Nantahala River. One said to the other, "Where's the water? I'm so thirsty that my apron gills hang down," which got them both into a laughing fit.

TUXEDO NY

Leni-Lenape Indians called the lake here *Tucseto*, meaning "place of the bear." It seems *to* or *tough* means "a place," and *p'tauk-seet* means "the bear," a name ascribed to an Indian chief. Together, it means "place ruled by the chief known as 'the bear.'" A 1754 survey calls it Tuxedo Pond; in 1769, the area was called Potuckett. By 1778, it was generally known as Tuxedo or Toxedo, although some sources from 1847 and 1875 refer to it as Duck Cedar.

In the 1880s, Pierre Lorillard IV purchased several thousand acres here as an exclusive playground for the fabulously rich. Mansions were built on large tracts of land, and the homes became the settings for elegant parties. The formal wear male guests wore to them became known as tuxedoes. It is fitting that Emily Post, the grand dame of American etiquette, once lived in nearby Tuxedo Park.

TWIN LAKES CT

Apparently, the larger of the two lakes once had the Indian name *Panaheconnok*. By 1743, however, the English called it North Pond, later, Northeast Pond. Similarly, the southwestern lake was said to have been called *Hokonkamok*. But neither of the Indian names appear in standard references. In 1847, Judge Samuel Church referred to the lakes as "Washinee" and "Washining" and implied that these were the true names. He claimed their meanings were "laughing water" and "smiling water." These meanings can't be verified, but at least they have a story: Washinee and Washining were the daughters of an Indian chief who both loved a brave captured by an enemy tribe. They tried unsuccessfully to secure his release. On the eve of his torture and death, the two women paddled away in a canoe and were never seen again. It is said that during a full moon, an empty canoe can be seen drifting on the lakes.

TYE RIVER VA

Allen Tye explored this region in the 1730s.

TYRE KNOB NC

Named for the biblical city on the Mediterranean Sea, Tyre (rhymes with *sour*), founded in 2750 BC. It is now a city of 250,000 in Lebanon.

TYRINGHAM MA

Settled in 1735 as Housatonic Township #1 and named for Jane Tyringham Beresford in 1762 by her cousin Francis Barnard, the governor of MA. This is the only town in the state named for a woman. Town citizens are aware that this namer, through his repressive policies, contributed greatly to the start of the American Revolution.

U

UNAKA MOUNTAIN NC/TN

Derived from the Cherokee word for "white mountains," referred to as such because of their quartzite cliffs.

UNDERMOUNTAIN ROAD
UNDERMOUNTAIN TRAIL CT

Also designated CT Route 41. The name refers to the road's construction, which tucked the roadbed so far into the mountainside that it's practically underneath it. The 2.7-mile trail, blazed by farmer and trail volunteer Ned Anderson, departs from Undermountain Road and terminates at Paradise Lane Trail. *See* Ned Anderson Memorial Bridge, CT.

UNICOI GAP GA

Originally an Indian trail, it became the route of the first road across the mountain (now GA Route 75), built circa 1812. *Unicoi* is Cherokee for "white," but it is not known if the name predates the turnpike or whether it was assigned by the traders who used it.

V

VALLEY WAY NH

The path was established by Appalachian Mountain Club originals E. B. Cook and Laban Watson in the 1880s. Later improvements were made by AMC founding president J. Rayner Edmands, who originated the now-common practice of planning trails to follow topographic contours. Once Edmands was done with the trail, it closely followed the valley of Snyder Brook. *See* Edmands Col, NH.

VAUGHN STREAM ME

Francis Vaughn was a guide, trapper, and taxidermist who lived in Greenville Township in the 19th century.

VERMONT

An anglicized version of the French phrase *les monts verts,* or "green mountains." The name was officially taken on June 30, 1777, and is credited to Dr. Thomas Young of PA. Before the American Revolution, the area now known as Vermont was part of the remote NH land grants. Delegates to a NH constitutional convention in the summer of 1776 voted for the counties between Lake Champlain and the Connecticut River to form a sovereign state—not a far-fetched idea, as each of the original 13 colonies declared similar status through the Declaration of Independence.

The NH delegates first adopted the name New Connecticut, but changed their minds when they discovered a similarly named place in PA. Young suggested the name Vermont as a way to honor the famed Green Mountain Boys. Another story gives credit for the name to Dr. Samuel Peters, who claimed he had named the region Verd Mont back in 1763. VT became the 14th state in 1791.

VERNON NJ

English admiral Edward Vernon (1684–1757) fought against Spain in 1739, but is perhaps better known as the inspiration for the name Mount Vernon, the eventual home of George Washington, in VA. The naming of the estate is credited to Washington's brother Lawrence, who had served under Vernon.

VIRGINIA CREEPER TRAIL VA

The trail takes its name from the railroad line whose corridor it follows, which took its name from the climbing vine with blue-black berries also known as woodbine. The line's name is a reference to the train's slow progress through this mountainous terrain.

VIRGINIUS ISLAND WV

This small 13-acre island in the Shenandoah River at Harpers Ferry was first called Stubblefields Island after the Harpers Ferry armory superintendent, James Stubblefield. In 1827, the town of Virginius was established here; its name is Latin for "from Virginia" (Harpers Ferry was part of VA until 1863). Between 1824 and 1935, various industries operated on the island, including saw and pulp mills, the last of which closed in 1935. The record flood of March 18–19, 1936, swept the mill away. Evidence of this record flood can still be seen from the AT at Harpers Ferry where the Potomac and Shenandoah rivers meet. Pillars are all that remain of two bridges swept away when the water rose 36.5 feet above flood level. Ferry service was restored until 1949, when the U.S. Route 340 bridge opened.

VONDELL SHELTER VT

Built in 1967 by the International Paper Company, the shelter is named for John Vondell, an active member of the Green Mountain Club in the 1950s and '60s.

W

WADE SUTTON PLAQUE NC
Wade Sutton died here on December 7, 1968, while fighting a forest fire.

WALASI-YI CENTER GA
Walasiyi, meaning "frog place," recognizes an odd Cherokee legend. After the Cherokee captured the magician Shawano, he convinced them to spare his life in return for his capture of Uktena, the evil serpent. When the Indians and their prisoner came into this place, they encountered a giant frog, which terrified the Indians. Shawano got a big laugh out of the fact that his ferocious captors were so frightened of a big frog. The point of the parable is lost.

The AT goes through the center of the building, constructed of American chestnut and local rock in the 1930s by the Civilian Conservation Corps. It is now on the National Register of Historic Places. *See* Mt. LeConte, NC/TN, and Neels Gap, GA.

Potomac AT Club

War Correspondents' Memorial, in Gathland State Park, MD, is the only known monument honoring war correspondents.

WALLINGFORD VT
The town charter was granted in 1761 to a group led by Capt. Eliakim Hall and his partners from Wallingford, CT, which got its name from the town in Berkshire, England, on the river Thames.

WALLKILL NJ
Named for settler Joseph Walling. The derivation is from the Dutch *kill,* or "stream"—making it Walling's Stream.

WALLPACK VALLEY NJ
From the Leni-Lenape *walpekat,* which means "very deep water."

WAPITI SHELTER VA
Wapiti is the Shawnee name for *Cervus canadenis,* the American elk, also called the gray moose, which no longer inhabits the area. This is another shelter donated by the family of hiker Robert Trimpi; it was built by the forest service in 1980. *See* Trimpi Shelter, VA.

WAR CORRESPONDENTS' MEMORIAL MD
Built by George Alfred Townsend, newspaper reporter turned amateur architect, at his Gapland estate at Crampton Gap. Erected in 1896 in memory of Townsend's fellow Civil War journalists, artists, and photographers, the memorial is inscribed with the names of 152 correspondents from both the North and the South. Included are all but one correspondent who covered the Civil War. (One fellow refused to have his name listed.) Contributors to the memorial included Thomas Edison, J. Pierpont Morgan, Joseph Pulitzer, and explorer Henry J. Stanley. *See* Gathland State Park, MD.

WARNER HOLLOW ROAD MD
Luther Warner lived on the road in the 19th century.

WARREN NH
Incorporated in 1763 and named for a British naval admiral.

WARREN TURNPIKE CT
Thought to have connected Falls Village and Warren, following the Housatonic River to Cornwall Bridge, then up the mountain to Warren. It alternately was known as Seven Crossings Road because it crossed the railroad tracks seven times. It also was called River Road along various stretches, and the name eventually referred to the entire length. Like Warren, NH, this CT town was named for Admiral Warren of the British navy.

WASHINGTON COUNTY MD
At MD's first state convention, in 1776, this county was created by carving off part of Frederick County. It became the first place name to honor George Washington; the county was renamed before he was elected president.

WASHINGTON MONUMENT MD
The first monument erected to honor the first president, built by Whig partisans from Boonesboro as a show of opposition to the new Democratic party and Andrew Jackson. Construction began on July 4, 1827; by that afternoon, volunteers had constructed a base of dry-stacked native stone 15 feet in diameter. When the inscription stone was laid later that day, three Revolutionary War veterans fired musket rounds in tribute. In the fall of 1827, 30 feet were added to complete the cream-bottle-shaped structure.

During the Civil War, the monument was used as an observation and signal tower by the Union Army. During World War I, it was mysteriously dynamited—some say by a German sympathizer, others say by a local farmer who didn't like his daughter hanging out with boys there. The monument suffered only minor damage, a hole at its base, but age and periodic minor vandalism left the monument in poor condition by the 1930s. The Civilian Conservation Corps then took it apart and rebuilt it from the ground up.

WATAUGA DAM AND LAKE TN
Although its meaning is unconfirmed, the name is said to be Cherokee for "beautiful river." Watauga once referred to two towns in Cherokee territory. The first was on Watauga Creek, a branch of the Little Tennessee River. The second was located at Watauga Old Fields, near present-day Elizabethton on the Watauga River.

WATEROAK GAP NC
The water oak is a tree, but it does not grow in this area. Perhaps it once did, or perhaps the namers called another tree species by the wrong name.

WATERVILLE BRIDGE PA
Built in 1890 by the Berlin Iron Bridge Company of East Berlin, CT, the bridge crossed Little Pine Creek in the town of Waterville until 1986. By then, the volume of traffic was too much for the old bridge. It was slated for demolition, but activists convinced the state to preserve it. They moved it 75 miles south to this spot, where it crosses Swatara Creek. The bridge is now listed on the National Register of Historic Places.

WATSON PATH NH
The trail was cleared here in 1882 by Laban Watson, who cleared many trails in the area to further the business of the Ravine House, a large hotel he owned in Randolph.

WAWAYANDA STATE PARK NJ
Derived from the Leni-Lenape *wai wai,* or "winding many times," and *anda,* meaning "action."

Edward Talone

A sign warns hikers at the approach of the long suspension bridge across Webster Brook in the White Mountains of NH.

WAYAH BALD
WAYAH GAP NC

Wayah is the Cherokee word for "wolf" and is thought to be imitative of the creature's howl. Red wolves were common in this area until the mid-19th century. In 1776, Gen. Griffith Rutherford led a rampage here against the Cherokee. The clash was a desperate stand for the Indians. Daniel Boone is thought to have taken part in the battle; his brother was killed in it.

WAYNESBORO VA

First settled in the 1730s when Joseph Tease opened a tavern here. It became known as Teaseville. The city's location, along the South River and near the Rockfish Gap passage of the Blue Ridge, was a great attraction. The town was laid out in 1797 by James Flack and Samuel Estill, and rechristened Waynesborough in 1801 in honor of American Revolution general "Mad" Anthony Wayne. It was incorporated as a town in 1824, becoming an iron- and steel-producing center when the railroad arrived and earning a reputation for the manufacture of railroad cars. Mad Anthony is also the namesake of Fort Wayne, IN. *See* Anthony's Nose, NY.

WEBSTER MOUNTAIN NH

The mountain and many features on it are named for politician and orator Daniel Webster (1782–1852). A NH native, he was elected to the House of Representatives from NH, then from MA. He also served two terms in the Senate, was a member of the Harrison-Tyler cabinet, then was re-elected to the Senate.

WELCH RIDGE NC/TN

With the number of Welches in the area, no one is sure which gave the ridge its name. The first Welches settled near Alarka Creek circa 1810, but not much is known of them, and there aren't any records of the name until much later. Washington Welch settled here in the 1850s.

WENTWORTH NH

Settled in 1774 along the Baker River and named for colonial governor Benning Wentworth.

WEST BRANCH PLEASANT RIVER ME

Once called *Mun-Olam'mon-Un'gun* by the Abenaki, but the meaning is unknown.

WEST HARTFORD VT

West Hartford and Hartford are named after the town of the same name in CT, which derives its name from Hertford, in Hertfordshire, England—a Middle English word for "a stag ford." The West Hartford area was first called Centerville, then Sucker City because the town was known for its White River fishing.

WEST HARTFORD–QUECHEE ROAD VT

The road leads from West Hartford to the village of Quechee, formerly known as Queechy. The name is transferred from Queechee Gorge and is derived from the Natick word *Ottauquechee*, meaning "swift mountain stream."

WEST MOUNTAIN NY
West of what, you might ask? Why, Doodletown, of course.

WEST POINT NY
In 1802, this site was chosen for a U.S. military academy to replace the old British fortification on Constitution Island. The old site was on a straight stretch of river and was tough to defend, but the new site was on a high bank above a sharp S curve on the west bank of the Hudson River. Even though the story of the name is not very interesting, the place has a fascinating history. In 1780, the colonial general in command of the new fort at West Point promised to divulge secret plans to a British general in exchange for 20,000 pounds. When the treachery was uncovered, British major John Andre was captured and hanged. The American involved in the scheme escaped, however. His name, Benedict Arnold, became synonymous with traitor.

WEVERTON MD
As a highway and railroad construction engineer, Caspar W. Wever laid out Pennsylvania Avenue in Washington DC and served as superintendent of the National Road, which was authorized by Congress in 1806 to run from Cumberland, MD, to the Ohio River. The road was completed in 1818 at Wheeling, VA (later WV). When Democrat Andrew Jackson was elected in 1828, he removed all Whigs from their government jobs, including Wever, who came to Washington County, a center for Whig sympathizers, and became superintendent of construction for the Baltimore & Ohio Railroad.

He purchased property along the Potomac River and Israel Creek, hoping to sell riverfront property to either the B&O or the Chesapeake & Ohio Canal. He also had plans for an industrial center called Weverton Manufacturing. But there were few takers on the building leases he offered because of the predatory rents he charged. He sold off some of the land, including lots for the town of Weverton. He died in 1849. In 1852, a flood ruined the wooden dams and industrial buildings he had built. In 1870 and 1877, other floods damaged more buildings. The property was eventually sold to C&O, which razed the buildings.

WHALEY LAKE STREAM NY
The Whaleys owned land at the south end of Whaley Pond, which was enlarged by a dam built by the Matteawan Company to power factories and mills. *Matteawan* is an Indian word said to mean "large water in the valley." Others claim it means "good beaver ground."

WHEELOCK STREET NH
Named for the Rev. Eleazer Wheelock, who founded Dartmouth College in a single log hut built in 1770.

WHISKEY SPRING PA
A whiskey still operated nearby during Prohibition using water from this spring.

WHISTLING GAP NC
One of the charms of toponymy is that the explanations of word origins are themselves invitations to search for word origins. Here's what Allen R. Coggins writes for Whistling Gap in his *Place Names of the Smokies:* "Whistling Gap may have been associated with a whistle punk or bell boy, a device used by the logging industry to provide whistle signals on a log skidder."

WHITE BROOK TRAIL ME
This trail was part of the AT until 1975. White Brook is named after nearby White Cap Mountain. *See* White Cap Mountain, ME.

WHITE CAP MOUNTAIN ME
It's usually covered with snow until late in the spring.

WHITE RIVER JUNCTION VT
The White River is known for long stretches of rapids and whitewater. The town was the junction point for three railroads.

WHITE ROCKS MD
Seen from below, the gray rocks contrast with the leafy hillside.

WHITE ROCKS MOUNTAIN VT
Outcroppings of milky white quartz give the mountains their distinctive appearance.

WHITE ROCKS RIDGE PA
Marking the northern terminus of the Blue Ridge Mountains, this ridge is named for its extensive outcroppings of white quartz.

WHITEOAK STAMP NC
A stamp is an open area where livestock were gathered in the 19th century after summers of grazing in the forest. The gathering point in this stamp was a great white oak.

WHITESIDE MOUNTAIN NC
Named for its white granite face, featuring sheer cliffs up to 750 feet high; formerly known as the Devil's Courthouse.

WHITETOP MOUNTAIN VA
At 5,520 feet, the second highest point in VA, and formerly called Iron Mountain. The new name refers to a 500-acre grassland on top that shimmers in the sunlight like a glacier. In the 1930s, before the AT crossed the mountain, there was a motel here called White Top Lodge. The toll road to the top cost a dollar for cars, but hikers could walk up for free.

WIGWAM MOUNTAIN VA
Visible from the blue-blazed former AT (1.7 miles north of USFS 63), it was named in the 1800s for a band of Cherokee Indians who camped here after being banished from Lexington because they had smallpox.

WILBUR CLEARING MA
This grassy open area in a red spruce forest is named for Jeremiah Wilbur, who pastured animals here on the Greylock range. Wilbur first started farming in 1767 at the age of 14 and later built the first road over the notch between Ragged Mountain and Mt. Greylock (the forerunner of Notch Road). Decades later, in his *Travels in New England and New York*, former Yale president Timothy Dwight recounts a visit to Wilbur's farm; he describes 1,600 cleared acres producing 100 tons of hay a year and enough maple trees to produce 1,800 pounds of sugar. There were also cattle and sheep and cider, grist, and saw mills on Notch Brook. Wilbur died in 1813.

WILDCAT MOUNTAIN NH
Named by professor Arnold Guyot of Princeton, who named dozens of Appalachian places—many of which had perfectly fine names before he arrived. Legend has it that either he or a friend once saw a panther here, an animal that is no longer found in these mountains. The mountain was formerly named Mt. Hight and East Mountain because it was located east of Pinkham Notch. *See* Mt. Hight, NH.

WILDER DAM VT
When residents of the nearby village of Olcott wanted a bridge built across the Connecticut River, Charles Wilder of Boston promised to donate his estate for the bridge fund when he died if the village name was changed to Wilder. The village agreed. Wilder died in 1898, and his bridge stood until the 1950s, when it was removed for the construction of Wilder Dam.

WILDER MINE HOLLOW TN
Union colonel John Wilder (1830–1917) held off Confederates during the Battle of Chickamagua in September 1863. After the Civil War, Wilder developed iron foundries in Rockwood and mined ore near the base of Roan Massif.

WILEY SHELTER NY
Built in 1940 with assistance from William O. Wiley of the Tramp and Trail Club of NY.

WILLEY HOUSE SITE NH
Named for the Willeys who died here in a flood in 1826. Believing that their home would be swept away by the rising floodwaters, they abandoned it. But they were engulfed in a landslide that pushed tons of debris into the notch. Samuel Willey, his wife and five children, and some hired hands all perished in the disaster. Ironically, the house somehow withstood what is now called the Willey Slide.

WILLIAM B. DOUGLAS LEAN-TO VT
Dr. Christopher Swezey was a dedicated member of the Green Mountain Club who in 1926 donated materials for a shelter, originally called the Buck Job Camp. Later it was renamed for Swezey himself. In 1973, it was renamed for William B. Douglas, a volunteer trail worker in the 1950s and '60s.

WILLIAM BRIEN MEMORIAL SHELTER NY
William Brien, the first president of the NY Ramblers, bequeathed $4,000 for a shelter that was built in 1958 at Island Pond. Its location made it prone to vandalism, however, and it was soon abandoned. But the name lived on when the former Letterrock Shelter was renamed in 1973.

WILLIAM PENN SHELTER PA
William Penn (1644–1718) was the son of English admiral Sir William Penn and founder of the PA colony. He is noteworthy to trail historians because he was an early believer in the concept of public land, having set aside tracts of land for hunting and wild-berry gathering.

WILLIAMSTOWN MA
A fort settlement situated here in the northwest corner of the MA colony in 1745 was originally called West Hoosac. The fort was intended to guard against the Dutch in NY. Ephraim Williams was the commander of a line of forts and stockades that ranged east to the Connecticut River; he was killed in the French and Indian War in the Battle of Lake George. His will included money to found a "free school," the equivalent of a public high school to day, with two stipulations. First, the town of West Township had to be renamed Williamstown (this was done in 1765). Second, the school had to be in MA (this one took time, because NY and MA were fighting over which state held title to the land that included Williamstown; the dispute was resolved in 1784 in MA's favor). In 1785, the school was established. It became Williams College in 1793.

WINDING STAIR GAP NC
Named for its precipitous series of switchbacks.

WINDSOR FURNACE PA
The site of an early pig iron works; the furnace was in operation before 1768 and was called Windsor Castle Furnace after King George's residence in England. A number of charcoal hearths in the area provided fuel for the furnace.

WINHALL RIVER VALLEY VT
There are several stories about the origin of this name, but none have been substantiated. A reasonable one is that the name came from the combination of surnames of two of the town's grantees: Winn and Hall. But there are no Halls in

the charter documents. Another account traces the name to a village called Winall in Herefordshire, England—a real place, indeed, but with no known connection to this VT town.

WINTTURI LEAN-TO VT
Loyal trail worker Mauri Wintturi is still a Green Mountain Club member.

WITHERLIE RAVINE ME
George Witherlie explored the Katahdin region extensively from 1880 until 1901.

WOLFPEN GAP GA
During frontier days, wolves were considered the scourge of the land. Domestic farm and stock animals provided easy pickings for the predators. And since nearly everyone had some animals, even if just a few chickens and a cow, wolves, in the eyes of settlers, could take food off the table of anyone's household. Various schemes offering cash for their hides were developed to encourage the wolves' eradication. A farmer who couldn't be bothered to turn in the hide would often nail the carcass to a tree or fencepost to show his neighbors that he was doing his part—today it is not uncommon to see coyote remains in a similar state. Wolfpens were deadfall traps commonly used by mountain settlers. A deadfall trap is constructed of heavy tree limbs and is triggered by the weight of the animal. When the limbs fall, they strike the animal in the head or pin it to the ground.

WOLFSVILLE ROAD MD
Sources disagree on which Wolf was the founder of Wolfsville. The local historical society credits David Wolf, Sr., and gives the date for the settlement as 1828. But others credit Jacob Wolf as the founder, whom records show was postmaster in 1834. The name Jacob D. Wolf is also associated with the founding of Black Rock Hotel, but the history of this establishment spans from roughly 1870 to 1880, when the hotel burned, and to 1907, when Wolf is said to have rebuilt it. It seems a stretch that Jacob could have been old enough in 1828 to found Wolfsville and still have the vigor to rebuild a hotel in 1907. The founder of Black Rock is usually referred to as Jacob D. Wolf—perhaps the *D* was for David, or perhaps he was a descendant of Jacob or David, or both. There also seems to be an interchangeable use of two spellings, Wolf and Wolfe. In any case, the road to Wolfsville was not built by Wolfs; it was a well-traveled old route from Frederick to Hagerstown thought to follow an even older Indian path. *See* Black Rock, MD.

WOODS HOLE SHELTER GA
Opened May 2, 1998, the only log shelter in GA is dedicated to Tillie Wood and her late husband, Roy. The Roswell couple had long welcomed hikers into their summer home in Sugar Run Gap for breakfast and provided shelter in a converted barn and farmhouse called the Woodshole Hostel. Tillie is still hosting spring thru-hikers.

WOODSTOCK VT
Transferred from Woodstock, CT, or directly from the old city of Woodstock in Oxfordshire, England. The ancient meaning is "a place in the woods."

WOODY GAP GA
There is little disagreement that the Woody family gave its name to the gap, but whether it was for a specific Woody remains a question. John was an early postmaster of Dahlonega. Arthur Woody (1884–1946) grew up on a farm in Union County. As a forest service employee, he advocated federal land acquisition in the GA mountains and became the first ranger of the newly formed GA National Forest (now the Chattahoochee National

Forest). He is credited with re-establishing the deer population in northern GA by bringing in fawns from other states after it had been decimated by overhunting. Woody is known to have kept a bear paw in his truck, a device he used to catch deer poachers. He would make tracks near hunting camps to lure hunters into the woods hoping to bag a bear, thereby distracting them from the deer.

WOOLY TOPS LEAD NC/TN
A wooly head is a knob or slope covered with a dense thicket of rhododendron, azalea, and laurel—known locally as "laurel hells." A lead is a spur coming off a larger mountain.

WYMAN MOUNTAIN ME
Named for the Wymans, who cleared land here about 1900.

Y

YANKEE HORSE RIDGE VA
A Union soldier's exhausted horse fell to its death here during the Civil War, according to legend.

YELLOW BREECHES CREEK PA
According to one story, the creek is named for the yellow pants worn by the PA militia during the American Revolution. Another story is somewhat baffling: A 1938 edition of the *Potomac AT Club Bulletin* reports that the stream was originally called Callapatick Creek and that the current name evolved through mispronunciation. The spelling was then changed to fit the new pronunciation. (I've tried dozens of accents out loud to discover the transformation without success.)

YELLOW CREEK GAP NC/TN
Smoky Mountains author Allen R. Coggins suggests that the gap is named for the autumn foliage of tulip trees and sugar maples. It's easy to imagine hunters sidling through the woods here along a stream bed painted yellow by fallen leaves.

YELLOW MOUNTAIN NC
Known by Native Americans as *Ta-loh-na* or *Da-loh-no-geh*, meaning "yellow" or "gold."

Z

ZITTLESTOWN ROAD MD
Michael and Magdelena Zittle settled on the western slope of South Mountain, below Turners Gap, in 1792. Their son Michael, Jr., was born shortly thereafter; he earned a reputation as a kind of witch doctor and was the inspiration for Madeleine Dahlgren's book *South Mountain Magic*. Michael, Jr., died in 1877. *See* Dahlgren Chapel, MD.

References

BOOKS

Abbott, Katherine M. *Old Paths and Legends of the New England Border.* New York: G. P. Putnam's, 1907.

Albright, Jack. *Appalachian Trail Guide to Central Virginia.* Harpers Ferry, WV: Appalachian Trail Conference, 1994.

Albright, Rodney, and Priscilla Albright. *Hiking Great Smoky Mountains.* 4th edition. Old Saybrook, CT: Globe Pequot Press, 1999.

Appalachian Trail Guide to Central and Southwest Virginia, 7th edition. Harpers Ferry, WV: Appalachian Trail Conference, 1974.

Appalachian Trail Guide to Central and Southwest Virginia, 8th edition. Harpers Ferry, WV: Appalachian Trail Conference, 1981.

Appalachian Trail Guide to Central and Southwest Virginia, 9th edition. Harpers Ferry, WV: Appalachian Trail Conference, 1986.

Appalachian Trail Guide to Central and Southwest Virginia, 10th edition. Harpers Ferry, WV: Appalachian Trail Conference, 1988.

Appalachian Trail Guide to New Hampshire–Vermont, 2nd edition. Washington, DC: Appalachian Trail Conference, 1964.

Appalachian Trail Guide to New Hampshire–Vermont, 3rd edition. Harpers Ferry, WV: Appalachian Trail Conference, 1979.

Appalachian Trail Guide to New Hampshire–Vermont, 4th edition. Harpers Ferry, WV: Appalachian Trail Conference, 1985.

Atwater, Francis. *The History of Kent, Connecticut.* Meriden, CT: Journal Publishing Co., 1897.

Avery, Myron H., ed. *Guide to the Appalachian Trail in the Southern Appalachians,* 2nd edition. Washington, DC: Appalachian Trail Conference, 1942.

Bearse, Ray, ed. *Massachusetts: A Guide to the Pilgrim State.* Boston: Houghton Mifflin, 1971.

Beebe, Levi. *Meteorology: How to Foretell the Weather for Each Season, for All Time and in All Parts of the World.* South Lee, MA: n.p., 1892.

Birdsall, Richard D. *Berkshire County: A Cultural History.* New Haven, CT: Yale University Press, 1959.

Bixby, William. *Connecticut: A New Guide.* New York: Charles Scribner's Sons, 1974.

Boltwood, Edward. *The History of Pittsfield, Massachusetts from the Year 1876 to the Year 1916.* Pittsfield, MA: City of Pittsfield, 1916.

Bond, C. Lawrence. *Native Names of New England Towns and Villages,* 2nd edition. N.p., 1993.

The Book of Berkshire. Springfield, MA: Clark W. Bryan & Co., 1887.

Boynton, Edward C. *History of West Point and Its Military Importance During the American Revolution.* 1863. Reprint, Freeport, NY: Books for Libraries Press, 1970.

Brooks, Robert R. R., ed. *Williamstown: The First Two Hundred Years, 1753–1953.* Williamstown, MA: McClelland Press, 1953.

Brown, Fred, and Nell Jones, eds. *The Georgia Conservancy's Guide to the North Georgia Mountains,* 2nd edition. Atlanta: Longstreet Press, 1991.

Bruce, Dan "Wingfoot." *The Thru-Hiker's Handbook.* Conyers, GA: Center for Appalachian Trail Studies, 1994.

Bruce, Dan "Wingfoot." *The Thru-Hiker's Handbook.* Hot Spring, NC: Center for Appalachian Trail Studies, 1997.

Bryant, William Cullen. *The Poetical Works of William Cullen Bryant.* New York: D. Appleton, 1913.

Buckingham, J. S. *America, Historical, Statistic, and Descriptive.* New York: Harper and Brothers, 1841.

Burns, Robert M. "Schunemunk Mountain." In *The Hudson Highlands.* New York: Appalachian Mountain Club, 1945.

Bushaber, Albert B. "Walk of the Nine Hills." In *The Hudson Highlands.* New York: Appalachian Mountain Club, 1945.

Byron, Carl R. *A Pinprick of Light: The Troy and Greenfield Railroad and Its Hoosac Tunnel.* Shelburne, VT: New England Press, 1995.

Campbell, Carlos C. *Birth of a National Park in the Great Smoky Mountains,* revised edition. Knoxville: University of Tennessee Press, 1969.

Chase, Jim. *Backpacker Magazine's Guide to the Appalachian Trail.* Harrisburg, PA: Stackpole Books, 1989.

Chazin, Daniel D. *Appalachian Trail Guide to New York–New Jersey,* 14th edition. New York: New York–New Jersey Trail Conference, and Harpers Ferry, WV: Appalachian Trail Conference, 1998.

Chew, V. Collins. *Underfoot: A Geologic Guide to the Appalachian Trail,* 2nd edition. Harpers Ferry, WV: Appalachian Trail Conference, 1993.

Clawser, N. Clair. *A Guide of Pennsylvania Towns.* Harrisburg, PA: AFC Press, 1998.

Clyne, Patricia Edwards. *Hudson Valley Tales and Trails.* Woodstock, NY: Overlook Press, 1990.

Coggins, Allen R. *Place Names of the Smokies.* Gatlinburg, TN: Great Smoky Mountains Natural History Association, 1999.

Cook, Joe, and Monica Cook. *Appalachian Trail Companion,* 1st edition. Harpers Ferry, WV: Appalachian Long Distance Hikers Association, Appalachian Trail Conference, 1994.

Corey, Faris Jane. *Exploring the Mountains of North Carolina.* Raleigh, NC: Provincial Press, 1972.

Coriell, Jack, Alan Duff, Dick Ketelle, and Nancy Shofner, eds. *Appalachian Trail Guide to North Carolina–Georgia,* 11th edition. Harpers Ferry, WV: Appalachian Trail Conference, 1998.

Crane, John Wright, and Benjamin F. Thompson. *A History of the Town of Washington, Massachusetts.* 1918. Reprint, Pittsfield, MA: Berkshire Family History Association, 1992.

De Hart, Allen. *North Carolina Hiking Trails,* 3rd edition. Boston: Appalachian Mountain Club Books, 1996.

DeFoe, Don, Beth Giddens, and Steve Kemp, eds. *Hiking Trails of the Smokies.* Gatlinburg, TN: Great Smoky Mountains Natural History Association, 1994.

Denton, James. *Circuit Hikes in Shenandoah National Park,* 12th edition. Washington, DC: Potomac Appalachian Trail Club, 1986.

Denton, Molly Tabor. *Guide to Appalachian Trail in Shenandoah National Park,* 6th edition. Washington, DC: Potomac Appalachian Trail Club, 1967.

Denton, Molly Tabor. *Guide to Appalachian Trail in Shenandoah National Park,* 7th edition. Washington, DC: Potomac Appalachian Trail Club, 1973.

Denton, Molly Tabor. *Guide to Appalachian Trail in Shenandoah National Park,* 8th edition. Washington, DC: Potomac Appalachian Trail Club, 1977.

Dohme, Alvin. *Shenandoah: The Valley Story,* revised 1st edition. Washington, DC: Potomac Books, 1973.

Donehoo, George P. *Indian Villages and Place Names in Pennsylvania.* Baltimore: Gateway Press, 1977.

Dunn, Durwood. *Cades Cove: The Life and Death of a Southern Appalachian Community.* Knoxville: University of Tennessee Press, 1988.

Dunwell, Frances F. *The Hudson Highlands.* New York: Columbia University Press, 1991.

Dwight, Timothy. *Travels in New England and New York,* vol. 3. New Haven, CT: S. Converse, 1822.

Dykeman, Wilma. *The French Broad.* New York: Rinehart, 1955.

Dykeman, Wilma, and Jim Stokely. *Highland Homeland: The People of the Great Smokies.* Washington, DC: National Park Service, 1978.

Eager, Samuel W. *An Outline History of Orange County, with an Enumeration of the Names of Its Towns, Villages, Rivers, Creeks, etc.* Newburgh, NY: S. T. Callahan, 1846–47.

Edgar, Kevin. *Appalachian Trail Guide to Tennessee–North Carolina,* 11th edition. Harpers Ferry, WV: Appalachian Trail Conference, 1995.

Emblidge, David. *Exploring the Appalachian Trail: Hikes in Southern New England.* Mechanicsburg, PA: Stackpole Books, 1998.

Encyclopedia of Tennessee. New York: Somerset Publishers, 1993.

Espenshade, Abraham. *Pennsylvania Place Names.* University Park, PA: Penn State Press, 1925.

Federal Writers' Project. *Connecticut: A Guide to Its Roads, Lore, and People.* Boston: Houghton Mifflin, 1938.

Federal Writers' Project. *Dutchess County.* Philadelphia: William Penn Association, 1937.

Federal Writers' Project. *Massachusetts: A Guide to Its Places and People.* Boston: Houghton Mifflin, 1937.

Federal Writers' Project. *New York: A Guide to the Empire State.* New York: Oxford University Press, 1940 (1976 reprint).

Federal Writers' Project. *North Carolina: A Guide to the Old North State.* Chapel Hill: University of North Carolina Press, 1939.

Federal Writer's Project. *Pennsylvania: A Guide to the Keystone State.* Washington, DC: Work Progress Administration, 1940.

Federal Writers' Project. *Tennessee: A Guide to the State.* New York: Hastings House, 1939.

Figliomeni, Michelle P. *E. H. Harriman at Arden Farms.* Arden, NY: Orange County Historical Society, 1997.

Fisher, Lee. *Footpath in the Wilderness.* Middlebury, VT: Middlebury College Press, 1941.

Floyd, Tom. *Lost Trails and Forgotten People.* Washington, DC: Potomac Appalachian Trail Club, 1981.

Gannett, Henry. *The Origin of Certain Place Names in the United States.* Washington, DC: Government Printing Office, 1905.

Garvey, Edward B. *Appalachian Hiker II.* Oackton, VA: Appalachian Books, 1976.

Georgia Appalachian Trail Club. *Friendships of the Trail: A History of the Georgia Appalachian Trail Club, 1930–1980.* Atlanta: Georgia Appalachian Trail Club, 1981.

Gilbert, David. *Where Industry Failed.* Charleston, WV: Pictorial Histories Publishing, 1984.

Goldthwaite, George E. "Constitution Island." In *The Hudson Highlands.* New York: Appalachian Mountain Club, 1945.

Golightly, Jean C. *Appalachian Trail Guide to Maryland and Northern Virginia,* 13th edition. Washington, DC: Potomac Appalachian Trail Club, 1989.

Golightly, Jean C. *Appalachian Trail Guide to Maryland and Northern Virginia,* 14th edition. Vienna, VA: Potomac Appalachian Trail Club, 1993.

Golightly, Jean C. *Appalachian Trail Guide to Maryland and Northern Virginia,* 15th edition. Vienna, VA: Potomac Appalachian Trail Club, 1995.

Golightly, Jean, ed. *Appalachian Trail Guide to Maryland and Northern Virginia with Side Trails,* 15th edition. Vienna VA: Potomac Appalachian Trail Club, 1995.

Gove, Doris. *Exploring the Appalachian Trail: Hikes in the Southern Appalachians.* Mechanicsburg, PA: Stackpole Books, 1998.

Griswold, Whit. *Berkshire Trails for Walking and Ski Touring.* Charlotte, NC: East Woods Press, 1979.

Gross, Wayne E., ed. *Guide to the Appalachian Trail in Pennsylvania,* 10th edition. Cogan Station, PA: Keystone Trails Association, 1998.

Guide to the Appalachian Trail from the Housatonic River to the Susquehanna River, 1st edition. New York: New York–New Jersey Trail Conference, 1934.

Guide to the Appalachian Trail from the Housatonic River to the Susquehanna River, 3rd edition. New York: New York–New Jersey Trail Conference, 1966.

Guide to the Appalachian Trail from the Susquehanna River to Shenandoah National Park, 6th edition. Washington, DC: Potomac Appalachian Trail Club, 1966.

Guide to the Appalachian Trail from the Susquehanna River to Shenandoah National Park, 9th edition. Washington, DC: Potomac Appalachian Trail Club, 1974.

Guide to the Appalachian Trail from the Susquehanna River to Shenandoah National Park, 10th edition. Washington, DC: Potomac Appalachian Trail Club, 1979.

Guide to the Appalachian Trail in Pennsylvania, 3rd edition. Cogan Station, PA: Keystone Trails Association, 1973.

Guide to the Appalachian Trail in Pennsylvania, 4th edition. Cogan Station, PA: Keystone Trails Association, 1977.

Guide to the Appalachian Trail in Pennsylvania, 5th edition. Cogan Station, PA: Keystone Trails Association, 1982.

Guide to the Appalachian Trail in Pennsylvania, 6th edition. Cogan Station, PA: Keystone Trails Association, 1985.

Guide to the Appalachian Trail in Pennsylvania, 9th edition. Cogan Station, PA: Keystone Trails Association, 1994.

Guide to Appalachian Trail in Shenandoah National Park, 5th edition. Washington, DC: Potomac Appalachian Trail Club, 1959.

Guide to the Summer Resorts and Watering Places of East Tennessee. Memphis, TN: Toof and Company, 1880.

Guide to Tuscarora Trail. Cogan Station, PA: Keystone Trails Association, 1979.

Hanna, Willard A. *The Berkshire-Litchfield Legacy.* Hanover, NH: Universities Field Staff International, 1983.

Headley, Russel, ed. *The History of Orange County, New York.* Middletown, NY: Van Deusen and Elms, 1908.

Hemperley, Marion R. *Historic Indian Trails of Georgia.* Atlanta: Garden Club of Georgia, 1989.

Herrick, Margaret E. *Early Settlements in Dutchess County, NY: A Compilation of the "Why . . . ?" Stories by Poughkeepsie Journal Feature Writer Helen Myers.* Rhinebeck, NY: Kinship, 1994.

Hiltz, Andy. *Guide to Appalachian Trail in Shenandoah National Park,* 11th edition. Vienna, VA: Potomac Appalachian Trail Club, 1994.

Hine, C. G. *The New York and Albany Post Road.* New York: C. G. Hine, 1905.

History of Berkshire County, Massachusetts, vols. 1 and 2. New York: J. B. Veers, 1885.

History of Litchfield County, Connecticut. Philadelphia: J. W. Lewis, 1881.

History of Tennessee. Nashville, TN: Goodspeed Publishing Company, 1886.

Holland, Josiah Gilbert. *History of Western Massachusetts,* vol. 2. Springfield, MA: Samuel Bowles, 1855.

Holmes, Lester L., ed. *Guide to the Appalachian Trail in the Great Smokies, the Nantahalas, and Georgia,* 1st edition. Washington, DC: Appalachian Trail Conference, 1971.

Hooke, David, ed. *Appalachian Trail Guide to New Hampshire–Vermont,* 9th edition. Harpers Ferry, WV: Appalachian Trail Conference, 1998.

Horowitz, Howard L. *An Encyclopedic Dictionary of American History.* New York: Washington Square Press, 1970.

Horton, James H., Theda Perdue, and James M. Gifford. *Our Mountain Heritage.* Cullowhee, NC: Western Carolina University, Mountain Heritage Center, 1979.

Howell, William Thompson. *The Hudson Highlands,* vol. 2. New York: Lenz & Riecker, 1934.

Huba, George. *Circuit Hikes in Shenandoah National Park,* 6th edition. Washington, DC: Potomac Appalachian Trail Club, 1963.

Hughes, Arthur H., and Morse S. Allen. *Connecticut Place Names.* Hartford, CT: Connecticut Historical Society, 1976.

Hunt, Elmer. *New Hampshire Town Names and Whence They Came.* Peterborough, NH: Noone House, 1970.

Johnson, Elizabeth. *Big Blue Trail Guide.* Washington, DC: Potomac Appalachian Trail Club, 1987.

Johnson, Thomas H. *The Oxford Companion to American History.* New York: Oxford University Press, 1966.

Julyan, Robert Hixson. *Mountain Names.* Seattle: Mountaineers, 1984.

Kaminkow, Marion J. *Maryland A to Z: A Topographical Dictionary.* Baltimore: Magna Carta Book Co., 1985.

Kasuba, Donna M. *The Berkshires: A Beacon of Beauty, Culture, and Commerce.* Montgomery, AL: Community Communications, 1997.

Keller, Allan. *Life Along the Hudson.* Tarrytown, NY: Sleepy Hollow Restorations, 1976.

Kennan, George. *E. H. Harriman: A Biography,* vol. 2. Freeport, NY: Books for Libraries Press, 1922.

Kenny, Hammell. *The Place Names of Maryland, Their Origin and Meaning.* Baltimore: Museum and Library of Maryland History, Maryland Historical Society, 1984.

Kephart, Horace. *Our Southern Highlanders.* 1913. Reprint, New York: Macmillan, 1929.

Knapp, Samuel L. *The Picturesque Beauties of the Hudson River and Its Vicinity.* New York: J. Disturnell, 1835.

Kodas, Michael, Glenn Scherer, Mark Condon, and Andew Weegar. *Exploring the Appalachian Trail: Hikes in Northern New England.* Mechanicsburg, PA: Stackpole Books, 1999.

Krakow, Kenneth K. *Georgia Place-Names.* Macon, GA: Winship Press, 1975.

Lanman, Thomas. *Letters from the Allegheny Mountains.* New York: G. P. Putnam, 1849.

Leckie, George G. *Georgia: A Guide to Its Towns and Countryside.* Athens, GA: Tupper & Love, 1954. Revised edition of the Works Progress Administration book of 1940.

Lederer, Richard M., Jr. *The Place-Names of Westchester County.* Harrison, NY: Harbor Hill Books, 1978.

Logue, Victoria, and Frank Logue. *The Best of the Appalachian Trail Day Hikes.* Birmingham, AL: Menasha Ridge Press, 1994, and Harpers Ferry,

WV: Appalachian Trail Conference, 1994.

Logue, Victoria, and Frank Logue. *The Best of the Appalachian Trail Overnight Hikes.* Birmingham, AL: Menasha Ridge Press, 1994, and Harpers Ferry, WV: Appalachian Trail Conference, 1994.

Malone, Dumas, ed. *Dictionary of American Biography,* vol. 5. New York: Charles Scribner's Sons, 1961.

Manning, Phillip. *Afoot in the South: Walks in the Natural Areas of North Carolina.* Winston-Salem, NC: John F. Blair, 1993.

Manning, Russ, and Sondra Jamieson. *The Best of the Great Smoky Mountains National Park.* Norris, TN: Mountain Laurel Press, 1991.

Marquis, Albert Nelson. *Who's Who in New England,* 2nd edition. Chicago: A. N. Marquis & Co., 1916.

Marshall, Ian. *Story Line: Exploring the Literature of the Appalachian Trail.* Charlottesville: University Press of Virginia, 1998.

McDaniel, Lynda. *Highroad Guide to the North Carolina Mountains.* Atlanta: Longstreet, 1998.

Mead, Albert S. *Five Hundred Miles A-Foot.* Self-published, 1900.

Means, John. *Maryland's Catoctin Mountain Parks.* Blacksburg, VA: McDonald & Woodward, 1995.

Melville, Herman. *The Piazza and Other Prose Pieces (1839–1860).* Evanston and Chicago: Northwestern University Press and the Newberry Library, 1987.

Melville, Herman. *Pierre—or The Ambiguities.* Evanston and Chicago: Northwestern University Press and the Newberry Library, 1971.

Michaels, Joanne, and Mary-Margaret Barile. *The Best of the Hudson Valley and Catskill Mountains,* 3rd edition. Woodstock, VT: Countryman Press, 1998.

Mooney, James. *James Mooney's History, Myths, and Sacred Formulas of the Cherokees.* Asheville, NC: Historical Images, 1992 (contains "Myths of the Cherokee" [1900] and "The Sacred Formulas of the Cherokees" [1891]).

Mudge, John T. B. *The White Moutains: Names, Places, & Legends.* Etna, NH: Durand Press, 1992.

Murkett, Peter, ed. *A Local History, Town of Monterey.* Monterey, MA: the town of Monterey, 1997.

Myers, Eloise. *A Hinterland Settlement.* Self-published, n.d.

Myles, William J. *Harriman Trails: A Guide and History.* New York: New York–New Jersey Trail Conference, 1992.

New Jersey Writers' Project. *The Origin of New Jersey Place Names.* Washington, DC: Public Works Progress Administration, 1939.

Nichol, Florence. *Guide to the Appalachian Trail in the Great Smokies, the Nantahalas, and Georgia,* 5th edition. Harpers Ferry, WV: Appalachian Trail Conference, 1973.

Older, Curtis L. *The Braddock Expedition and Fox's Gap in Maryland.* Westminster, MD: Family Line Publications, 1995.

Peattie, Roderick, ed. *The Berkshires: The Purple Hills.* New York: Vanguard Press, 1948.

Pelletreau, William. *History of Putnam County, New York.* 1886. Reprint, Brewster, NY, 1988.

Pennsylvania Rail Trails, 4th edition. Washington, DC: Rails-to-Trails Conservancy, 1998.

Phillips, W. H. *Pathfinder to Greylock Mountain, the Berkshire Hills, and Historic Bennington.* Amherst, MA: Massachusetts Historical Society, 1910.

Pollock, G. F. *Skyland: The Heart of the Shenandoah National Park.* Washington, DC: Chesapeake Book Company, 1960.

Powell, William S. *The North Carolina Gazetteer.* Chapel Hill, NC: University of North Carolina Press, 1968.

Ramp, A. T. *The Wagonauts Abroad.* Nashville, TN: Southwestern Publishing House, 1892.

Rand, Christopher. *The Changing Landscape: Salisbury, Connecticut.* New York: Oxford University Press, 1968.

Raymor, Mrs. Ellen M., and Mrs. Emma L. Petitclerc. *History of the Town of Cheshire.* Holyoke, MA: Clark W. Bryan & Co, 1885.

Reeder, Jack, and Carolyn Reeder. *Shenandoah Heritage: The Story of the People Before the Park*, 5th printing. Vienna, VA: Potomac Appalachian Trail Club, 1995.

Reynolds, T. W. *High Lands.* N.p., 1964.

Reynolds, T. W. *The Southern Appalachian Region*, vols. 1 and 2. Self-published, 1966.

Rice, Mallard Milburn. *This Was the Life.* Baltimore: Genealogical Publishing Co., 1984.

Ritchie, David, and Deborah Ritchie. *Connecticut: Off the Beaten Path.* Old Saybrook, CT: Globe Pequot Press, 1998.

Rockwell, Francis W. *The Glory of Greylock: Written as a Souvenir of an Excursion.* Boston: Seaver-Howland Press, 1921.

Rudd, Malcolm Day. *An Historical Sketch of Salisbury, Connecticut.* New York: n.p., 1899 (includes "History and Explanation of Indian Names in Salisbury, Connecticut," by Irvin Wilbur Sanford).

Rutherford, Philip R. *The Dictionary of Maine Place-Names.* Freeport, ME: Bond Wheelwright Company, 1970.

Rutterber, E. M., and L. H. Clark. *History of Orange County, New York.* Philadelphia: Everts and Peck, 1881.

Salmon, Emily J., and Edward D. C. Campbell, Jr. *The Hornbook of Virginia History*, 4th edition. Richmond: Library of Virginia, 1994.

Scharf, J. Thomas. *History of Western Maryland.* 1882. Reprint, Baltimore: Regional Publishing Company, 1968.

Scherer, Glenn. *Vistas and Vision—A History of the New York–New Jersey Trail Conference.* New York: New York–New Jersey Trail Conference, 1995.

Scherer, Glenn, and Don Hopey. *Exploring the Appalachian Trail: Hikes in the Mid-Atlantic States.* Mechanicsburg, PA: Stackpole Books, 1998.

Schlotterbeck, Judith A. *The Pen Mar Story.* Funkstown, MD: Tri-State Printing, 1977.

Sealock, Richard B., Margaret M. Sealock, and Margaret S. Powell. *Bibliography of Place-Name Literature.* Chicago: American Library Association, 1982.

Sellers, Helen Earle. *Connecticut Town Origins.* Stonington, CT: Pequot Press, 1942.

Sills, Norman, and Robert Hatton, field eds. *Appalachian Trail Guide to Massachusetts-Connecticut*, 10th edition. Harpers Ferry, WV: Appalachian Trail Conference, 1996.

Skelton, William H., ed. *Wilderness Trails of Tennessee's Cherokee National Forest.* Knoxville: University of Tennessee Press, 1992.

Smeltzer-Stevenot, Marjorie. *Footprints in the Ramapos.* Ashland, OH: Bookmasters, 1993.

Smith, Chard Powers. *The Housatonic: Puritan River.* New York: Rinehart, 1946.

Smith, J. E. A. *History of Pittsfield, 1734–1800.* Boston: Lee and Shepard, 1869.

Smith, Philip H. *General History of Dutchess County.* Pawling, NY: n.p., 1877.

Spitzer, Carroll F. *A Pictorial History of Pen Mar Park.* Hagerstown, MD: Tri-State Printing, 1986.

Starr, Edmund C. *A History of Cornwall, Connecticut.* New Haven, CT: Tuttle, Morehouse, and Taylor, 1926.

Strain, Paula. *The Blue Hills of Maryland.* Washington, DC: Potomac Appalachian Trail Club, 1993.

Stephenson, Jean, ed. *Guide to the Appalachian Trail in the Great Smokies, the Nantahalas, and Georgia,* 1st edition. Washington, DC: Appalachian Trail Conference, 1963.

Stephenson, Jean, ed. *Guide to the Appalachian Trail in Tennessee and North Carolina: Cherokee, Pisgah, and Great Smokies,* 1st edition. Washington, DC: Appalachian Trail Conference, 1963.

Stephenson, Jean, ed. *Guide to Paths in the Blue Ridge,* 4th edition. Washington, DC: Potomac Appalachian Trail Club, 1950.

Sternfield, Jonathan, and Lauren R. Stevens. *The Berkshire Book: A Complete Guide,* 4th edition. Lee, MA: Berkshire House Publishers, 1997.

Stevens, Lauren R. *Hikes and Walks in the Berkshire Hills.* Lee, MA: Berkshire House Publishers, 1998.

Stewart, George R. *American Place-Names.* New York: Oxford University Press, 1970.

Stone, R. C., comp. *The Gold Mines, Scenery and Climate of Georgia and the Carolinas.* New York: National Bank Note Company, 1878.

Swift, Esther Munroe. *Vermont Place-Names, Footprints of History,* 2nd printing. Brattleboro, VT: Vermont Historical Society, Picton Press, 1996

Thomas, Vaughn. *Appalachian Trail Guide to Southwest Virginia.* Harpers Ferry, WV: Appalachian Trail Conference, 1994.

Thompson, Harold W. *Body, Boots and Britches.* New York: Dover Publications, 1939.

Thoreau, Henry David. *A Week on the Concord and Merrimack Rivers.* Reprint, Princeton, NJ: Princeton University Press, 1980.

Turco, Peggy. *Walks and Rambles in Dutchess and Putnam Counties.* Woodstock, VT: Backcountry Publications, 1990.

Turco, Peggy. *Walks and Rambles in the Western Hudson Valley.* Woodstock, VT: Backcountry Publications, 1996.

Van West, Carroll, ed. *The Tennessee Encyclopedia of History & Culture.* Nashville: Tennessee Historical Society, 1998.

Van Zandt, Roland. *Chronicles of the Hudson: Three Centuries of Travel and Adventure.* Hensonville, NY: Black Dome Press, 1992.

Waterman, Laura, and Guy Waterman. *Forest and Crag: A History of Hiking, Trail Blazing, and Adventure in the Northeast Mountains.* Boston: Appalachian Mountain Club, 1989.

Williams, Byron L. *The Old South Mountain Inn: An Informal History.* Shippensburg, PA: Beidel Printing House, 1990.

Williams, Thomas J. C. *A History of Washington County, Maryland.* 1906. Reprint, Baltimore: Regional Publishing Company, 1968.

Wilson, James Grant. *Memorial History of the City of New York and the Hudson River Valley.* New York: New York History Company, 1892.

Wise, Kenneth. *Hiking Trails of the Great Smoky Mountains.* Knoxville, TN: The University of Tennessee Press, 1996.

Zeigler, Wilbur G., and Ben S. Grosscup. *The Heart of the Alleghanies or Western North Carolina.* Raleigh, NC: Alfred Williams & Co., 1883.

Zinn, Howard. *A People's History of the United States.* New York: HarperCollins, 1980.

MAGAZINES, PAMPHLETS, AND OTHER PUBLICATIONS

"Above the Clouds: Mount Greylock Summit." Pamphlet from the Massachusetts Department of Environmental Management (no date).

"Advocate's Guide to the Northern Berkshires." Published by the *Berkshire Advocate,* 1999.

"Buyers at Lenox Preserve Forest." *The New York Times,* October 26, 1947, p. 25.

"CCC Camps Made Lasting Contribution to Berkshires." *The Berkshire Eagle,* May 15, 1961, p. 10.

"Eaton's Report for Mt. Everett Reveals Great Interest in Laurel Week." *The Berkshire Eagle,* July 15, 1936.

"Indian Traditions of Monument Mountain." *The New-York Mirror,* vol. 11, no. 18, November 2, 1883, p. 141.

"October Mountain, State's Largest Park, Is Opened." *The Berkshire Evening Eagle,* June 15, 1935.

"To Keep Autos off Mt. Everett to Preserve Natural Beauty." *The Springfield Sunday Union and Republican,* January 22, 1928.

"Hiking Trails in Clarence Fahnestock Memorial State Park and the Hubbard-Perkins Conservation Area." New York–New Jersey Trail Conference pamphlet, 1997.

"Hiking Trails in the East Hudson Highlands." New York–New Jersey Trail Conference pamphlet, 1997.

"Southern End of Trail Is Springer Mountain." *Appalachian Trailway News,* vol. 20, no. 1, January 1959, p. 8.

"The Civilian Conservation Corps: Shaping the Forests and Parks of Massachusetts." Pamphlet by the Massachusetts Department of Environmental Management, prepared in cooperation with the DEM Office of Historic Resources, 1999.

"Whitman Statue Dedicated at Bear Mountain." *Appalachian Trailway News,* vol. 2, no. 1, January 1941, p. 8.

Appalachian Trail Guide to Maine, vol. 1. Maine Appalachian Trail Club, 1934.

Appalachian Trail Guide to Maine, vol. 2. Maine Appalachian Trail Club, 1936.

Appalachian Trail Guide to Maine, vol. 5. Maine Appalachian Trail Club, 1953.

Appalachian Trail Guide to Maine, vol. 6. Maine Appalachian Trail Club, 1964.

Appalachian Trail Guide to Maine, vol. 8. Maine Appalachian Trail Club, 1975.

Appalachian Trail Guide to Maine, vol. 12. Maine Appalachian Trail Club, 1993.

Appalachian Trail Guide to Maine, vol. 13. Maine Appalachian Trail Club, 1996.

Appalachian Trailway News, vol. 1, no. 1. Appalachian Trail Conference, January 1939.

Appalachian Trailway News, vol. 11, no. 1. Appalachian Trail Conference, January 1950.

Appalachian Trailway News, vol. 19, no. 2. Appalachian Trail Conference, May 1958.

Appalachian Trailway News, vol. 20, no. 2. Appalachian Trail Conference, May 1959.

Appalachian Trailway News, vol. 22, no. 1. Appalachian Trail Conference, January 1961.

Appalachian Trailway News, vol. 28, no. 3. Appalachian Trail Conference, September 1967.

Appalachian Trailway News, vol. 44, no. 5. Appalachian Trail Conference, November 1983.

Appalachian Trailway News, vol. 48, no. 1. Appalachian Trail Conference, March 1987.

Appalachian Trailway News, vol. 54, no. 3. Appalachian Trail Conference, July 1993.

Appalachian Trailway News, vol. 55, no. 5. Appalachian Trail Conference, November 1994.

Avery, Myron H. *The Appalachian Trail in Pennsylvania's South Mountain.* October 1936.

Avery, Myron H., and Kenneth S. Boardman, eds. "Arnold Guyot's Notes on the Geography of the Mountain District of Western North Carolina." *North Carolina Historical Review,* vol. 15, no. 3, July 1938.

Bascom, John. *Greylock Reservation.* Pittsfield, MA: Sun Printing Co., 1907.

Beauchamp, William M. "Aboriginal Place Names of New York." New York State Museum, Bulletin 108, Archeology 12. May 1907.

Best of American Canals, no. 2. American Canal and Transportation Center, 1984.

Best of American Canals, no. 3. American Canal and Transportation Center, 1986.

Bicentennial History of Dalton, Massachusetts, 1784–1984. Printed in 1984.

Browne, C. A. "Elder John Leland and the Mammoth Cheshire Cheese." In *Agricultural History* 18:145–53, October 1944.

Browne, William B. *The Mohawk Trail: Its History and Course.* North Adams, MA: n.p., 1920.

Browne, William B. *Over Pathways of the Past: Familiar Features of Our Valley—How They Originated—What Happened Along the Way.* North Adams, MA: North Adams Transcript, 1938.

Calhoun, Newell Meeker. *Litchfield County Sketches.* Litchfield County University Club, 1906.

Chapman, Gerard. "The Dome of the Taconics." *The Berkshire Eagle,* August 31, 1977.

Chapman, Gerard. "The Grandeur of Monument Mountain." *Berkshire Week,* August 17, 1995, p. 28.

Chapman, Gerard. "Noble Monument." *The Berkshire Eagle,* April 21, 1977.

Cilley, Dean, and Susan Cilley. *Guide to the Appalachian Trail in Maine,* vol. 9. Maine Appalachian Trail Club, 1978.

Dalzell, Robert F., Jr. "Solving the Puzzle of Ephraim Williams' Surprising Vision." *Williams Alumni Review,* Summer 1993.

Davidson, Donald. *The Tennessee,* vol. 1: "The Old River, Frontier to Succession." New York: Rinehart, 1946.

De Sousa, Rebecca. "Finding the Osborn Loop and the 'AT.'" Manitoga newsletter, n.d.

Drew, Bernard A. "The Mysterious and Grand Whitney Estate." *Berkshire Sampler,* September 30, 1979.

Drew, Bernard A. "An Upland Home for Wildlife." *Berkshires Week,* September 12, 1996.

Eno, Joel Nelson. "Ancient Place-Names in Connecticut." *Connecticut Magazine,* vol. 12, no. 1, January–March 1908.

Fink, Paul M. "Smoky Mountains History as Told in Place-Names." *Potomac Appalachian Trail Club Bulletin,* January 1936.

Giddings, Ted. "Mohhekennuck Club." *The Berkshire Eagle,* August 6, 1982.

Guide to Paths in the Blue Ridge, vol. 1. Washington, DC: Potomac Appalachian Trail Club, 1931.

Guide to Paths in the Blue Ridge, vol. 2. Washington, DC: Potomac Appalachian Trail Club, 1934.

Hale, Edward E. "Dialectical Evidence in the Place-Names of Eastern New York." *American Speech,* December 1929.

Hodge, Frederick Webb. *Handbook of American Indians North of Mexico,* part 1, Bulletin 30, 3rd impression. Washington, DC: Smithsonian Institution, Bureau of American Ethnology, 1911.

Hodge, Frederick Webb. *Handbook of American Indians North of Mexico,* part 2, Bulletin 30, 2nd impression. Washington, DC: Smithsonian Institution, Bureau of American Ethnology, 1912.

Hull, Richard. *People of the Valleys* (photocopy forwarded by librarian at Albert Wisner Public Library, Warwick, NY).

Jewell, William C. *Southeastern New York, Putnam County,* vol. 2. New York: Lewis Historical Publishing Company, 1946.

The Maine Naturalist, vol. 8, no. 2. Maine Naturalist Co., June 1928.

The Maine Naturalist, vol. 8, no. 3. Maine Naturalist Co., September 1928.

The Maine Naturalist, vol. 9, no. 3. Maine Naturalist Co., September 1929.

The Mohawk Trail Region, 1999–2000. Charlemont, MA: Mohawk Trail Association, n.d.

Musey, Reuben L. *It Happened in Washington County.* Washington County (MD) Bicentennial Committee.

Newman, Marc. "General Richard Montgomery First National Hero." *Montgomery Day Journal,* vol. 1, no. 1, September 12, 1992.

O'Brien, Tom. "Beartown State Forest." *Monterey News,* September 1987.

Official Souvenir Book, Old Home Week, September 5–11, 1909. Published by the Publicity Committee of North Adams, MA.

PATC Bulletin, vol. 2, no. 4. Potomac Appalachian Trail Club, April 1938.

PATC Bulletin, vol. 3, no. 1. Potomac Appalachian Trail Club, January 1934.

PATC Bulletin, vol. 3, no. 3. Potomac Appalachian Trail Club, July 1934.

PATC Bulletin, vol. 4, no. 1. Potomac Appalachian Trail Club, January 1935.

PATC Bulletin, vol. 4, no. 3. Potomac Appalachian Trail Club, July 1935.

PATC Bulletin, vol. 5, no. 4. Potomac Appalachian Trail Club, October 1936.

PATC Bulletin, vol. 5, no. 4. Supplement. Potomac Appalachian Trail Club, October 1936.

PATC Bulletin, vol. 6, no. 3. Potomac Appalachian Trail Club, July 1937.

PATC Bulletin, vol. 7, no. 2. Potomac Appalachian Trail Club, April 1938.

PATC Bulletin, vol. 7, no. 4. Potomac Appalachian Trail Club, October 1938.

PATC Bulletin, vol. 9, no. 3. Potomac Appalachian Trail Club, July 1940.

PATC Bulletin, vol. 11, no. 2. Potomac Appalachian Trail Club, April 1942.

PATC Bulletin, vol. 14, no. 3. Potomac Appalachian Trail Club, July 1945.

PATC Bulletin, vol. 21, no. 4. Potomac Appalachian Trail Club, October 1952.

Pawling Nature Reserve pamphlet and map.

Scott, Rev. Charles. "Shawangunk, Its Meaning and Origin." *Olde Ulster* 1:19–20 (January 1905).

Shearn, Evelyn. *A History of Mount Washington, Massachusetts.* N.p., 1976,

Stotelmeyer, Asa P. "The Black Rock Hotel on the Bagtown-Jugtown Trail." *Baltimore Sun Magazine,* November 15, 1970.

The Sun, Pittsfield, MA, April 19, 1900. Vertical file of Pittsfield, MA, Public Library.

Swaen, A. E. H. "Dutch Place-Names in Eastern New York." *American Speech* 5:400 (June 1930).

Tuten, Rebecca L. "The Rich History of Beech Mountain." Photocopy sent by the Beech Mountain Chamber of Commerce.

Virginia Magazine of History and Biography, vol. 7, n.d.

Wolfinger, James R., comp. *Washington County Maryland Post Offices, When Established and Discontinued, Postmasters.* 1940.

Wyand, Jeffrey A. "The Hundreds of Washington County." *Maryland Historical Society Magazine,* Fall 1972.

OTHER SOURCES

"A Little Shady Valley History." From website www.geocities.com/Heartland/Ranch/1185/history.html, February 2000.

"Early Putnam County History." Hope Farm Press and Bookshop website.

"Greenbrier State Park." Maryland Department of Natural Resources website.

"South Mountain State Park." Maryland Department of Natural Resources website.

"The History of Orange County." Orange County website.

"The Long Path." New York–New Jersey Trail Conference website.

"Town History." Town of Tuxedo website.

"Track Information." Lime Rock Park website.

"Visitor's Guide to Salisbury." Salisbury Association website.

Amicalola Falls State Park website, March 3, 2000.

Bailey, Stella, town/village historian of Highland Falls, NY. Correspondence dated April 12, 2000.

Bast, Doug, Boonesboro (MD) historian. Conversation with K. Clark, January 10, 2000.

Bistrais, Bob. *Place Names on Vermont's Long Trail.* University of Vermont graduate thesis, 1995.

Bloom, George. Conversations with postmaster of Glencliff, NH.

Burstein, Nancy. Author correspondence with curator of the Williamstown House of Local History.

Cherokee National Forest website. February 2000.

Coriell, Jack. E-mail correspondence, March 28, 2000.

Crowder, Orville. "Gapland: A Ghost on the Trail." *Potomac Appalachian Trail Club Bulletin,* April 1934 (reprinted on Potomac Appalachian Trail Club website).

Daniels, Walt. Correspondence of December 20, 1999.

Doyle, Brian. Author correspondence with AT overseer at Bear Mountain–Harriman State Park. December 21, 1999.

Doyle, Patrick. Conversation with former president of Old Dominion Appalachian Trail Club.

Ellenwood, Bob. Conversation with member of Natural Bridge Appalachian Trail Club.

Fadner, Raymond. Conversation with Edward Talone, April 2000.

Frye, John. Conversation with curator of Western Maryland Room, Washington County Public Library, Hagerstown, MD, January 3, 2000.

Gannett, Henry. *A Gazetteer of Maryland.* Washington, DC: Government Printing Office, 1904.

Garvey, Edward B. Interview conducted by Edward Talone, 1999.

George Washington and Thomas Jefferson National Forests website, May 2000.

Griggs, Thurston. Correspondence, January 18, 2000.

Hanover town calendar, 1995.

Haynes, Rebecca. "Bear Mountain State Park." Reprinted on Hudson River website.

Haynes, Rebecca. "Explore the Hudson Valley's Rich History." Reprinted on Huson River website.

Henneberger, Karel, and Alfred Henneberger. Correspondence, March 12, 2000.

Historical Society of Frederick County. Conversation with librarian, February 24, 2000.

Hopson, Emily. Correspondence with K. Clark of the Kent Historical Society, November 12, 1999.

Kirby, Ed, Norman Sills, and Jeanne Majdalany. Conversation with Sharon, CT, town historian, November 29, 1999.

Maine Atlas and Gazetteer, 17th edition. Freeport, ME: DeLorme Mapping Co., 1994.

Majdalany, Jeanne. Correspondence with Sharon, CT, town historian, December 3, 1999.

Massachusetts Department of Environmental Management files. Regional Office, Pittsfield, MA.

McKeen, Nate. Correspondence with regional manager of the Vermont Department of Forests, Parks, and Recreation, March 2, 2001.

Miller, James. Correspondence with director/archivist/researcher, Mark Dewey Research Center, Sheffield Historical Society, Sheffield, MA, January 4, 2000.

National Register Nomination for Mount Greylock Summit, Section 7, September 4, 1997, draft. Massachusetts Department of Environmental management files.

Niedzialek, Carol. Correspondence with member of the Potomac Appalachian Trail Conference, February 3, 2000.

Pennsylvania Atlas and Gazeteer, 3rd edition. Freeport, ME: DeLorme Mapping Co., 1990.

Pinna, Gail. Conversation and correspondence with Dalton Historical Commission, Dalton, MA, January 2000.

Schoolcraft, Henry R. "Comments, Philological and Historical, on the Aboriginal Names and Geographical Terminology, of the State of New York, Part First: Valley of the Hudson." In *Report from the Committee on Indian Names, etc.* Proceedings of the New York Historical Society, 1844.

Slick, Charles. Conversation with the president of the Smithsburg (MD) Historical Society, January 10, 2000.

Sonne, Christian R. Correspondence of the historian of the town of Tuxedo, NY, April 14, 2000.

Spofford, Horatio Gates. *A Gazetteer of the State of New York.* Albany, NY: B. D. Packard, 1824.

Springfield Republican, April 9, 1950. Vertical file of Pittsfield, MA, Public Library.

Stimpson, Donna. Correspondence with the Massachusetts Department of Environmental Management, October 20, 1999, relaying information from Carl Curtin, assistant forests and parks coordinator, Division of Forests and Parks.

Sypher, Sallie. Correspondence with Putnam historian, December 22, 1999.

Talone, Edward. Interviews conducted in April–June 1999 and January 2000.

Temple, Jean. Conversation with postmaster at Etna, NH.

Vermont Atlas and Gazeteer, 8th edition. Freeport, ME: DeLorme Mapping Co., 1988.

Wilk, Joseph Addison. *A History of Adams, Massachusetts.* Ph.D. diss., University of Ottawa, 1945.

Williams, Lisa. Correspondence with the Georgia Appalachian Trail Conference, March 28, 2000.

Wismar, Bishop Cyril. Conversation with the Falls Village historian and resident of Barrack Mountain, November 29, 1999.

www.appalachian.org. February 2000.

www.damascus.org. "A Brief History of Damascus, Virginia," February 2000.

www.fs.fed.us. U.S. Forest Service website, March 2000.

www.georgia-atclub.org. Georgia Appalachian Trail Club website, March 2000.

www.georgiatrails.com. "Byron Herbert Reece Access Trail," April 2000.

www.gorp.com. February 2000.

www.hotspringsnc.org. February 2000.
www.mdarchives.state.md.us. Maryland State Archives website.
www.ngeorgia.com. Website for communities of northern Georgia, March 2000.
www.nps.gov/grsm. Great Smoky Mountains National Park website, April 2000.
www.r8web.com/cherokee. Cherokee National Forest website, April 2000.
www.silasgriffith.com. Silas Griffith House, Danby, VT, website, March 2001.
www.smnet2.net/users/nhc. Nantahala Hiking Club website, March 2000.
www.tehcc.org. Tennessee Eastman Hiking and Canoeing Club website, February 2000.
www.wilderness.net/nwps/wilderness.cfm. National Wilderness Preservation System website, April 2000.